D0407087

TOM HANKS

TOM HANKS

DAVID GARDNER

BLAKE

Published by Blake Publishing Ltd,
3 Bramber Court, 2 Bramber Road,
London W14 9PB, England

First published in 1999

ISBN 1 85782 3273

British Library Cataloguing-in-Publication Data:
A catalogue record for this book is available
from the British Library.

Typeset by BCP

Printed in Great Britain by
Creative Print and Design (Wales), Ebbw Vale, Gwent

1 3 5 7 9 10 8 6 4 2

Pictures supplied by courtesy of Axis Entertainment,
Columbia Tri-Star Films (UK)/Kobal, DreamWorks/Kobal,
TriStar/Kobal, Paramount Pictures/Kobal,
Touchstone/Kobal, 20th Century Fox/Kobal, Universal/Kobal,
Warner Brothers/Kobal, Camerapress

CONTENTS

To Michelle

Acknowledgements

M y heartfelt thanks to the following people who helped make this book possible: John Blake, Rosie Ries, Betty Black Duval, Hilda Bauquier, Wayne Melton, Vincent Dowling, Winifred Martinez, Jon Finley, Melissa Marsh, Lawrence Hanks, Roderick Brown, Tim Miles, Wendy Henry, Jean Gardner, my wife, Michelle, and children Mickey, Jazmin and Savannah.

In addition, two books, *The Films of Tom Hanks* by Lee Pfeiffer and Michael Lewis (Citadel Press, 1996) and *The Devil s Candy: The Bonfire of the Vanities Goes to Hollywood,* by Julie Salamon (Houghton Mifflin, 1991), provided some valuable information.

PROLOGUE

It had been raining non-stop for three days and the eight men shivered under their single blankets as the temperature dropped below 40 degrees in the makeshift campsite in anonymous countryside about one hour north of London.

The men hadn't been told where they were in case they tried to run away. But they might as well have been on another planet.

None of them had reckoned on this. If war was hell, this was a special version of Hades. They suffered so much they even thought about mutinying, and were inches away from packing up their squalid, muck-lined tents.

Only one man held them together.

It all started wonderfully. It was sunny. They set up their tents. The countryside, even if it was in the middle of nowhere, was lush and green. A camping break would be a good chance for some male bonding. They could probably sneak some beers, maybe play some cards. Then it started to rain.

It didn't stop for seven days. The men soon realised their tents were so small their feet stuck out the end. And the harsh reality of boot camp dawned early — before dawn, in fact, when each man awoke to a sharp kick to the heel and an order to assemble outside in the rain.

They had been asleep just three hours and their clothes were already soaked. 'You had this skinny little fucking thing they called a blanket, which wasn't fit to cover a squirrel,' one related. 'You could either put it on top of you or put it under you. If you put it on top, you're sleeping on the ground. And the ground — you could literally feel it suck the life out of your body.'

Climbing out of their tents, any thoughts of a jolly camping trip washed away, they came face to face with the man who was there to make them miserable.

Captain Dale Dye, a 21-year veteran of the American Marine Corps, America's toughest soldiers, collected three Purple Hearts and a Bronze Star in Vietnam and served in war-torn Beirut. Wounded by shrapnel and bullets, it was his job to take the 'sissy-boys' and turn them into fighting men. 'My training is tough,' he said. 'Deprivation is what soldiers live with all the time.' Dye called all the men turds — but one, singled out because of his status, had to endure a refinement: he was 'turd number one'.

The day began with a gruelling set of exercises as dawn came up over the pastoral setting. Then came a five-mile run with the men carrying a full kit on their backs. On their return they may or may not have been fed breakfast depending, as Dye put it, on 'whether they pissed me off or not'.

They ran, hiked and fought mock battles in mud, cold and wet. Food was war rations, which, said one of them, looked like dog food and smelled like vomit.

Halfway through the boot-camp torture, they began to get sick. One twisted an ankle. Others suffered diarrhoea, cramps, high fevers, nausea from lack of sleep and rheumatism.

The leader of the group had his own tent, separate from the rest. Three days into the ordeal, the others called a meeting. They wanted to take a vote on whether to continue — or go home. They had taken enough. All of them voted to cut their losses and leave. Except for the leader. Insisting on a second vote, giving them time to think harder about their decision, he reported up the line.

'We have a small problem,' he said. Part of the reply was, 'You're a leader — solve it.'

So, going back into a huddle with the others, the leader once again told them he was staying and left them in no doubt what he thought they should do.

'You know enough to be a Marine? Then you can leave,' he

Perhaps his public could be forgiven for believing that Tom Hanks has always had it made. It is only natural that people would assume their American-as-apple-pie hero had an upbringing befitting his *The Right Stuff* persona.

But they would be very wrong. The reality was a childhood full of doubts, confusion and loneliness. By the time he was ten, Tom had had three mothers, gone to five different schools and lived in ten different homes. At one stage, he had so many siblings and stepbrothers and stepsisters that he was known simply as 'Number Eight'.

He would joke later: 'My parents pioneered the marriage dissolution laws for the state of California. I think a couple of clauses, in fact, are called The Hanks Family Clauses in the penal code.' But there wasn't much to laugh about at the time.

The complex emotions arising from such an unsettled start in life even spilled over into adulthood, with an unplanned pregnancy and a doomed marriage fitting the pattern of thwarted ambition set by Tom's father, an intelligent, determined man whose dreams were ultimately buried under the burden of responsibility.

Even after Tom's acting career took off, with the astonishing success of stock family films like *Splash* and *Big*, his path seemed to be heading down the burnt-out cul-de-sac favoured by many of Hollywood's once blazing stars.

With the collapse of his first marriage, and the guilt of failing his two young children just as his parents had failed him by separating when he was a boy, came an unseemly divorce battle and the obligatory Californian therapy sessions to attempt to lift his despair.

The fact that Tom turned his life around in such a huge way, both as an actor and as a man, was, I think, due primarily to two factors.

The first was Rita Wilson, the wife he says 'saved' him. She gave him the kind of security all of us crave — the security to be himself. Bubbly, extroverted and popular, Rita comes from a close-knit, conventional — if that is still the case in these dysfunctional times — family. She was always going to be an actress, growing up in Hollywood and even sharing the same school as such screen told them. 'And those of you that don't think you know enough about what it means to take that beach and be a Marine — you stay.'

The second vote was a landslide in favour of continuing with boot camp. 'It was like yeah, yeah, yeah ... all of us,' said one. 'So this time he turned to me and said, "There doesn't seem to be a problem here." And I said, "No, there doesn't," and we walked away.'

It could so easily have been a scene plucked straight from a classic war movie. But these were not soldiers and, even though the eight boot campers were actors, no cameras were rolling as they got their brief glimpse into the grim — and grimy — realities of conflict.

The camp was, in fact, director Steven Spielberg's idea to help prepare his hand-picked actors for the realism he saw as a necessary backdrop for his film, *Saving Private Ryan*.

While no audience will ever get the chance to see this dramatic episode on screen, the character and bearing of the leader who offset the mutiny will already be familiar to many. In life, as on film, he is a man whose strong, understated qualities make him a force to be reckoned with, a role model who leads by example.

Ladies and gentlemen, starring as himself, Turd Number One: Tom Hanks.

To his millions of fans around the world, Tom is Hollywood's Mr Nice Guy, an image that is so pervasive it has become just about the only thing that irritates him in interviews when asked time and again: 'How does it feel to be so nice?'

He is the rightful heir to the celluloid throne vacated by the two movie stars he is most often identified with — James Stewart and Cary Grant.

He has a wife to die for, four children he worships and a filofax full of Hollywood friends that would turn a Los Angeles plastic surgeon green with envy.

Oh, and he is the world's biggest and most bankable movie star — a double Oscar winner and one of an elite group of two or three actors who can not only command up to $20 million per film, but still give their studio paymasters value for money.

sirens as Judy Garland, Lana Turner and Linda Evans.

The second factor in the making of Tom Hanks was his own convoluted family. It is Tom's sense of family, both his alienation from it and his desperate need for it, that provides the central theme to this book.

From Tom's father's unpublished memoirs, written shortly before his death in 1991, we get a unique perspective on the formative influences on the life of one of the biggest names of our times.

From stories about his relatives and ancestors — including the tragic murder of his grandfather and his ancestral links to Abraham Lincoln — we can better understand his roots and genealogical make-up.

And from this first, detailed look behind the curtains of a man who has lived much of his life in the spotlight, yet still hidden in plain sight, we are able to see just how many hurdles he has had to overcome in his personal life to achieve such unparalleled success, both on and off the screen.

Some of that private pain, Tom will openly admit, has helped him as an actor. Initially, acting offered a lost, mixed-up teenager an escape from the unhappiness of his home life and, later, it would benefit from a reservoir of loneliness in which he could occasionally immerse himself for inspiration.

It is interesting to note that many of Tom's lighter, fluffier roles came at a time he was going through tough periods at home, striding to get on in a business that is notoriously stressful on young families. When he had found fulfilment away from the set, many of the parts he chose took on a more dramatic, serious tone.

Of one thing we can be certain about a Tom Hanks film. Be it the physical comedy of *Big*, the emotional pathos of *Philadelphia*, the sentimental quirkiness of *Forrest Gump* or the intensity of *Saving Private Ryan*, they are all immensely watchable movies. Even the bad ones generally have a good performance by their star.

We read about Tom's Oscar triumphs. We have watched him grow up as an actor before our very eyes. He has repaid his primarily baby boomer audience by reflecting its interests in the choices he makes.

But he is still a most unlikely hero.

He has few of the physical attributes of his A-List rivals.

There's the slightly bulbous nose, the tight, curly black hair that perches on top of his prominent forehead, and the pale blue, restless eyes that flicker behind his small, almost Oriental, eyes. He tells directors that one profile is Richard Gere and the other is Richard Nixon, although a double chin is always threatening to unbalance the more attractive side of the equation.

He doesn't do blockbuster action movies, although he boasts he could play a James Bond 'baddie' in his sleep. Nor does he do sex scenes.

And he has been uniquely successful at keeping his private life largely a closed book to the public without anyone ever really realising it.

Tom would argue that his 'crack team of showbusiness experts' are amply rewarded for keeping him the most secretive of superstars. Yet this star, more than most, has much to be proud of in the way he has handled his immense fame.

To him, all the money, the adulation and the golden statuettes are secondary. His wife and children come first. 'I have no best friend,' he says. 'The family takes up the vast amount of time.'

And family leads us back to Tom's antecedents, particularly his great-grandparents, Selina and Amos, a couple to whom Tom owes a great deal more than he knows. From them, he has inherited many of the gestures and mannerisms that are now so familiar in his performances, particularly in his comedy roles.

Tom's aunt, Hilda Bauquier, now in her 80s herself, is his only relative who can still clearly remember the 'glint' in her grandfather's eye as he sat with his family around the kitchen table. She sees the same deprecating sense of humour in her famous nephew.

'The family always has had a great sense of humour,' she said. 'His great-grandfather had that same offhand way of putting himself down that Tom has.

'The movement at the back of Tom's head reminds me of his father and he moves like him. We all wave our arms around and we stand with our hands on our hips. I have a picture of a whole group of relatives standing in exactly that same way. Tom does it too.'

Over the years Tom has, ever so politely, distanced himself from the rest of his family. He gets an invitation every year to the reunions, and relatives have tried to send him details of the family tree. But, so far at least, he has shown little interest.

Perhaps that is because he no longer wants to look back. Approaching middle age, he has conquered the demons from his past and is comfortable with his role as our saint-next-door.

As he puts it: 'My dad was a guy who grew up on a farm during the Depression. I think there's a degree of communicative skills that my dad did not have. I knew he didn't have them, and for the longest time, I didn't have them either.

'But at my age I think I'm done with wrestling the ghosts of my dad, or my parents in general.

'Somebody once said to me that by the time you are 40, you'd better quit complaining and get on with your life. So now I'm in the "shut up, just do it" phase of my life and it feels right.'

Tom Hanks is larger-than-life proof that a nice guy really can finish first.

And therein lies the key to his success. He is not a comic-book hero with impossibly big muscles or telepathic powers of deduction. Up there on the screen, he is someone his audience can relate to; an ordinary man with all the hopes and fears and doubts that all of us carry around with us. If it seems unlikely that a man who describes himself as having 'a big ass, fat thighs, a goofy-looking nose, ears that hang down, eyes that make me look part-Chinese and a gut I've got to keep watching' can win the heart of a Meg Ryan or a Robin Wright Penn, then we are happy to suspend our cynicism for the space of 90 to 120 minutes or so. After all, we are all allowed to dream. And if Tom can do it, perhaps we can too.

Besides, extraordinary things do happen in life. It takes an extraordinary actor of the calibre of Tom Hanks to make them seem real in a place like Hollywood, where artifice so often takes precedence over accuracy.

Behind every successful person, be it in business, in entertainment or any other field, there is another side to the story that will tell you how full their lives are. As much as Hollywood, with its controlling publicists and cash-hungry agents, may try to persuade people otherwise, the sum total of an actor cannot be counted on his work alone. The reason actors and actresses are paid countless millions while nurses and teachers toil twice as hard for a pittance is not just because they are easy on the eye or good at making pretend or, more often, both. It is because a huge number of people around the world identify with them as people. It is not just about the characters they play.

It is only fair then, that the audience that pays these vast salaries can hold the stars they worship to account.

There is no excuse for hounding anybody, but it is important to know where he or she has come from, to understand how they behave when the cameras stop rolling, to see how they are perceived by their friends and to gauge how they have coped with success and failure.

As much as these sentiments may irritate or even anger the artists, be sure that if a superstar did do something in his or her private life that upset or antagonised the public, their stock — and their fee — would quickly fall. Be sure, too, that the now-wealthy, high-living megastar was once a hungry actor, grateful for any morsel of publicity that came his or her way.

The impressive thing about Tom Hanks is that he has succeeded on both sides of the coin. We know much of his on screen successes. What many do not now is how hard he worked to hone his craft. He didn't hurtle into Hollywood on the back of a kids' TV show or an offbeat improvised cult comedy show. He spent years in the theatre, working his way up from the carpentry shop to centre stage, leading one senior director to call him the best comic Shakespearean actor he had ever seen. He did the rounds of forgettable bit parts in established television shows, where the proven stars jealously guarded all the best lines. And he worked his way through a kaleidoscope of movies before finally hitting his stride. To Tom, it is not all about being a movie star. It is all about being an actor.

In his life away from the spotlight, Tom is more of a mystery to his fans. He doesn't punch photographers or frequent trendy Hollywood showboating restaurants. His own experiences have taught him that he is happier caring for his own loved ones than carousing with someone else's. *Pretty Woman* director Garry Marshall says the actor is one of the Hat Pack — 'because the wildest thing he does is to occasionally put on a hat'.

If Tom commits to a project, you can be sure he will be out there on the promotional circuit in the weeks running up to its release. Having signed on to a (usually lucrative) deal, he feels obligated to do everything he reasonably can to make it a success.

If he sees a well-wisher or even a press camera in the crowd while shooting a film, he is more likely to offer a friendly wave than try to hide his face. While some stars go to the ridiculous lengths of covering their faces with umbrellas in between scenes on set, Tom will usually find the whole circus faintly amusing.

Early in his career, in particular, he spoke at some length about his childhood and his self-perceived shortcomings. While he quickly learned not to invite a magazine writer right into his home and thus avoid critiques on his carpets, furniture, colour schemes, etc., he nevertheless continued to give frank, sometimes quirky interviews.

Perhaps it is for these reasons that the entertainment press has largely given him a comfortable ride and has never pried too deeply into his private life, as with other stars of similar popularity.

To interviewers he is both courteous and understanding of their needs for an interesting angle. He understands the game and how to play it to his best advantage.

His determination to live as ordinary a life as possible under very abnormal circumstances has given him a more philosophical outlook on his fame, and an attitude many of his contemporaries would do well to heed. He told *USA Weekend*: 'I have been getting cuts in line at airports for quite some time, so it has its advantages. It is not so much the loss of privacy, it's how you protect what privacy you have. I made my peace with that a long time ago.

'I go to a restaurant and people take pictures. I go on a vacation and people come up and introduce themselves. Some things I just don't do any more, like go to the bank, because it's too much trouble. I try to go to the same restaurants and stores, so they are used to me. Every once in a while I will go to a new one and all hell will break loose. Sometimes it's funny and sometimes it's a hassle. But if the tragic loss of being a celebrity is that I don't get to go to baseball games as much as I would like to, that's a price I can pay without much difficulty.'

At an age many people are only just reaching their stride in their chosen careers, Tom has been dancing around the spotlight so long it is easy to overlook his early struggles, both as an actor and as a man.

For he has indeed come a long way. He successfully plotted a path through an emotional minefield to emerge a phenomenon. And he has pretty much found his own way through the maze with little help from anyone else.

It wasn't always an easy journey. For the first time, this book will take Tom's fans along for the ride.

1

A Family Secret

Clutching the wooden deck rail on the rolling ship taking her from everything she knew in England to the perilous promise of the New World, Selina Scoble Ball was suddenly so overcome by a sickening dread that she could scarcely breathe. On the horizon halfway across the Atlantic, she had spied another ship steaming in the opposite direction, returning to the familiar bustle of 1881 London.

It wasn't homesickness. She hadn't been able to wait to start her North American adventure. Nor was she ill, although the cramped, dirty conditions on board made the long journey a griping nightmare for many. The awful truth behind the wrenching heartache that had remained with her as she watched the other ship sail out of sight didn't dawn on Selina until she arrived with her newborn baby and three young children at their destination, more than 3,000 miles from home …

Selina had been in love with the dashing Amos Ball from the moment he tenderly replaced a little locket she was wearing around her neck with one of his own. The discarded locket had been given to Selina by her fiancé in England, before she left to work as a maid for a wealthy family in St Helier, Jersey, in the Channel Islands. But as he clasped the new chain around her neck, Amos laughed: 'Now, I have taken his place.'

The adoring couple married and returned to Devon, where they quickly had three children. It was while Selina was expecting their fourth child that she and Amos decided to try their luck in the burgeoning Americas. He would go on ahead to Canada to find work while she had the baby and sold up their house and property. In time, she would follow Amos out with the rest of the family.

It was a sensible arrangement, the kind of route people follow to this day if they are considering emigrating to an exciting, if uncertain, new life.

But Amos was miserable in Canada on his own. He fretted about his children. He missed his wife. And eventually, he couldn't stand it any longer; he booked a passage back to England on the next ship.

Meanwhile, at home in Newton Abbot, Devon, Selina was finding life without Amos unbearable. There were no problems with the pregnancy and she gave birth to her second son, George. But she desperately missed her husband.

Unable to wait any longer to be with Amos, she ushered the children to London and caught the first ship across the Atlantic.

It was only when Selina arrived in Canada, exhausted from the trip and not knowing a single soul, that she discovered Amos had indeed been on that passing ship she had seen in the middle of the Atlantic Ocean. It would be several more months before he was able to get back to Canada to finally be reunited with his family.

Such a plot could easily come from a Tom Hanks film. A similar story about moonstruck lovers missing each other until the final frame is probably sitting in the actor's in-tray at this very moment, with Meg Ryan's name pencilled in as co-star.

It has everything: love, longing, a large slice of destiny and, of course, a happy ending.

What is so fascinating about this particular romantic farce is that not only is it all true, but it is also how Tom Hanks's family came to America.

The extraordinary addendum to the story is that this is probably the first time Tom has heard about it.

For an actor famed for his thorough and intelligent research into a part, that may seem unusual. But then Tom Hanks is an unusual man.

The first known members of the Hanks family lived in Buckland,

England, in the mid-1400s. Little of the canvas of their lives can be coloured in, but the Hanks family tree, titled 'Bent But Unbroken', provides at least an outline, telling how John Hanks had a son, George, born in 1505, who moved to Malmesbury, Wiltshire. His son, Thomas, was born in 1536, and when he was 34 he had a boy, Thomas II, who moved on to neighbouring Stow.

Thomas, it seems, was a popular name in the Hanks family — a tradition Tom's father was determined to keep — and it was Thomas III, born in Stow sometime before 1630, who set sail in 1653 with his wife, Elizabeth, on the dangerous trip to the New World. Undertaken just 33 years after the *Mayflower* docked in America, the journey would have been painfully slow and uncomfortable. Travelling at a little over three miles an hour, the ship took nearly three months to make the crossing.

Thomas arrived in Virginia with a patent for 'one hundred acres of land situated in Gloucester County in woods upon the north side of a swamp on the east side of the Matapony River.' The Englishman prospered in his new home and became the owner of more than 2,000 acres. He is thought to have had four children, all born in America: William, George, Robert and Peter.

It was William, born in about 1650, who is the central link between Abraham Lincoln and Tom Hanks.

For he had three sons; Luke, William II and John, all born in Richmond, Virginia.

Tom's line in the family dates back to the youngest son, John, born in 1690, a genealogical journey which took eight generations to get to the movie star.

According to evidence compiled by Hanks historian Adin Baber, author of *Nancy Hanks, Destined Mother of a President* and *The Hanks Family Legacy*, John's elder brother, Luke, born 1685, was Abraham Lincoln's great-great-grandfather.

Luke's son, Joseph, born in Kentucky in about 1730, fathered a boy, Abraham, in Carolina when he was 29 years old.

It is said to have been this Abraham's daughter, Nancy Hanks, born in 1784, who was Lincoln's mother. After marrying Thomas Lincoln, she gave birth to the future President on 12 February 1809. 'All that I am, or hope to be, I owe to my Angel mother,' Lincoln is said to have told his law partner.

When Abraham Lincoln was seven, his father, Thomas, had moved the family from Kentucky to Indiana, where he built a one-room cabin. Then just two years later, his mother Nancy died, at the age of 36, from a fever called 'milk-sickness'. The boy carved the pegs for her coffin from green wood and helped bury her in the woods next to a deer run, without the benefit of a funeral.

Neither Nancy nor her husband could read or write and, for a while, the future 16th President of the United States and up to a dozen of his family lived together, crowded into a small, primitive cabin.

Curiously, one of America's most treasured Presidents and one of its most beloved film stars had some interesting parallels in their respective upbringings. Both were separated from their mothers at an early age — Lincoln by death and Tom by divorce — and both were brought up in cramped homes surrounded by step-siblings. The young Abraham Lincoln and his sister would be introduced to their new stepmother without any explanation other than: 'Children, this is your new ma.' Tom and his brothers and sister would have an identical experience when their father remarried. Furthermore, both men would go on to make the most of their meagre beginnings.

While today's politicians and film stars may feel that the scandal sheets are a modern-day invention, Lincoln faced question marks over both his legitimacy and that of his mother. So vicious were the rumours about his own birth that Lincoln sent a commission to Kentucky to find proof of the marriage of his parents. Unfortunately, they went looking in the wrong place and it wasn't until the turn of the century, in 1901, that proof was found that Nancy Hanks and Thomas Lincoln were indeed wed in 1806, three years before Abraham was born. Claims over Nancy's parentage were also rebuffed.

In a very different age, Tom Hanks now shares his time between a £2 million home in exclusive Pacific Pallisades, a luxurious, rambling ocean-front mansion in Malibu close to his friend Steven Spielberg, and a plush apartment in New York. He spares no expense to give his family everything they could possibly need. His four children have travelled first class around the globe with their father on fun-filled holidays and accompany him to exotic film locations.

For Tom's ancestors, however, it was a very different story.

The impish little boy looked close to tears as he walked purposely across the windswept cemetery, studying the names on the carefully tended headstones. It was his first visit to the family burial plot and the usually high-spirited six-year-old seemed particularly struck by the solemn serenity of the graveyard. Stopping at each stone bearing the name of his grandparents and generations of his ancestors, he dropped to one knee and elaborately crossed himself, looking for all the world like he would himself die of grief.

Only after finishing his grave task did the boy allow himself a glance at his watching family. And that proved his undoing. He couldn't help the big smile from destroying the dramatic moment he had created and his father, brother and sister were soon falling about laughing at his antics.

It was Tom Hanks's first performance and a lifelong lesson he would never forget — that he could ease people's pain by making them laugh. The sombre trip to the Hanks burial ground had been transformed into a precious family memory, particularly for Tom's father, Amos, who tried to hide the feelings of anger and resentment that were stirred every time he went back to the cemetery by Thomes Creek in the small northern California outpost of Paskenta.

To Tom, big brother Larry, then nine, and sister Sandra, 12, the trip brought to life a colourful family history that had always been something of a mystery to them. But Amos had his own reasons back then for keeping some of the family secrets from his young children.

The oldest headstone in the Hanks burial plot at Paskenta marks the grave of Tom's great-grandfather Daniel Boone Hanks, who was born in 1847 and joined the pioneer trail west from his home in Kentucky in 1873 with his wife, Mary Catherine. His granddaughter, Wanda Hanks Morning, submitted a letter written by her mother to the Hanks family history describing the gruelling journey to pre-Hollywood California.

It reads:

'In 1873 they came across the plains with oxen and six horses. They were six months on the way. They came across Donner Pass and first settled in or near Bakersfield. Mary Catherine got malaria so they went to Modoc County. At that time there was just one small store the size of a small room in Cedarville and it sold everything. The building is still standing in a small park.

'Daniel and Mary decided to go back to Missouri and got as far as Flournoy, Tehama County. They were to travel with a group of people. Everything was arranged to leave a certain day and two of Daniel's horses got sick. They had sold the oxen. They were camped just west of the Flournoy bridge near the creek. They had to stay, so they went to live on small cabin on the sheep-shearing place and spent the winter there. They were told about 160 acres with a one-room cabin on it and they moved there and filed papers to homestead. All they had to start house keeping were several large wooden boxes, barrels, bedding and their dishes and cooking utensils.

'Daniel made a table and benches out of some of the boxes. One of the barrels was used for the flour with a heavy board on top for a work table.

'At first they cooked outside on a campfire. The beds were small oak trees cut down and put in the corners of the room, then laced back and forth with buckskin for springs. Their big ticking bags were filled with wild straw for mattresses ...

'They killed deer and quail and cotton tails for fresh meat and got fish in season from Stoney Creek. The first cow was just a calf when Mary got it and she worked for a lady who had a baby to pay for it. This is also the way they got their first two pigs ...

In spite of their tough times, Daniel and Catherine still found time to have 14 children. It was the fate of their eighth child, Tom's grandfather Ernest Beauel Hanks, that has caused so much anguish to the family that it lingers on even now.

Visiting Paskenta Cemetery that day in 1963 with his own three children, this was one particular story that Amos Hanks kept to himself. The painful memories had almost reduced him to tears before Tom's graveside performance broke the spell drawing him back to his childhood.

It would be years before Amos finally told his children that their grandfather had been murdered.

And, with a romantic yearning for the kind of rough justice lauded in books by his heroes Ernest Hemingway and Jack London, he went to his grave wishing he had been able to avenge his father's untimely death.

Members of the family had been slightly taken aback when Ernest Beauel, known as 'the fastest sack sewer in the Sacramento Valley', married elegant, well-educated librarian Gladys Hilda Ball in rural Willows, California, in 1915.

The schoolmarm with a rebellious streak had long had her eye on the handsome man who drove a horse to class, and who also happened to be the brother of her landlady. She had gone to the World's Fair in San Francisco early in 1915 and unbeknownst to her, Ernest had decided on a whim to go the same day. It was one of only two times he ever left the Willows area — the other time was a cattle drive to the neighbouring state of Nevada. Although they spent the day apart, the unlikely couple met up on train on the way home and Ernest plucked up the courage to ask for a date.

Her rather snooty siblings insisted Gladys was mistaken in agreeing to marry the local 'hillbilly' and the expectant bride was almost forced to agree on the day of her wedding. For the groom wasn't just minutes or hours late for the service — he was two whole days late!

Ernest had been hunting in the mountains with a friend, who had fallen and badly hurt himself. Knowing he couldn't leave the wounded man behind, even to get to his own wedding, he slowly carried the man down to safety. When he was finally able to get to a telephone, which he had never used before, he managed to get word through to Gladys. According to him, she fainted when she heard his voice. According to her, she told him: 'The wedding is just waiting for the groom!'

After tying the knot and celebrating at an aunt's house, the strapping farmer and his well-to-do, bespectacled bride settled happily into married life and had four children; Gladys Hilda, Ernest Beauel II, Amos Mefford and Mary Catherine.

Ernest struck up a friendship with Elisha Best, the former superintendent of the county hospital, and they worked together in the fields for almost 17 years. But their partnership came to a tragic end on the afternoon of 14 May 1935. According to a local newspaper report, the two men were working together digging hay on the Lester Killebrew Ranch in Willows when they got into a fiery argument over the horse team pulling their hay wagon.

The *Willows Daily Journal* recounted the fight, saying Hanks, who was on the wagon, jumped on Best's back and knocked him down. 'Best got up and warned Hanks not to get near him. He grabbed a pitchfork,' it reported. 'But Hanks made a rush for him and Best hit him with the pitchfork handle.

'Hanks sank to his knees and then got up and made another rush. Best hit him again. Hanks said: "You have drawn blood. I am going to have you arrested." Hanks got into the wagon and started for the house. Best climbed into the wagon and started driving. Hanks fell into the hay.'

When the wagon arrived back at the Hanks' house, Amos, then just eleven, was on his own with his sister Mary. Their father stumbled to the front door with blood gushing from his head wound as Best told the children: 'We just had a little scrap.'

By the time a Dr J.L. Rowhauser had arrived, Hanks had sunk into a coma, from which he ever recovered, and died four hours later from loss of blood. He was just 45.

But the trauma of watching his father die in front of him was just the beginning of the ordeal for Amos. For what the Hanks family thought would be a straightforward murder trial turned out to be anything but. Best was tried in court three times and Amos was a witness in the first two trials. The jury couldn't reach a verdict in the first hearing and brought a manslaughter verdict in the second. Finally, with Amos and his mother watching helplessly in the public gallery, Best was acquitted in the third trial.

The decision shocked and infuriated the young Amos. In his unpublished autobiography, he wrote: 'In the last days of his trial they seemed to be trying my father rather than his killer. They made much of the fact that he was not a man known for his piety or politeness.

'My father was misrepresented as some sort of monster by the defense attorney.'

The boy was so angered by the injustice he threatened to shoot Best, saying he would gladly swap his freedom to protect his dead father's good name, and his mother was worried enough to send Amos to stay with relations in another town at the end of the trial.

Best, he argued, was in his 60s, while his father was 'strong and agile.' Hanks had collapsed before being able to give his version and Amos remained convinced it could not have been a fair fight.

'It was a tough time for the family,' said Amos's elder sister, Hilda. 'I was 17 and it happened just before I graduated from high school, but my mother had to bring up myself and the three younger children by herself. My little sister was only eight when dad died.

'Amos, or Bud as we always called him, had to testify at a trial at 11 years old. Now all the children in a school would get counselling if something terrible like that happened. It was bound to effect him.

'Tom's father had very strong feelings about Best not being convicted. Bud was a very intense person and couldn't forgive easily.'

Hanks's widow went on to be elected county tax collector in Willows, serving for three terms, and had a leg amputated before she died in 1966. She is buried alongside her husband in Paskenta Cemetery.

It was Gladys's parents, Amos and Selina Ball, who had left England towards the end of the 19th century on that farcical, sublimely romantic Atlantic ocean journey which opens this chapter. The roots of the Ball side of Tom's family warrant further investigation, both because they make fascinating reading and because of the obvious legacy they bestowed upon Tom.

Amos Ball, Tom's great-grandfather, was born in Launceston, Cornwall on 13 May 1849, and left as a young boy to live in the relatively prosperous Channel Islands in Jersey. He grew up to become a local preacher in the Jersey Young Man's Christian Association and worked in a bakery. At the age of 14, he was thrown from the baker's cart he used to deliver bread to Elizabeth Castle and cut his face so badly that he wore a beard for most of his life to cover the scar. He later worked as a French translator.

When he was 25, he married a young maid whose heart he set out to win with long romantic walks along the beach — even though she was already engaged to a suitor back home in England. Her acceptance of his locket, as described already, signified her changed allegiance and the handsome couple was married in St Helier in 1874.

After the wedding, the Balls moved back to the mainland and settled in Kingsweek, Devon, where Amos worked for the Great Western Railway between 1874 and 1875. They moved on to Newton Abbott, Devon, the following year and Amos went back to working in a bakery.

By this time they already had three children: Amos II, Blanche and Elsie, and a fourth, George, was on his way. Still young, adventurous and madly in love, Amos and Selina decided to try their luck in the Americas, where they had been told they would be able to own their own land.

When they finally met up in Canada, in a small town along the coast, they were informed that there were better opportunities further south in America and given a contact to head for in Toledo, Iowa, where they hoped to open their own store. Unfortunately there was yet another mishap on the journey when they were misdirected and ended up in Toledo, *Ohio*, where once again they knew nobody, and so had to uproot and start off once more for Iowa.

Having opened a small feed store in the *right* Toledo, Amos and Selina settled down to have another three children: Evelyn, John Wesley and Gladys Hilda, Tom's great-grandmother. Another two girls, Lucy Emily and Violet Pinkham, died during childbirth

'I think that they had a very romantic life together,' said Tom's

Aunt Hilda. 'I am the only one left who can remember my grandfather very clearly. He would tell stories about what happened in England and talk about grandmother.'

There was never very much money, but the family always had enough food and soon became a popular fixture in Toledo. Even then, Amos was opposed to the use of tobacco, but he sold it nevertheless as it was one of the most sought after products at his shop, which had become a popular meeting place for the local farm community.

The children, particularly Amos II, had hated working in the store, but they weren't given any choice. Eventually Amos left, going on to become Vice President of Standard Oil of Indiana. His son, George, would become an Under Secretary of State and work for the United Nations. Blanche, the eldest daughter, married the brother of the famous heavyweight boxer 'Gentleman' Jim Corbett.

When Selina fell ill there was little anyone could do for her in the small town and she went to Chicago, where she died in 1907. Heartbroken over his wife's death, Amos decided to move across to California where several sisters were by now settled, having themselves emigrated from England.

Closing down his feed and grocery store in 1914, he travelled west with several of his children for the tiny Northern California outpost of Willows, a day's ride from the state capital of Sacramento. Maria, his spinster sister from England, was to meet them there and help care for her widowed brother, who had made just enough money from the sale of his shop to retire in relative comfort.

Maria, once a dressmaker for Alfred Lord Tennyson's sisters, ruled the roost in her new-found home with an iron will, insisting that the children and grandchildren being raised as English gentlewomen. 'My mother was the next-to-youngest in the family and they would all have to drink their tea just right and hold their napkins the correct way. It was a very proper upbringing,' said Hilda.

Gladys had remained in Iowa where she had a teaching position, but she followed her father to California, where she got a job at the Flournoy School in Willows. After she was married, her father and Maria moved in with them, living there for more than a decade before moving to Long Beach, Southern California, to the home of his eldest daughter, where he lived out his final years, still with Maria at his side. He was buried alongside Selina in Toledo, Iowa.

With four adults — Amos, Maria, Ernest, Gladys — and four children — Hilda, Ernest, Amos, Mary — squeezed in, the house was very cramped. There was no hot water, no telephone, just one large room upstairs and two downstairs with the kitchen slotted into a section of the porch.

'My mother was always a rebel and grandfather loved that about her,' said Hilda. 'Nevertheless, we were all raised in a very proper way too. She was a responsible rebel. Dad was a very good-looking, debonair man. My brothers were extremely fond of father, and so was my sister, but I didn't feel so close to him. I was closer to my mother. Tom's father and I were more Ball than Hanks.

'Mother was a wonderful Christian woman, but dad didn't have any interest at all. It wasn't until I started going to high school that dad started going to church.'

Hilda added: 'My brother Amos was different than the rest of us. He was a rebel from the church. He said he had been spoon-fed religion and blamed mother for forcing it on him.

'In those days, children did as they were told. But as soon as Bud was old enough to go his own way, he went his own way.

'Watching Tom now, it is very clear to me where he came from.'

Always a dreamer and an avid reader, Amos — or Bud as he was known to his friends and family for the rest of his life — tried his hand at a string of occupations, including logging, ranching, writing and an enforced spell in the US Navy during World War II, when he served in the New Hebrides Islands, near Australia. Returning to California, he went back to college, determined to graduate and become a writer. To help pay for his studies he would work in restaurants and bars in the California Bay area and planned to save enough money to go to Australia and write for a living.

But while working in a small restaurant in the college town of Berkeley, just across the bay from San Francisco, Amos met a pretty young waitress called Janet Frager, from nearby Livermore. Within a year they had eloped to Reno, Nevada, and married on 4 September 1950. Less than a year later, on 30 July 1951, their daughter, Sandra Lynn, was born.

His dreams of a new life in Australia dashed by the responsibility of providing for his young family, Amos threw himself into the catering business, working long hours to build a reputation as one of the best paid chefs in Northern California.

The couple's first son, Lawrence, was born in Livermore on 26 January 1953. Amos was a chef at the Sea Wolf in Oakland, turning over 200 tables at dinner each night, when three years later, on 9 July 1956, in Concord, California, they had a second boy, Thomas Jeffrey.

The family moved north to Redding, where Amos got a job as chef-owner of the food operation in one of the town's larger hotels. To outsiders at least, everything seemed calm in the Hanks household, and Amos and Janet did their best to keep their arguments from the children. A snapshot taken at the Hanks family reunion in 1961, with little Tommy wearing a cowboy hat, offers no clue to the domestic turmoil between the parents.

The birth of a fourth child, Jimmy, later that year on 15 June did nothing to ease the strain.

But it was all about to change. After ten years of marriage, Amos and Janet had reached breaking point. And Tom Hanks was to discover that his first five years would be the most stable period of his extremely unconventional childhood.

HANKS PEDIGREE CHART

John Hanks
b. 1470 in Buckland, England

George Hanks
b. 1505 in Malmesbury, England

Thomas Hanks
b. 1536 in Malmesbury, England

Thomas Hanks II
b. 1570 in Stowe, England

Thomas Hanks III
b. bef. 1630 in Stowe, England

William I
b. about 1650 in Richmond Co., VA

SONS OF WILLIAM I

Luke Hanks
b. about 1685 in Richmond Co., VA.

William Hanks
b. 14 Feb 1679

John Hanks
b. 1690 in Richmond Co., VA.

Joseph Hanks
b. about 1730 in KY.

John Hanks II
b. 4 May 1728 in Richmond Co., VA.

Abraham Hanks
b. about 1759 in North Carolina

Abner Hanks
b. 1763 in Richmond Co., VA.

Nancy Hanks
b. 5 February 1784

Capt. Thomas Hanks
b. 11 March 1791 in KY.

Abraham Lincoln
b. 12 February 1809

Thomas Hanks
b. 5 May 1819

Daniel Boone Hanks
b. 10 September 1847 in KY.

Ernest Beauel Hanks I
b. 1890 in Flournoy, Tehama Co., CA.

Amos Mefford Hanks
b. 4 March 1924 in Willows, Glenn Co., CA.

THOMAS JEFFREY 'TOM' HANKS
b. 9 July 1956 in Concord, CA.

2

A Broken Family

A ll Tom Hanks can remember about the night his cozy world caved in was wanting to take all the toys in his closet when his father knocked on his bedroom door and told him to gather his belongings. He was told he could only take one or two, and to hurry into the pick-up truck his father had parked in the driveway outside the family's Redding house.

Amos had left the home abruptly a month earlier without telling the children where he was going. In fact, he had gone to Reno, Nevada, to get a quickie divorce. His long working hours had taken their toll on the marriage, but relatives blamed Janet for the final split. Tom's uncle, Loyal Brummet, a 73-year-old retired San Francisco bus driver, recalled: 'Amos loved his first wife, but he couldn't forgive her for running around. He gave her three or four opportunities, but it didn't work.'

An apparently still bitter Amos wrote in his memoirs: 'Chronically dissatisfied and agog with the blandishments of one more in a series of attentive admirers, she decided, or was persuaded, that she would prefer to be separated not only from me, but also, within a few weeks, from the children.'

Now Amos had returned for the kids, having found a new job at the Mapes Hotel in Reno, a celebrity hotspot at the time, and a small basement apartment. Still unaware of what was happening, first Sandra, then Larry and little Tommy threw what few belongings they could carry into the back of the truck and drove off into the night with their father. The youngest child, Jimmy, then just a few months old, was to stay with his mother.

'Separating the children was not what I wanted to do,' wrote Amos later,' but needing some vestige of responsible parenthood to cling to, she would not have given Jimmy up easily.

'I had neither the time nor the money to fight with her for his custody even if I had a way to care for him. The older three were hampering her in her new life. Sandra was ten, Larry was eight and Tom was five.'

The Hanks children never were told their parents' marriage was over. But arriving in Reno in the early hours of the morning on 23 February 1962, they stopped outside a large corner house at 529 Mill Street, in a down-at-heel neighbourhood near an old brothel. Ushering them into the dusty basement flat, Amos told them: 'Welcome to your new home.'

The tiny, 600-square-foot apartment was owned by mother-of-eight Winifred Finley, who lived upstairs and had herself been left to bring five children up alone after her marriage failed. Her three older children had already married and left home and she desperately needed money to supplement her wages as a bookkeeper at the Guy Reade department store in Reno. So when she met Amos through her next-door neighbour, who worked at the same hotel as the cook, she offered him her basement to rent.

Both 38, with eight kids to care for between them, Winifred and Amos quickly became friends and then lovers. Shaken by the belated failures of their first attempts at marriage, they turned to each other for comfort at a particularly difficult time in their lives.

Besides, Amos needed someone to take care of his kids.

Amos was again spending long hours at work as the Mapes expanded to become the world's first hotel/casino. As well as running the catering operation, he served personal meals to such big stars as Judy Garland, who performed there, and Marilyn Monroe and Clark Gable, who stayed at the hotel while filming *The Misfits*.

As the youngest, Tommy couldn't be left alone at home for long hours and was booked into the Holy Child Day Care Center, a nursery run by nuns on Reno Avenue, close to the neon lights and round-the-clock action of the casino district.

Wayne Melton, now a society and entertainment columnist for the *Reno Gazette Journal*, went to nursery school with Tom. 'It was run by Catholic Irish nuns and it was pretty strict. They used to slap me and Tom on the hand when we misbehaved.

'Tom and I were little buddies and we used to get into a little bit of trouble together. Tom used to spend the whole day there while his father was at work. We were both five years old — I am one month older than Tom — and he was always great fun and rather mischievous. We were always goofing around. He was very energetic and had a great sense of humour.

'His older brother also went to the school. I remember Tom was from a home where they didn't have very much. I know there was quite a number of children, but he moved away before I got to know him any better.'

Holy Child teacher Bonnie Miller, now in her seventies, remembers Tom being a very curious boy and 'a little devil.'

On 19 April 1962, a Judge Thomas Craven granted Amos a divorce from Janet on the grounds of 'extreme mental cruelty'.

Divorce records in Reno show Amos gave all 'community property' to his ex-wife, claiming she treated him with 'a coldness and indifference' and starved him of love and affection.

Asked whether they quarreled, he answered: 'We did.'

Did she complain and criticise? 'She did,' he replied.

Was this continuous? 'It was.'

Was it difficult to do anything to please her? 'Impossible, I would say.'

Quizzed over the effect of the marred relationship on his health, Amos added: 'I have never experienced any sort of breakdown but it was detrimental.'

It made you extremely nervous? 'It did.'

On the same day, Winifred was granted her divorce from railway worker Theo Finley, the father of her eight children, and four days later, on 23 April 1962, she married Amos at the Reno Register Office with the kids all watching on, wondering how their lives had so quickly been turned upside down.

In the space of two short months, Tom, Larry and Sandra had a new home, a new mother and five new brothers and sisters. And still nobody had actually sat them down and explained how it came about. Tom said later that he felt 'lonely and in the dark' over the dramatic changes he was forced through.

But, at first at least, it all seemed to work out. Tom, in particular, got special treatment as the 'baby' of the brood. His stepbrothers and sisters, Melissa, Maureen, Norma, Debra and Jon helped take care of him and all eight children shared an 8 foot-by-18 foot bedroom in the basement, using curtains as dividers.

There were so many children running around that they were all given a number so their parents would know they hadn't left anyone behind. Tom was number eight.

'Suddenly, it was like, bang, zoom! — and there were kids all around,' recalled Tom in a 1989 *Playboy* interview. 'We were total strangers, all thrust together. I remember in school we had to draw a picture of our house and family and I ran out of places to put people. I put them on the roof. I drew dad in bed, sleeping, since he worked so hard in the restaurant.'

He added later: 'There was a stepbrother and four stepsisters whom I would not recognise now if they walked into a room. Then there were three or more step siblings in another place. It seemed like there was always someone new coming or going. It was the odd, '60s dysfunctional version of the extended family.

'When he and she split up, I never saw those people again.'

At the time of the wedding, Melissa was 13, Maureen, 12, Norma, 11, Debra, ten and Jon was eight.

'It was just like the *Brady Bunch*,' said Jon, now a father-of-four who works for the fire department in Richland, Washington. 'When that programme came out, we were saying, "That was us!" It was chaotic — but it was fun too.'

Winifred, in her 70s and suffering from a serious heart condition, always had a soft spot for little Tommy. 'When we were first married, I remember Tom coming in and jumping on my lap and saying, "So you're my new mum, eh?"'

The house in Mill Street had the same shabby appearance as most homes in the working-class neighbourhood and the big basement bedroom, with its tatty, worn-out carpet, became the ideal stage for Tom to follow up his cemetery acting debut.

The other children's shining faces would collapse with laughter at his antics. So they happily encouraged the five-year-old to think up more sketches and plays. Suddenly, he had an audience.

Said Winifred: 'My kids would love to put on shows, but it was always Tom who was the star. He had something that was very special ... and you could see it even then. The others would be captivated. Tom was a ham from the start. Even then, you could see where his future lay. It was definitely in his nature and he was wise enough to develop it when he got older.'

The oldest stepsister, Melissa, now a married mother-of-six living in Auburn, California, said: 'We all took care of Tommy. He was a sweet, friendly little kid.

'We used to do little plays and sketches and Tommy was right in there among us. It was only a small place. There were two bedrooms upstairs and the basement was filled up with kids. We used to pretend there was a 100-year-old man in the basement and Tom would get as scared as the rest of us. We all got along great as kids.'

Winifred now lives in Carewood, Idaho, with her third husband, Grady Martinez, who used to work with Amos at the Reno hotel.

She said: 'When I met Tom's father he had just separated from his wife. We were both in a pinch at the time. I was single and raising five kids and I had gone to Reno to get a divorce. We met through the next-door-neighbour, a lady who worked with Mr. Hanks at the hotel. She said, "There is this man who I am working with and he needs a place to live. Why don't you rent him the basement?"

'I kept saying I didn't want anybody in the house. But when we met we hit it off right away and he moved in there and then. I think he needed me at the time. As soon as we realised we had something to work on, he brought the children up from Redding to Reno. He brought the children to me because he needed a place for them. Tom was five.'

After a while, the new family left the cramped house in Reno for a more spacious home in Pleasant Hills, California.

'When we moved to Pleasant Hills there was a ton of kids in the neighbourhood,' recalled Jon. 'Larry was very quick and I was the scrapper. There was a lot of lads around and we'd all look after Tommy. I remember saving his bacon in the neighbourhood a few times.

'It was a small house with only three bedrooms. I remember mum and Bud converted the garage into a room for us boys. I remember in pillow fights I used to pick on Tommy and pound on his chest — perhaps that's why he has never called!'

'Their dad was a pretty good guy, but he always tried to keep us kind of separate.'

'Tommy would have Larry and I in stitches. He would really make us laugh. He had this way of getting what he wanted. Tommy was always theatrical. He was the little kid who knew how to push all the right buttons. He was just a natural '60s kid growing up.'

But as the honeymoon period wore off, the cracks in Amos and Winifred's rebound relationship began to show.

Winifred had become a Mormon while married to Amos and that soon became a source of conflict with her new husband, who was suspicious of religion in most forms. 'When we met his kids were Catholic and mine were Protestant and that had its difficulties,' said Winifred. 'Then I became enamoured of the Mormon Church and Mr Hanks didn't.

'It was funny because the kids enjoyed going to church. But after we had split up, Mr Hanks and I were at a friend's wedding and Tom ran up to me and said, "Mum, mum, guess what? I'm not a Mormon any more. Now I am a darned old Catholic!"'

She went on: 'Tom got on very well with my children. But Sandy felt the loss of her mother. To her I was always an intruder.

'Larry was much quieter than Tom, but he would hold his own. I don't think anything was really difficult for Tom. He was one who could roll with the punches.'

The inevitable end, when it came, was just as dramatic and abrupt as Amos's first marriage collapse. He said only that he married 'hurriedly'. But, once again, the Hanks family saw Amos as the victim. 'The second marriage was like jumping from the frying pan into the fire,' said Amos's brother-in-law Loyal Brummet. 'It was never going to last. In the end, Bud got right out of that one.'

Winifred remembers things differently. A self-educated man and an avid reader, Amos was determined to give his own children the best education possible. He had no such aspirations for his stepchildren and remained distant and slightly aloof from them throughout the short-lived marriage.

Said Winifred: 'I loved Tom's father and he loved me. We needed each other very much. We had a wonderful time together. When I broke up with him it was heart-rending for everyone.

'It was very hard for Bud to be married to me because he couldn't see how he was going to send all eight children to college ... and education was very important to him.

'I understand why my marriage to Tom's father didn't work out and there was never any bitterness over him leaving with his children. I had the greatest respect for him.

'I did worry about Tom and Larry and Sandy after they had gone, but I knew they were in good hands.

'Some reports I have read make it seem like Tom's father was some kind of itinerant cook. But that was not true. He was the best at what he did. He ran big hotels and banqueting halls. He was very highly regarded and a very intelligent man.'

The marriage had lasted less than two years when Amos once again instructed his three children to gather together their belongings and climb in the truck. Although the scenario was no longer novel to Tom, Larry or Sandra, it was no less unsettling. With the possible exception of Sandra, they had made friends, tried their best to put down some new roots and found solace in the topsy-turvy world of a big family. Tom felt strongly enough to call Winifred 'mum', and she in turn felt very protective of the baby of her extended family.

Tom's stepbrother and stepsisters were deeply shocked at the sudden parting.

'We missed him when he went,' said Melissa. 'It was kind of abrupt. They went just like that and we didn't really see Tom again. My mother never told us why they left and I haven't talked to him since he was six years old.

'I liked Bud. He wasn't really warm, but he was always there to answer questions. He wasn't unpleasant as a stepfather.

'I hadn't really thought of Tommy for years and I was watching the TV show *Bosom Buddies* one night when I realised it was Tommy on the screen. Now I have got most of his movies. I am proud of him. I guess he is our one claim to fame. I would like to talk to him about what it was like living in Reno back then and all of the things we used to do.'

Added Jon: 'I know mum used to worry about the kids after she split up with Bud. I was told that Tom's favourite sandwich is still peanut butter, mayonnaise and lettuce. I don't know if he remembers, but that was my favourite sandwich and I used to make them for him too.

'I remember it being a good time for all of us. Our mum really was a good mum to Tommy, Larry and Sandra. She treated them exactly as if they were her own. The way he is acting now is a testament to how he was brought up. Growing up he has been able to maintain his perspective.'

Winifred would dearly love to speak to the former stepson she hasn't seen or heard from since shortly after the breakdown of her marriage to Amos in 1964. Until this interview, she had never spoken publicly of her days as Tom Hanks's 'mum'.

Tom has never made any attempt to contact his 'secret' family and has been dismissive of them in interviews. Asked by the American entertainment magazine US in 1984 whether it was a Brady Bunch home, he replied: 'Oh, nooo. I wouldn't remember their names if they showed their faces today.'

In another interview, he said: 'My first stepmother was somewhat flaky. Her love of the Mormon Church was just one of the reasons I think dad left her. Dad did kind of rebel against it. She's not a Mormon now. She's probably into astrology or something.'

Just in case she was in any doubt, Winifred was saddened by a more direct snub when she tried to get in touch with Tom. 'I wrote to Tom through his agent, but I didn't hear from him.

'Then I heard him say on TV that so many people tried to bother him and claim they were related. I didn't want to be thought a nuisance.'

With her ailing heart, Winifred is resigned to never seeing Tom again. But she follows his career closely from afar. 'We want him to understand that we don't want anything from him. We just want to tell him how proud we are of him. I suppose we are the missing link in his family. My current husband even knew Tom as a boy because he used to work with Mr Hanks.

'I would love to be able to see him and talk to him again after all these years. But I understand he must be very busy with his own life. I respect his privacy. I have always kept a very close eye on how Tom was doing. We are all very proud of what he has done with his life. He appears to be such a nice man. I'm very glad how things turned out for him. And he doesn't really look a lot different today to the way he looked all those years ago.

'Before he died, Amos phoned me and asked if I was surprised that Tom was doing so well as an actor.

'I told him, "I am not surprised at all. Tom was always the star of the family."'

3

Home Alone

'Did you hear what the little creep said?' Sandra shouted scornfully from the back of the car. 'Tommy heard a stupid bird and he said, "Hark, a mourning dove!"'

While his brother and sister made fun of this latest example of young Tom's thespian affectations, he was very pleased with himself. He amused himself for the rest of the 100-mile journey to his mother's home by working the line for all it was worth. 'After that, it was, "Hark, a big red truck. Hark, some cows in a field. Hark, I have to go to the bathroom,"' remembered his father, who titled his typed-out memoirs 'Hark, A White Mule.'

The children also had a portentous game they would like to play. 'We based it on Disneyland,' recalled Sandra, 'with the brothers playing paparazzi and Tom playing the obnoxious star. It was just another home movie, but it was fun.'

Throughout his childhood, Tom would spend most of the holidays and periodic weekends with his mother and younger brother at their modest house in Red Bluff, Northern California. If he was working, Amos would drop the three children off at the bus stop in Oakland and their mother would be waiting for them at the other end. Otherwise, he would drive them upstate, going on to stay with relatives in Paskenta while the children spent some time with their mother, who was still working as a waitress. Although Janet married three more times, she at least remained in the same area and this offered some small stability to her increasingly nomadic elder children. Pressed on his 'hometown', Tom will often say Red Bluff, recalling bike rides down to the Sacramento River and stops at the Foster Freeze ice cream shop on the way home. But, in truth, his relationship with his mother was never close and the visits to Red Bluff would, if anything, underline he fractures in the family that were magnified by the fact that Jimmy lived there all the time.

One visit ended in floods of tears when Sandra, nearing puberty, heard Jimmy giving his mother's surname at the time as his own, forsaking the Hanks name. As the baby of the family, Jim would often be the brunt of his sister and brothers ill humour. He complained later that Tom was an unlikely 'bruiser' as a boy, picking on him so much that when he locked Jimmy in the wardrobe, as was his wont, it came as a relief to the smaller child because it meant he couldn't hit him any more. Such dramas were not unusual.

Janet tried her best to make her wandering children feel at home on their visits. She would paint eggs with them at Easter and organise hunts in the garden and around the house, paying the eager egg seekers 50 cents a time for finding the hidden prizes. At Christmas, she would make sure there was turkey with all the trimmings. Tom had a Christmas stocking with his name on it hung over the fireplace.

'He was always entertaining,' she recalled. 'During his visits he would turn a sock into a puppet and put on a little show. When he said something cute and adults reacted to it with amusement, he'd repeat it endlessly, milking the line for all it was worth. Tom had a natural love of the limelight.'

Tom would never be close to his mother, but Janet did the best she could in difficult circumstances, ensuring the children all knew she loved them, even if she wasn't always there for them. In return, Tom held kinder memories of Janet than his father had of his first wife, saying later: 'Essentially, my dad could afford and wanted to have the kids and mum couldn't. She could really only afford to have the baby at the time.'

Meanwhile, the Hanks children were back on the move with their father. Leaving behind their stepfamily for good, they were taken to live with Amos's strongly religious sister, the late Mary Brummet, and her husband, Loyal.

For Tom, used to the freedom and anonymity of a big, loose pseudo-family, it was a difficult period. Aunt Mary was a devout Nazarene and the children's antics were often at odds with her strict faith, an orthodox Wesleyan Christian church with a hard-line doctrine. 'That's a pretty hard-line religious thing,' Tom told *Première* magazine in 1989. 'We weren't allowed to watch the *Three Stooges*; there were an awful lot of rules … awfully long prayers.'

And there wasn't a lot of space. Tom's grandmother and his two nephews were already living in the four-bedroomed house in San Mateo, California, so Amos slept in a trailer in the back garden and the children shared a bed.

'They came to live with my wife and I for a while before Bud got an apartment,' said widower Loyal, who was married for 48 years. 'But it was rather crowded.

'Tom was very close to his dad. All the kids were. Bud worked very hard, but he always took care of his kids.'

The family moved after a couple of months to the first in a long succession of tatty flats in the Bay area. 'We moved about every six months,' said Tom. 'We must have moved a million times.' For a period of two-and-a-half years, the Hanks children pretty much raised themselves. There was little parental guidance or discipline, no one to ask for advice, no directions through the minefield of puberty.

For most of that time, they were home alone.

Like many single parents, Amos was caught in a dilemma. Determined to take good care of his children and obsessed with ensuring they had every chance of a good education, he had to work long hours to pay the bills. The price he paid was having barely enough time to spend with them once he was home, a Catch 22 he was painfully aware of when he decided to leave his second wife.

'Leaving was going to require new measures of self-sufficiency on the part of the kids. I would be working long hours. They would be alone,' he wrote. 'People expressed surprised disappointment that I didn't hire a housekeeper or a baby-sitter, but the kids didn't want to have any outsiders among us. I didn't either.

'They ate a lot of cold cereals, TV dinners and canned soup. The milkman had a key to the apartment and maintained the inventory at six quarts (years later I heard about milk-drinking competitions in our kitchen).'

While their father worked, Tom, Larry and Sandra took care of themselves, doing their own cooking, their own cleaning and laundry, their homework if and when they felt like it, watching whatever bad TV shows they chose and dealing with any crisis that may have arisen.

Inevitably, Tom was alone a lot of the time and suffered from a sense of loneliness that remains with him to this day. But it is the one part of his childhood he seems to remember fondly in interviews. Perhaps the funny sitcom-style stories of growing up without any parents around appeals more to his self-protective comic skills than the more serious, long-buried memories of deeply felt abandonment.

He told *Playboy*: 'We liked it because it was the first time we had lived alone with our dad. There were these TV shows like *Bachelor Father* that showed kids living with their father in this neat home. We used to think they were crazy. We lived in these ripped-up, stained apartments that we completely destroyed in the course of living there. And we had no Philippine house boy.'

But it was one of the many moves, this time to Oakland, that Tom recalled really growing up. He was nine at the time. 'Dad would work until 10 o'clock, so we were on our own,' he continued. 'We made our own dinners, which was more comical than anything else. I remember throwing away frozen peas and carrots and spinach so dad would think we'd eaten them. We'd burn a steak and have some bread with it and make some instant mashed potatoes and that would be our dinner. I still can't eat tomato soup because of the constant smell of burned tomato soup that hovered over our electric stove.

'We gained something from our lack of nutrition. We learned a lot, we became really independent. We did our own laundry. We supposedly had to keep the house clean, though it never was. That house was a shambles, too, by the time we left. We were completely unsupervised, but we got into surprisingly little trouble.'

Tom had similar tales of kitchen chaos for *Première*, saying: 'Culinary experts we were not. We were always supposed to have the four basic food groups, of which we would have maybe one by the time we ate the meal. That meant frozen packages of peas that we would eat plain. We didn't know about sauces or butter or spices or things like that. And brussel sprouts — you know how they look like the brains of rats? Roll 'em over on their sides and they kinda look elongated, like you can almost see the skull encasing? I can't eat that stuff, just because for about two-and-a-half years, that was all there was.'

But, as he confessed, the premature freedom he enjoyed came at some emotional cost.

With his inquiring, understated intelligence, Larry was the inventor, collecting and squirreling away anything that set off his curiosity. At that time, Larry was also the comedian in the family. His famous brother would say years later: 'People used to say, "Tom's loud." And then they would say, "But Larry — Larry's funny." I used to steal the stuff Larry said at the dinner table and take it to school the next day and get a laugh out of it.' Sandra, bright and energetic, was just discovering the endless temptations of being a teenager in the late '60s. As the oldest, she was usually the sibling with the last word. Sandra was always the leader, devising games and ultimately ruling over who won or lost. As Tom would later attest, she was the sibling who held the boys' childhood together with her strength of character. As a result of Amos's long hours at work, it was Sandra who effectively brought up the two elder Hanks boys.

For Tom, there was always the television. It was switched on around the clock and, when he wasn't at school, Tom was a fixture in front of it, devouring everything from sappy comedies to cooking programmes to lengthy documentaries.

His long hours in front of the baby-sitting box gave him an encyclopaedic TV brain. The *Apollo* space programme became an obsession — an infatuation he was to put to good use in true *Boy's Own* fashion in the film *Apollo 13* and his self-produced television series *From the Earth to the Moon* — and he refused to miss a single moment of the extensive coverage. He coveted all 26 episodes of *The World at War*. Even now, he can describe the six-panel black-and-white logo for one of his early-60s favourites, *Biography*, which was illustrated with thumbnail pictures of Einstein, Gandhi, Greta

Garbo, Winston Churchill, Franklin D. Roosevelt and baseball hero Babe Ruth. He watched *Fireball XL-5*, the *Batman* TV show, and Jacques Costeau, and devoured the Charlton Heston and Burt Lancaster epics when they eventually reached the small screen.

He still remembers sitting absolutely still for three-and-a-half hours watching Kurosawa's *The Seven Samurai*, his eyes transfixed by the subtitles and the scope of the film classic.

Tom was part of probably the first generation to have its political and social views coloured by television. And there were some subjects that struck home more deeply than others. 'There was always a vicious imbalance between two prevailing images of marriage,' he told *GQ* magazine in 1988. 'One was the fucking commercials, where marriage was waffle irons and "Love — American Style", and there was the reality of growing up in post-war America when my folks were divorced.

'I remember in grammar school and junior high, there were very few kids who came from multiple marriages, who had more than one mother and step siblings. No one at school knew about that stuff.

'I don't think you can have children at an early age and enjoy them the way they are enjoyed on fucking TV commercials. It was the same for my father — he turned around and he had all these kids and he said, "Jesus Christ holy cow ..."'

In spite of everything, Tom continued to get As and Bs at a succession of schools where he became well used to being the new boy. One of his teachers became so attached to the mop-haired Tom that she wanted to take him on a holiday trip to Britain and Europe, but the idea fell through when her favourite pupil moved on to another school and yet another teacher.

Had his grades dropped alarmingly or had there been a domestic disaster more serious than burned soup, the law may have taken a dim view of Tom being left alone for such long periods of time. It is quite conceivable he could have been taken from the family home. Fortunately, there were no major mishaps. But there were a couple of occasions, both involving Tom, when Amos feared the worst.

'One afternoon,' he wrote in his memoirs,'I got a panicking call from Sandra. 'The house door has slammed on Tom's fingers.'

Racing back from work, Amos was already preparing himself for the torrent of criticism he was likely to face for allowing such an accident to happen by leaving his young children on their own. He needn't have worried. 'I got back to find that Tom had a blood blister on the tip of his index finger ... he was sitting there watching TV, eating a banana,' recalled Amos.

The second emergency call Amos received at work was much more serious. He wrote:'I came home to find Sandra and Larry afraid and Tom in real distress. He was wheezing, struggling for breath. I had had experience with children with croup — using a humidifier in their bedroom and taking them into a closed bathroom with the shower running.

'This was more acute than anything I had seen. I bundled him up and ran red lights and exceeded speed limits all the way to the hospital. At the emergency room, both he and I were in such a state that they took us in ahead of other patients.'

There was no history of any breathing problems in the family and, for a while, Amos feared for Tom's life, so bad was his son gasping for air. But he said: 'The doctor administered a large shot with a needle into Tom's skinny little buttock. In seconds, as if by magic, his breathing became normal, his wheezing and struggling stopped. His expression of stricken terror changed back to his usual alert acuity.

'The doctor said this was probably the beginning of an ongoing problem. But there has been no recurrence.'

There was only one other time Amos could remember his son being in real peril. 'Tommy came in to go wee wee. He was just out of diapers and I saw the lid start to fall. I couldn't catch it. It was going to smash his little member like the flat of a cleaver does an *escalope de veau* on a meat block.

'But with masterful, unconcerned economy of effort, he thrust his little, round stomach forward to intercept it.'

On the rare occasions Amos could get time off work he was intent on teaching his sons some of the more manly pursuits he prided himself on as a young man. Tom was enrolled in judo classes and Little League baseball and the whole family was taken on camping trips to Grindstone Canyon, California.

When he got the chance, Amos would go hunting with a

group of friends, but his children showed little interest in following suit. Tom's only encounter with wildlife came on a camping trip when his father woke in the middle of the night to find Tom outside the tent screaming. 'Hey dad,' he shouted. 'There's a deer here. It's got horns. I could hit it with my BB gun.' By the time Amos had stumbled into the darkness the deer had disappeared. He recalled little Tom telling him in a baby voice: 'I was weally sca'wed.'

Another important ritual on these trips was learning to drive. The older two learned very quickly, chiefly because they were able to reach the pedals. For Tom, it was a bit more difficult. Wrote his father: 'Tom was too small to reach the pedals or see over the dashboard. I would sit him on my lap and steer while I did the necessary thing with the foot pedals and gear shift lever.'

It seemed the nine-year-old was a natural. 'He handled the wheel with authority and conviction,' his proud father boasted. 'I compared his skill with Sam Hanks, the famous driver of racing cars, a distant relative.'

Sandra recalled in an interview with OK! magazine: 'Our dad would throw a mattress in the back of a pick-up and on summer nights we'd sit in the back and go to a drive-in movie. Dad never even bothered to check what was playing — we'd just go.'

The snapshots of a regular family life were, however, few and far between. Although he dearly loved his father, Tom wrote a touching letter to his big sister 20 years later, in 1986, thanking her for 'holding it all together.' While all three were jokers, he said, they took their cue from Sandra. She was the one who made it fun.

In all, Sandra said she moved 31 times in 28 years. But she said: 'We never felt unloved or out in the cold. There were no foster homes, and we weren't shipped off somewhere or abandoned. I think we became flexible and closer to each other. Even if we weren't brothers and sisters we'd be friends — that's if we could find each other. We moved so many times.' Sandra remembers Tom as 'always a ham'. One of her abiding memories of Tom was his irritating, squeaky-voiced impressions of radio DJs.

Larry said they all made it up as they went along. 'We didn't really know what we were missing. That was just the way it was,' he said. 'We were almost feral children. We were probably the terrors of the neighbourhood. We certainly didn't have much in the way of parental control.

'We were quite young and there were the three of us and my father worked long hours in the restaurant business. So the three of us just took care of ourselves, basically.'

Larry remembers being very close to his brother and sister. 'We were siblings. There was just us. Nobody was famous at that time, with the complications that brings. Everybody was very equally loud when we were kids. There was no competition or anything like that.'

Although Larry did add: 'Tom has always been outgoing, always liked talking to people. And he could always talk to people better than I could.

'In high school, he used to borrow my tape recorder and do kind of his own radio news reports. They were pretty awful. I only discovered them later. For instance, he would announce urgently that an earthquake was coming, saying something like, "Leave the city immediately" and that type of thing.

'I have the tapes — it's great bribing material that might come in handy someday.'

Through adversity, the Hanks children became very close. But they couldn't always be right there for each other. At school, they were often on their own. 'It's not a great life for a kid to be the new kid in school all the time,' said Larry. 'And we did a lot of that.

'I don't think any of us particularly enjoyed that bit of it.'

'You could get lost in the shuffle,' said Tom, 'or you could be a loudmouth. I chose the latter route. My apprenticeship years, I called them.'

Tom told *US* magazine: 'The coolest place to be was at home because we were always cracking each other up. I was surrounded by goodness. No one was hitting me or telling me I was stupid or drinking themselves into oblivion. My dad was not a guy who had his fingers on the pulse of his own feelings, but he was a good guy.

'And my mum, even though she was far away, was always concerned about my well-being and always happy to see me. The skeletons in our closet were only a couple of femur bones.'

Reminiscing to *Première*, Tom went on: 'It wasn't that bad. We were wild, of course. I know I yelled a lot. But as I recall, it was two-and-a-half very pleasant years. Didn't get into any real trouble, and was very tight with my brother and sister throughout.'

But all that was about to change. If the gypsy years were the best of his childhood, the worst were those that followed. Amos had asked a Chinese waitress to become his third wife — and the freewheeling Hanks family would never be the same again.

4

A Family at War

'Trouble was brewing from the very start,' recalled Amos, who had met Frances Wong at the Jack London Square tourist spot in Oakland, where they both worked — Amos as a chef, Frances as a waitress. In the early throes of passion, he had dreamed of his children's lives being 'enriched by the blending of cultures.' At last, he thought, they would have a steady, secure home life with a house-proud stepmother more than happy to cook and clean for them. Being the youngest, Tom in particular would benefit from the belated stability.

He quickly discovered he could not have been more wrong. Within days of the wedding, Tom, Larry and Sandra had all assumed a sudden, intense dislike of Chinese food — and it went downhill from there.

Amos saw Frances as the 'romance of a lifetime'. To his children, at first she seemed the stepmother from hell.

Tom's father was now 40 and had got a job as a teacher in the Oakland school district — always a keen reader, he had taken correspondence courses to educate himself. It was Frances's second marriage and she had her own three second-generation American-Chinese daughters. The youngest, Debbie, aged five, stayed with her mother while the two older girls, Chris and Cheryl, went to live with their father in San Francisco.

From doing exactly as he pleased, ten-year-old Tom now found he had to ask to go out or stay up late. Cleaning his room was no longer an abstract concept. Mealtimes were held around a table rather than the television.

Frances, shocked at the wild ways of her new stepchildren, tried her best to tame them. She failed.

Up to now, despite all the moves, the new schools, the new brothers and sisters, the new friends, Tom had gone along, uncomplainingly, with his father's wanderlust. Any unhappiness or loneliness he felt he had largely kept to himself.

Now, older and unwilling to submit to the alien, new domestic regime, Tom, his brother and sister all rebelled. Sandra, by now 16, began getting in trouble for staying out late. After an explosive series of rows, Tom and Larry refused to speak to their embattled stepmum.

'The friction began then, in 1966. Everything started going crazy at that time,' Tom told *Playboy*. 'We had lived alone for two-and-a-half years. We had called our own shots. Now there was this woman telling us what to do. We weren't about to suddenly be told to make our beds when we hadn't made our beds for two-and-a-half years. Or to be told we couldn't go somewhere.

'This split the family right own the middle. My sister left and went to live with my mum. My brother and I lived by ourselves in the downstairs of the house. We talked to the rest of the family only at mealtimes, and barely even then.'

In a 1994 *US* interview, Tom called Frances the love of his father's life. But he said she most definitely did not raise him, even though he went to live with her when he was ten.

'I was already raised,' he said. 'You gotta understand, this union they had was very personal. For a few years, we tried to do family dinners. But it was a very ugly time. She had a daughter, and we're friends. But they were Asian — Frances is Chinese — and there were differences there.

'And this came on the heels of three of us kids being on our own for the better part of three years. You can't just change that.'

Added Sandra: 'After spending so much time on our own, looking after each other, it came as a shock to us suddenly living with these Chinese stepsisters. On top of that, dad's Chinese wife was really traditional. We went from a steady diet of pizza to being served Chinese dishes at every meal.'

The situation came to a head when Tom let fly at his younger stepsister with an uncharacteristic attack. Realising the family feud was getting out of hand, Amos tried to make peace. 'I called a conference hoping to nip this thing in the bud. I failed. The conference became a shouting match,' he added.

Sandra went to live with her mother in Red Bluff. She hardly spoke to her father for the next five years.

After graduating from high school, Larry followed his sister to Red Bluff, leaving just Tom and Debbie at home in Alameda, a suburb of Oakland. An uneasy truce was called, but Tom, parted for the first time from his siblings, was earnestly looking for a way out.

At Bret Harte Junior School, he began taking his role as class clown seriously. Even then, his disarming sense of humour kept him out of any real trouble with the teachers. 'I was horribly, painfully, terribly shy,' he said. 'At the same time I was the guy who would yell out funny captions during the filmstrips.' But he was still learning to cover up his insecurities. And not everyone was fooled. 'Tom was appalled by the divorce. It hurt him, but he covered it up,' said his then best friend, Kent Mulkey. 'My mum always said that Tom was so funny because he was crying out for love. He survived by making jokes.'

Years later, Tom revealed what he really thought of his years at Bret Harte — it was 'pure hell.'

'It's just too painful a time to remember,' he said. 'A miasma of emotions, hormones and fears.

'It's like a way station, like waiting for a bus for three years. That's what I remember — pure, absolute hell. Three years of frustration, pain and loneliness.'

It was at Skyline High School that Tom found the escape he had been searching for and took the first unsteady steps on a path that would eventually lead to Hollywood. With a breathtaking, panoramic view of the Bay area, the busy school with its rich ethnic mix prides itself on the diversity of its studies.

To Tom, settled physically if not emotionally at home, the high school provided him with a source of friends and community he had never stayed anywhere long enough to find before.

Pouring over *The Catcher in the Rye* and immersing himself in the loneliness and isolation felt by J.D. Salinger's anti-hero Holden Caulfield, or glued to the faithful cathode tube, he was often sullen and uncommunicative with what remained of his family. Frances had given up trying to impress her will on the moody youngster, despairing of his obvious resentment towards her.

At school, a very different character began to emerge. The jokes were no longer necessary to make instant buddies and his confidence grew with his popularity. Most importantly, he saw himself as just another 'normal' student, earning mostly Cs but not having to prove himself to a fresh new set of faces every other term.

That doesn't mean he didn't still test his teachers with his quick wit. Recalling his schooldays in *Parade* magazine, he graded himself sternly: 'Math? Oooh — dead. Science? If they were talking about space I was interested.

'In the 6th grade we had to study South America. My question was always: Why? What does Simon Bolivar have to do with us? They said we studied American history in 5th grade. So like, we know everything there is to know about American history? Can't we go back and maybe just look at the Civil War once more?

'But I was not a troublemaker. I would only toy with authority up to the point that authority would get mad at me and then I would back off. If the teacher wasn't laughing, I'd shut up.'

While he was bombarded with the bohemian hippie urgings of the late 1960s and early 1970s, particularly where he lived in the Bay area, the home of the peace and love movement, Tom was looking in exactly the opposite direction.

He had had his share of freedom and he was too painfully shy in his early teens to even think about girls. Besides, he never much liked the music.

He tried playing soccer and running track, looking spindly and rather out of place among the high-school 'jocks'. Although his wacky humour would ensure acceptance, sport didn't provide the anchor he was searching for. Nor did the anti-authoritarian militancy sweeping the campus at that time. He had quite enough of that at home.

'It was big, urban public school. Two thousand kids. A big drug culture. Very well integrated,' Tom told *Playboy*. 'The rules were being completely redefined. As a matter of fact, I think everybody had given up by then. By the time I got there, the attitude was do whatever you want, just don't burn the place down, which, actually, some people still tried to do.

'I mostly just wanted to get out of the house; the house wasn't a good place to be.'

The path Tom took was to religion. A club at school led him to the First Covenant Church, just down the hill at Skyline, and a faith that would dominate his life for the next four years.

The church would provide friends, a girlfriend, structure, later even surrogate parents and a car. In return, the young recruit simply had to believe and to conform — two things born-again Tom was more than happy to do.

Sister Sandra remembers her brother as being 'self-righteous' around his Fundamentalist Christian period, 'as if he had seen the light and the rest of us were in the dark'.

His father was equally dismissive, saying Tom suffered 'an adolescent faith attack'.

But although he admits to being 'a geek, a spaz' as he entered his teens, the church answered a very real need in Tom at a time he was having trouble shrugging reality off with a ready quip.

He had already tried being a Catholic, a Mormon and a Nazarene. But those had always been forced on him by circumstance. Here was a religion that wanted him for himself, irrespective of who his mother happened to be.

'Because of all the people I lived with, I had a chequered religious upbringing. Then, when I was in high school, I had a serious born-again experience,' Tom explained in a *Los Angeles Times* interview. 'A great group of people ran a church near where I lived, and they provided a safe, nurturing atmosphere at a time there wasn't much else I could count on.

'The beliefs I embraced at that time don't mean the same thing to me now. When you're young and idealistic you tend to view things in absolute terms, and the absolutes didn't pan out, even within the confines of that place. You begin to see the contradictions without looking too closely.'

It was a while though, before Tom started looking back to the secular world. For now, he was enjoying his own, contradictory rebellion. While other kids his age were straining at the leash, growing long hair, pubescent moustaches, playing truant from church, and testing authority, Tom was joining the congregation youth group and choir and faithfully attending both the morning and afternoon Sunday services at the Oakland church that had become his second home. In time, he wasn't just joining Bible readings, he was leading them.

He says he was 'a Jesus freak', the sort of boy who would approach other students in the hallways at school and invite them to his house after class to discuss passages from the Bible.

But he couldn't grow his hair long if he tried. Emmy Perry, whose son D.J. also belonged to the church, clearly remembers Tom's odd Afro hairstyle. 'Tom had very curly hair,' she said. 'And it would never grow beyond his shoulders like the real Jesus freaks, no matter how much he plastered it down.'

The actor told *Vanity Fair* in 1994: 'It was not a Holy Roller place. They didn't speak in tongues. The only thing that was a little odd was that they really frowned on dancing ...

'You did have to accept Jesus Christ as your saviour. You did have to pledge your life to Christ. You did need to accept Him into your heart. I was 14 and I needed something very badly — not just something to believe in, not just some sort of faith. I needed a brand of acceptance that would combat the loneliness I had felt all the way up to then. I wanted to belong to a group. I was young and scared and the world was fucked up.'

Apart from the church, the other main influence on Tom's life at the time was director Stanley Kubrick's classic *2001: A Space Odyssey*. Tom first saw it when he was 13 and he went on to see it an incredible 22 times at the cinema.

'It was probably the most influential film, movie, story, artistic package, whatever, that I ever saw. It was just bigger. It affected me much, much more than anything I had ever seen,' he said. 'There was just awe. Every time I saw it, I saw something new, something else that Kubrick had put in. He was able to suspend my disbelief. I just felt, "We are in space."'

As he was preparing to enter his senior year at high school in 1973, with his sister and brother long gone, Tom decided to make a break of his own. A family from the church, with a son in Tom's grade, offered to take him in. The house was much nearer to Skyline school than the houseboat Amos and Frances were living in at a marina in neighbouring Alameda. But the real reason was that relations between Tom and his stepmother had continued to deteriorate.

When his attempts to dissuade his 17-year-old son from leaving fell on deaf ears, Amos had little choice but to let him go.

During this period, when he became involved with the Christian Fellowship drama section, he stayed with Bertie McColloch, a single mother with three children. Her little boy, Spike, suffered from Bell's palsy and it was Tom, remembers Bertie, who changed her son's life forever by encouraging him to overcome his handicap and go out and face the world.

'Tom would talk to the kids for hours,' she said. 'He would gently tease Spike and make him laugh at himself. Spike was so self-conscious that he didn't even want to go to school or out to play. But Tom convinced him through his sense of humour that there was nothing to be ashamed of.'

Sadly for Tom, he was still struggling to attract girls at school. 'I was death with women in high school — absolutely strikeout king,' he said. 'I was a little too geeky, a little too gangly, and much too manic.'

But, with time, his true personality began to shine through.

A more confident Tom had made many more friends, both inside and outside the church. Now he used his joker's mask to hide his unease with girls. But, with one girl in particular, Tom gradually found he was able to drop the comedy charade and share the kind of feelings he had kept locked inside for so long.

Carol Wiele was in the same year at Skyline as Tom and equally committed to the First Covenant Church. She was Tom's first love and his only real high-school girlfriend.

Now married and living near Sacramento, Carol remembers first meeting Tom in English class, when they had desks next to each other. 'Then we got to know each other better through the church. He wasn't a ladies man then at all. If he had been, I would never have dated him.

'He was a really nice guy. He was easy to be around and a lot of people liked him. But he was actually a very serious person underneath. He had a lot of things going on inside his head.'

Carol was Tom's date for the Skyline Senior Prom Night, the big party marking the end of school. 'We were the Class of '74 and Tom wasn't a turkey at all. He was delightful. We double-dated with some other friends and the guys worked very hard to make it a success. It was a trend at the time for guys to wear light blue tuxedos, but Tom chose a nice navy one.

'He was the perfect gentleman and we went out to a lovely dinner before going on to the prom.'

It was Carol's now brother-in-law who got Tom a job as a bellman at the Oakland Hilton hotel. The actor's hilarious tales of being a hotel gofer would later make him a big hit with chat show audiences in America. Late-night host David Letterman chose Tom for his final show with the NBC network because he wanted to hear more about his bellboy antics.

'That was the quintessential perfect job for somebody like me. I recommend it,' he said. 'It's a great job. Not much is expected of you, but you have to be smart. You can't be an idiot. Usually the bellman is unseen, the invisible employee. You can observe human behaviour as if you're looking through a keyhole.

'And you meet famous people. I met Cher when she was married to Greg Allman. I met Chris Evert. I told that story on some talk show Billie Jean King was on, because I had also carried Billie Jean's bags. It got back to Chrissy and she sent me a nice note asking if she had tipped me. There was a lot of stuff like that. I only worked three or four days a week because I was the late guy on weekends. But there was one time in the summer when I had to work regular business hours to fill in for a guy on vacation and I thought I was going to die!'

Other high points in Tom's bellman career included driving Sidney Poitier to the airport in the hotel limousine and carrying bags for Harry Belafonte and the Los Angeles Lakers basketball team.

There were few dull moments in that job, according to Tom, but the most bizarre occasion was when Elvis Presley and his entourage took 100 rooms for one night. 'Elvis's fans were absolutely crazy,' he said. 'There were entire families in 1942 DeSoto cars descending on the hotel to gawk at him.

'There must have been a thousand people jammed into the hotel lobby hoping for a glimpse of him. I only saw him for a few seconds in the lobby, as his bodyguards practically knocked me down to clear the way for him. The curtains in Elvis's suite were closed, but we fished at least ten stark naked women out of the swimming pool.'

'I don't know how much actual work they did, but they certainly seemed to have a good time there,' said Carol.

Although both Tom and Carol went on to the same college, they gradually drifted apart. 'We were friends for a long while, then we started dating. The truth is, it was probably better when we were friends. After he graduated, Tom was around for a couple of years and we would see each other around, but it wasn't the same.

'When he left to go to university, we kind of lost touch.'

The relationship broke up with Tom's virginity intact. 'It's this loneliness thing — it still kicks in,' he admitted in *Vanity Fair*. 'The confidence I had was in very few sides of my life. When the sex thing started happening, I was totally crippled when it came down to confidence with members of the opposite sex or ... well ... with ... you know, people that thought I was sexually attracted to or thought were neat.

'The sexual revolution didn't land on my shoulders quite so squarely. But I do think that a sense of humour gets you much farther in the movies than it does in real life. There was a long period of time where I swear to God being funny just didn't get you laid no matter how funny you were.'

For years, the only contact Carol had with her high-school sweetheart was through his films. 'He would have videos coming out and there would be pictures of Tom in the store,' she said. 'It would totally surprise me. I would think, What's Tom doing up there?"

While she was in San Francisco with her husband recently, Carol discovered she was staying at the same hotel as Tom and his wife, actress Rita Wilson. 'We got together over breakfast and talked about old times. It was really nice to see him and meet his wife and his two older children. They were all so charming,' she said.

Tom's split with Carol coincided with his cooling interest in the church. Although he had embraced religion to bring more focus to his jumbled life, he now found himself filled with more questions than answers. He decided to go back and live with his father.

'After about a year, Tom came home,' wrote Amos. 'Grateful as he was to the friends who had taken him in — they had even provided him with a car — they had expected commitment of which he was not capable. His adolescent religious zeal had run its course. He was no more receptive to fundamentalism than I had been.'

Tom is grateful to the church to this day. In 1994, he told the *Chicago Tribune*: 'It was an evangelical Christian youth group, and it was one of the best things I ever did. I made friends that I still have today. I had been a confused kid ... Religion helped me.'

The church had played its part. But the impressionable teen had a new love, one he had been waiting his whole life for. Tom had discovered acting.

5

Thespian Tom

Tom's high-school yearbooks offer a clue to the teenager's growing interest in drama. As a member of the track team, where he ran the 440 metres in a respectable 61 seconds, and in the line-up for the soccer team, where he had struggled earnestly with the no handling rule, he was listed as Tom Hanks, or perhaps Thomas Jeffrey Hanks. The following year, as a budding member of the school's drama group, he had become Thom Hanks, the name better befitting his new thespian status.

'For a while,' he would later confess, 'I spelled my first name Thom, but decided that spelling my last name Hanx would be rather dumb.'

Skyline put on two plays a year, a musical in the spring and a play during the autumn term. While he was still trying to make his mark as a sportsman, Tom sat in the audience for a production of *Dracula*, starring one of his friends, Daniel Finnamore. 'I was into our high-school drama department before Tom was,' said Finnamore. 'I was Dracula and Tom wasn't really into acting, but he came to two performances and he was really excited about it.'

Tom remembers being 'utterly envious' of the actors on stage. He told *Interview* magazine in 1994: 'I sat in the audience and thought, 'How come I'm not up there doing that.' When they opened the curtain, it was all just so full of life; friends of mine were on the stage and running the lights, and I knew most of the people backstage.

'Up until then I'd had no clue that acting was ever an option. The next year I signed up for the drama class and tried out for all the plays, and got into them, and had more fun than I could possibly imagine. It was an incredible group of people, some of whom are still my friends.

'I got into this eclectic group that was kind of rootless and clique less.'

For Tom, it was a group of people who, for a variety of different reasons, shared his sense of being apart. Like him, they were looking for a way to escape the mundane. They included a driven, flamboyant, bearded actor and designer called John Gilkerson, and Trudi Stillwell, who both formed close friendships with Tom. But the key to the dramatic new world of acting was Skyline's drama teacher, Rawley Farnsworth.

Farnsworth, a Kansas farm boy who had done monologues and readings at community get-togethers in his youth, had taught drama in Wichita and in the Shawnee Mission district outside Kansas City before falling in love with San Francisco and moving to Skyline, the 'crown jewel' of the Oakland School District, in 1968.

Coming from the conservative Mid-West, Farnsworth had good reason to enjoy the free-spirited bohemia of San Francisco. For he was gay and happy to live in a more liberal climate.

But across the bay in Oakland, the drama teacher chose to keep his homosexuality to himself. As we shall see later, the arrival of a 16-year-old Tom Hanks in his class in 1972 would one day have considerable consequences on the teacher's career-long decision to remain, as he puts it, a 'closet queen'.

Back then, Tom was left guessing along with the rest of his enthralled classmates over their charismatic teacher's sexuality.

'I had always been somewhat closeted. I never told my classmates that I was gay. My private life was not for discussion,' said Farnsworth. 'I was a different person when I walked into the school building in the morning than the person who left it at night.'

He hid his homosexuality not because he feared losing his job, but because 'my biggest fear was the reaction of the kids. I thought they might blow things out of proportion, get carried away and write nasty things on my door. My discipline would have flown out of the window.'

Farnsworth's adoring pupils, however, had their suspicions. Tom later recalled studying his teacher in class and thinking he 'couldn't believe he was a "homo".'

Whatever his sexuality, Farnsworth brought the subject alive for his impressionable young student.

'Tom came along and took every course I offered,' said Farnsworth, who retired in 1985 after teaching for 14 years at the school. 'I do remember him clearly. He was always very open and happy-go-lucky. The yearbook voted him the class clown, but he was not a cut-up, just very witty. He was great fun to work with and a delightful teenager.'

While most of his best friends were happy to work off camera, Tom soon found that he was most comfortable in the footlights. The stage offered him a refuge from his problems at home, from the spectre of loneliness that haunted his quieter moments, from the trials and tribulations of being a teenager. More than that, it was fun.

'He had tremendous stage presence and wonderful timing. He needed very little direction. It all just came out naturally,' said Farnsworth.

He remembered quickly spotting Tom's comic ability. 'But I always preached to him that a good actor was a versatile actor — and Tom has been very smart in that respect.'

Even at school, Tom appeared to heed his mentor's advice, appearing first as Andrew Aguecheek, a self-infatuated fop in Shakespeare's *Twelfth Night*, then starring as a high-tempered, very intense stage director in *The Potboiler*. He was cast in *The Night of the Iguana* and, as a senior, he won the coveted role of Luther Billis in *South Pacific*. 'He was dressed in a grass skirt and had a tattoo of a battleship on his stomach — and he had a hoot. 'He won our own little Academy Awards for best actor,' said Farnsworth. 'Little did I dream that 20 years later, almost to the day, he would win the Academy Award. If I'd known, I would have passed out.'

Irrespective of his singing voice, Tom certainly made an impression in his one and only musical. 'I think it was probably after his third or fourth movie, ' his sister Sandra told *Première*, 'that my parents finally stopped referring to how good he was in *South Pacific*.'

Larry remembers being astonished at how impressive his kid brother was up on stage. 'It wasn't until we were in high school that I really had an inkling that he had any talent in that respect,' he said. 'It was when he was in *South Pacific* wearing an outfit with coconuts that it hit me. Before that I didn't even know he was interested in acting. His performance was so good that during the break everyone was talking about him. I remember thinking, 'Well, there is something going on here.' It really kind of blew me away. I knew he was dabbling in that sort of stuff, but I didn't know he was so serious about it.'

Did his first drama teacher know his lippy young pupil was bound for stardom? 'It crossed my mind,' said Farnsworth, 'but I had other students who I felt the same way about and they didn't do anything. I don't mean to put Tom down at all. He was just smart enough and did all the homework. And he must have had a terrific manager and agent. You have so many students that it is difficult to say who will make it and who won't. But Tom certainly went right to the top.

'And watching that ascent has been one of the biggest thrills of my life.'

Although Tom was the joker in the pack of students who hung around the drama department, it was his friend, John Gilkerson, who was widely thought to be the star-in-the-making. The talented, soft-spoken student was never in any doubt that his future lay in the stage.

'If I had to predict back then,' added Farnsworth, 'I would have expected John to have gone on to bigger acting roles than Tom. He was a tremendously gifted artist.'

It was Gilkerson who badgered Tom into joining Skyline's acting troupe and he kept cajoling his friend to keep involved in drama.

While drama had been fun and a good way to meet like-minded friends, it had never occurred to Tom that he might make a living from acting. Knowing the long hours his father had worked, he had no intention of following him into the catering trade. But, other than a life in the church, which he once considered and later rejected, he had no real clue what he was going to do with himself once his studies were over.

For now though, that wasn't a pressing problem. His bellman job gave him enough pocket money to keep him in petrol for his clapped-out VW and buy tickets to baseball games. And Amos's insistence that he continue his education gave him at least a couple of years reprieve from having to make any tough choices.

While his high school grades weren't bad, they weren't going to interest any Ivy League universities. So Tom signed on for two years at the Chabot Community College in nearby Hayward. Now back at home, although still generally at odds with his stepmother, Tom initially chose a smorgasbord of courses. As a treat to himself, he took one drama class a term.

Then one day he bumped into John Gilkerson, who was also going to Chabot. 'He asked me what I was doing with myself,' said Tom. 'I told him I was a bellman at a hotel and he said, "Shame on you! You're not doing anything. You should try to do plays!"

'And that was really the beginning.'

The bug had already bitten. He had been going off to the theatre for months, seeing whatever production was being performed locally, from Shakespeare to Chekhov, at the American Conservatory Theater in San Francisco and the Berkeley Stage Company and the Berkeley Repertory Theater. Often, he would go alone, particularly when his friends were skiing or watching basketball games, two passions Tom never warmed to as a youngster. A devoted baseball fan — he loyally followed the Cleveland Indians team which became a national joke with its woeful record and even now makes a point of watching games at the nearest stadium when on location — he says he could never be bothered with a game where you can score 100 and still lose. And he was always more drawn to the beach than to the mountains.

He wouldn't take dates with him to the theatre. It became a ritual to drive there alone, buy his ticket, take his seat, read the programme from cover to cover and then immerse himself totally in the play. 'I spent a lot of time like that,' he recalled, 'seeing Brecht, Tennessee Williams, Ibsen and all that.'

At Chabot, it gradually dawned on Tom that this was something he wanted to do. Not only did it seem to fit his personality, he was really good at it. Early in 1975, he decided to audition for the school play, a production of Thornton Wilder's *Our*

Town. He won the leading man role opposite fellow student Pamela Naibert, who played Emily Webb in the story of two turn-of-the-century New England families.

Apparently, Tom's chemistry with Pamela was a powerful portent of his celebrated partnership with the likes of Meg Ryan and Sally Field.

In Tom's first rave review in the college newspaper, the *Chabot Spectator*, stage critic Charles Sawyer wrote: 'Thom Hanks as George Gibbs was convincing in a role that required him to be almost as decorous and virginal as Emily. Their best interaction together was undeniably the second act scene at the soda fountain. Talk about gentleness and warmth!'

That's not to say it went entirely without mishap. Sawyer went on: 'There were a few glaring foul-ups during the performance however, and they all seemed to be due to the confusion of the technical crew. Someone ought to take away their smocks for a week or until they promise to respond to the right cue with the right effect at the right time.

'But all-in-all, last Friday's performance of *Our Town* by the Chabot College Humanities Division was an enlightening and stunning treat. If you are the least bit sensitive to the human condition as interpreted by one of the foremost playwrights of all time, then DON'T MISS *OUR TOWN*.'

Thinking it was another acting class, Tom then signed up for lecturer Herb Kennedy's Drama in Performance class. He was surprised to discover the course was designed to encourage students to read play literature. In ten weeks, he saw five different types of theatre and found his calling.

He had already been to see Brecht's *The Good Person of Szechwan* and Albee's *Tiny Alice* when he was asked to read O'Neill's *The Iceman Cometh* in readiness for seeing the play. 'This,' he said later, 'was the big turning point.'

He told *Connoisseur* magazine in 1988: 'I literally couldn't wait to finish that play. I read the last page curled up on the front steps of my house. Then I went to see it at the Berkeley Repertory Theater — 150 seats, three-quarter staging. You were right on top of the stage, transported back to the Lower East Side of New York.

'This was the most magical thing that has ever happened to

me. I came out of the theatre enthralled with what those people had done that night. Four hours of concentration. I had never seen that anywhere else.

'And I wanted to do something in the theatre, something as immediate and personal as that.'

'It was an epiphany moment for Tom,' said his old Chabot drama teacher Herb Kennedy, now retired and living in the Oakland area. 'When Tom came into the class, he really didn't know what it was about. But he stayed with it. He told me that after watching *The Iceman Cometh*, he knew that this was what he wanted to do.

'He was at Chabot for a relatively brief time. He did some backstage work and some acting. He's kept in touch over the years. The thing most of all about Tom, then and since, is that he is the original Mr Nice Guy. He is one of the few Hollywood big shots who you could say that about.

'A few years later, Tom got a job on a TV series called *Bosom Buddies*. But after the first season, the show was put on hold and I had the idea to bring Tom back to Chabot for a summer season to do *Charley's Aunt*. In the meantime, he had learned to juggle, so we worked that into *Charley's Aunt*. We had Tom up on stage juggling.

'He was great fun and a real professional.'

Now Tom was set on his path, he set out to graduate in drama at the Sacramento State University, about 60 miles from his home in Oakland, and the only higher-education institute he could get into where he could do plays. He never would get his degree, dropping out after one-and-a-half years — just six months from graduation — and has since turned down offers of an honorary degree. But he worked hard on the groundwork that would be so vital to his success as an accomplished, well-rounded actor.

Professor Larry Shumate taught two of Tom's classes. 'He was in my stagecraft group, which dealt with the building of sets, and theatre graphics, which involved things like set design and make-up.

'He was a typical student. In fact, he was a bit like the characters he played in his earlier roles. He was the class comic. He always had a quick comment or a joke. He had a buddy and the two of them used to play of each other all of the time. It's funny how things turn out. Tom made it — but his friend didn't.

'I know Tom was doing a lot of technical courses. He did lighting and acting classes. He has always remembered us very kindly and when I retired he sent me a very nice letter of thanks.'

For a while, Tom considered going into production and stage management rather than performing. After having worked backstage on several campus productions as a set builder, lighting technician and stage manager, however, he auditioned for and won a role in guest director Vincent Dowling's staging of Chekhov's *The Cherry Orchard*. Taken by the young actor's enthusiasm and intuitive understanding of his character, Dowling, then artistic director of the Great Lakes Shakespeare Festival in Cleveland, Ohio, recruited Tom in 1977 for the summer season.

'I think this is where he decided that this was his life's work,' said Bob Smart, another of Tom's old lecturers.

Tom is still remembered as the sound man who made all the stagehands laugh. The guy who hosted cast parties at his sparse midtown apartment on T Street, where he had a big sign reading 'Platypus Arms' hanging in the living room.

He was the theatre major who didn't particularly like school — a straight Bs student.

The only evidence that Tom ever acted in a university production is a photograph hanging in the hallway at the school's theatre arts department. Even then the picture of the 1976 cast of *Enrico Four* has a barely recognisable Hanks in the corner, with the brown hair and cap in blurry profile.

'Tom was a fresh-faced kid from Oakland and didn't want to act,' said his old friend Randy Fector. 'He wanted to teach dramatic art to kids — until he found out that it was possible to support himself acting.'

'I don't think Tom would have ever imagined he would become so successful,' said John Ickes, who runs his own PR firm and worked with Tom on the Civic Center's 1977 production of *The Cherry Orchard*.

'We used to talk about making it as an actor, about how hard it was going to be, and we talked a lot about money,' he added. 'Actors never have enough money.

'It couldn't have happened to a nicer guy. I will always remember Tom as a nice, funny guy who was always very professional. He did it because he loved the work.'

But as serious as he was about his chosen profession, Tom could still never resist a gag. Miriam Gray was auditioning with Tom for *The Cherry Orchard*, which was seen as a big deal at the time because an out-of-town director, Vincent Dowling, was in charge.

'Everybody was so serious,' said Miriam, who now owns an acting studio. 'Remember this was Chekhov, one of the big guys. We were all acting as if we were auditioning for the Royal Shakespeare Theatre, for God's sakes. We were so, so serious. Then Tom walks up the steps and pretends to trip. He hit himself and said, "Shake it off, don't get nervous." Everybody cracked up. He made fun of everybody being so serious. That was so Tom. He's a natural, a born stand-up comedian.'

Tom got the part of the manservant Yasha. In the opening night review, by *Sacramento Bee* critic William Glackin, he was described as making 'a valuable, clear-cut contribution'.

As well as performing, Tom also worked as an assistant stage manager, in charge of set design and construction. He once used a stapler to fix a broken strap on actress Phyllis Cupparo's platform shoes in the middle of *Death of a Salesman*. Moments before Cupparo was to head back on stage, Tom told her: 'If it breaks, that's OK. Play it.'

But Cupparo recalled: 'I was terrified. He could say that because he was a natural ad-libber, he was so quick. Anything could happen and he would go right along ... I could not do that. Fortunately, the staple didn't come out.'

The TV culture Tom grew up with remained a major part of his life. Les Cockayne, a lighting and staff technician while Tom was at university, said: 'I remember he was running lights for a show and he was a Trekkie ... You know, a *Star Trek* fan. Everything was, "Beam me up, Scotty," and that kind of stuff. It was funny when I saw his film, *Bachelor Party*, some years later. Tom was definitely *Bachelor Party*. He liked to have a good time.'

While the fledgling actor was putting in his groundwork, he also found a new social scene, which revolved around the drama department. Living away from home, he spent every spare moment in the student lounge nicknamed the Green Room, after the reception areas where actors and guests are entertained while they wait to go on TV shows.

Surrounded by 'luvvies' and drama queens, Tom was in his element. 'It was a place where everybody had an entrance, everybody was a star. It was a great mix of people,' he remembered.

There was one fellow student who especially caught Tom's eye. While he had settled quickly into his role as the Green Room joker, he found himself suddenly at a loss for words when theatre-studies student Susan Dillingham made her entrance.

Pretty and self-confident, Susan shared Tom's dreams of a life on the stage. It wouldn't be very long before they shared much more than that. College had been a happy playground where Tom was finally able to shed some of his loneliness and revel in the unconditional company of friends who asked nothing from him.

After plucking up the courage to ask Susan out, Tom would soon discover that he must grow up very fast.

6

In the Family Way

Susan Dillingham was the leading lady Tom had been searching for. For years he had been complaining to his friends that being funny never got him laid. With his bush of brillo-pad curls, his doughy face and tall, gangly frame, he was never going to be a stud. He would happily admit his sexual confidence was rated around rock bottom.

But at Sacramento, his personality all began to click into place with women. Suddenly, being funny was sexy. Then along came Susan, who was about to become the first of millions to discover Tom's talents as a leading man. What he lacked in rampant sex appeal, he more than made up for in a kind of trusting vulnerability — and, of course, in laughs.

In public, they were the perfect pair, hosting parties and living the student lifestyle to the max. In private, Susan offered Tom the stable relationship he had never before experienced with a woman. He had been taken away from his real mother and forced to live with two stepmothers. Now he chose to move in with Susan.

For a while it seemed that everything was going their way. Both were actors just starting out on their great adventure with dreams of Broadway, fame, fortune and, dare they admit it, Hollywood.

But halfway through their first year at university, the sky fell in. Susan realised as March turned into April in 1977 that her period was late. Her doctor soon confirmed her suspicions. She was pregnant with Tom's child. They were both 20 years old.

For Tom, it was as if he was reliving his parents' mistakes. Burdened by the toil of providing for his young family, Amos had forsaken his dreams to buckle down in the arduous catering trade. Just as he was certain what he wanted to do with his life, Tom feared he too would become too weighed down by responsibilities to succeed as an actor.

With Susan's profile swelling by the day, Tom took up director Vincent Dowling's offer to make some money that summer with the Great Lakes Shakespeare Festival in Cleveland, Ohio.

For the next three summers, Tom would return to Cleveland, paying his dues alongside other jobbing actors and actresses, winning his equity card and working as a paid, albeit poorly paid, performer.

After Tom's audition for *The Cherry Orchard* back in Sacramento, Dowling had been more impressed with Tom than he let on. 'When I came home that afternoon,' said the director, who now lives in Chester, Massachusetts, where he founded the Miniature Theater, 'I told my wife there was one kid there who had star quality.

'I said, "He's like a young Tony Curtis, but I think he has even more potential."'

'A friend of mine ran the Eaglet Theater in Sacramento and I had finished my second season as artistic and production director of the Great Lakes Shakespeare Festival and I was looking around America for promising young directors. He asked me to direct a play there and I agreed.

'To my horror, when I got there, he told me it was not a professional company but they were wonderful people from the university. I had a sinking feeling I can still remember now. But he was right. There was an extraordinary group of both faculty and students who had a lot of talent.

'Curiously enough, after I noticed the similarity with Tony Curtis, Tom went on to do *Bosom Buddies*, which was very much based around Tony Curtis's *Some Like it Hot*.

'Even before we started on the performance, I was very taken with Tom's presence and his understanding of the whole thing. It was that stance of his and his attitude.'

When he offered him an internship with his Cleveland-based company for the following summer, Dowling warned Tom there was little money in it for him.

'I told Tom, "In my view, it is the last form of legalised slavery. There is no money."

'But Tom was not rich and he said he would need some money. I said there was housing and a stipend for food and the odd drink.'

Tom was not alone on his acting pilgrimage to Ohio. Six of his friends were also offered jobs as interns and they would all become quickly known in Cleveland as the 'Sacramento 7'.

'Tom was undoubtedly the leader of the whole group. Whatever he did would have to be the best,' said Dowling, who was himself an actor for 23 years with the Abbey Theatre in Dublin.

He also started a ritual at the opening party, where the whole company met together for the first time at a firehouse just outside Cleveland. 'Tom started the tradition of sliding down the fireman's pole, including doing it headfirst,' said Dowling. 'Tom kept everyone amused and kept morale up.

'At the end of the second season we did a benefit and we decided we would have an intern section. Tom came and he said he had an idea. It was for a court sketch all in rhyme. He put it all together himself, with a judge and jury and it was terrific — very funny, in rhyme and very fast.'

Tom played mostly small roles in a score of productions. Among the more showy parts were Grumio in *The Taming of the Shrew* and Proteus in *The Two Gentlemen of Verona*, for which he earned the Cleveland Critics Circle Award as best actor of the year in 1978. It was the last time Tom played anything remotely resembling a bad guy.

He also worked on the company's lighting and set crews.

Tom very quickly found himself a paid, professional actor. Dan Sullivan, who has directed some top Broadway shows, was directing *The Taming of the Shrew* for the company, but was having trouble finding anyone with the right comic skills to be cast as Grumio. As it would be necessary for the actor to tour with the show around Ohio after the summer season, whoever played the part would really need an Equity union card.

TOM HANKS

Said Dowling: 'Dan came to me and I said, "There is an intern here. I know he is something extraordinary and would be perfect for you. Will you at least audition him?"

'Well, he cast him and I knew that when the time came to tour I was going to have to either replace him or make him Equity. It was the only time in nine years I was there that I made an intern Equity.

'I knew he had star quality. I knew he was going to make it. He had that something special.'

Interns would help with the changeovers on stage and generally do odd jobs around the theatre which the professional actors would not do. On Tom's last night as an intern, the day before going on tour for the first time as a professional, he walked off stage at midnight and refused to help with his usual chores.

'He said, "I am an Equity actor now chaps, thank you very much,"' laughed Dowling. 'The next morning he was out there with his bags, waiting for the bus.'

Tom still has clear, fond memories of his time with the company.

'It was like learning to play the violin on a Stradivarius,' he said. 'This wasn't just singing and dancing. This was the Bard. It automatically gave me a professional attitude. You had to be disciplined. You had to do your homework.

'This was really my equivalent of being in the armed forces. A time when you just put your head down and did it until you said, "OK, now I'm done. I'm done here, thanks very much. I'm finished with this."'

After the first summer in 1977, Tom and Susan went back to university for the autumn term. But Tom, tiring of his studies and painfully aware of his looming financial responsibilities, dropped out to take an $800-a-month (£500) job as assistant stage manager at the Sacramento Civic Theater.

On 24 November 1977, Susan gave birth to a son, Colin.

With very little money, the couple managed to get by on Tom's meagre salary until the following summer, when the actor again headed for Cleveland.

Actor Holmes Osbourne, who was six years older than Tom, also starred in *The Two Gentleman of Verona*, and remembered sharing dingy motel rooms and cramped dressing quarters with his friend when they took the production on tour.

'Tom was so clean-living; he had no bad habits other than an addiction to peanut M&Ms. We were a pretty hard-drinking company, but Tom never drank, never even did tobacco.'

With a newborn baby at home in California, Tom could scarcely afford nights out on the town. But that didn't mean he had lost his sense of humour.

'Once I mentioned to Tom that I had played a role in a Navy recruiting film called *A Day in the Squadron*. So he snuck down to the Cleveland recruiting office and asked to see the film; then at a party he surprised me with this brilliant spoof of my entire performance. From that one viewing he had memorised my lines and my gestures.

'His sense of humour was what I enjoyed most,' added Osborne. 'It was always there — not in a frenetic Robin Williams way, but in a carefully calculated, mischievous way.'

Vincent Dowling remembered Tom and Osborne making a dashing pair of young actors as they toured together on *The Two Gentlemen of Verona*. There would often be a crowd of young women waiting by the stage door, particularly after putting on shows for students.

There was one production at the Victory Theater in Dayton, Ohio, that still stands out in the director's mind. 'I shall never forget it,' he said, 'There were all these girls waiting outside after a student matinee and they were saying how wonderful Tom and Holmes were. Then one girl said to me, "We understood every word in the play today. But that's because you weren't doing it in Shakespeare, you were doing it in English." I thought that was a great tribute to the way they were able to bring it alive for young people.

'I have honestly never known a Shakespeare clown as brilliant as Tom.

'I have met few actors who have had the focus about their future that Tom had. It was not ruthless or damaging to anyone else. It was just his eyes set on the work to be done.

'My only complaint against him is that he has never come back to the theatre since his film stardom. The loss to Shakespeare is very considerable.'

There were still occasions, however, when the concentration slipped. The director recalled one time when an almost empty house at a theatre in America's Amish country led to the two leads 'messing around.'

'My wife was stage managing that season and she told me only recently that she went backstage and read the riot act to Tom and Holmes after the first act. They came out for the second act and were back to their normal, good performances. It was a lesson that Tom may well have remembered.'

The Cleveland company offered Tom the security of an acting 'family' where he could thrive. Once offstage, there were barbecues, parties, swimming in the lake, and the baseball games watching his beloved Cleveland Indians. Each year, the group would select a quiet pub and crowd it out for the whole summer season. The next year, another equally out-of-the-way hostelry would be chosen for an instant, but short-lived revival.

'I can still see Tom now, arranging a baseball game between the actors and the techies. It's as clear as if it was yesterday,' said Vincent Dowling.

After the 1978 summer season, Tom decided that another winter in Sacramento had little more to offer. Friends he had met in Cleveland suggested that he try New York, where he could get work with the Riverside Shakespeare Company. After a long talk with Susan, they decided to try their luck in the Big Apple, hoping that the greater opportunities would give Tom his big break. Their savings amounted at that time to a grand total of $35.

A more obvious starting point would have been Hollywood, but coming from Northern California he confessed to 'an inbred hatred' of Los Angeles. Tom thought he would disappear in LA and vowed never to move there unless he had a job waiting for him. 'We always said LA was like San Jose except 16 times as large, so there was no reason to go there unless you wanted to work in a bank or wait tables. Which I never had to do.'

So New York it was. Tom sold his beloved Volkswagen and hitched a ride east with fellow company member Michael John McGann in November, 1978, just after Colin's first birthday, with the idea of finding a flat and sending for his wife and child. For a few weeks, he slept on the couch in McGann's large, busy apartment. 'He was heavenly,' recalled McGann, an actor who still lives in Brooklyn, New York. 'He was and still is the kindest man I have ever met.'

But life wasn't easy in New York for a young family without a job. They moved into a small, roach-infested walk-up tenement close to the railway in the notorious Hell's Kitchen neighbourhood — with no carpet or linoleum on the floor, just bare boards — and Tom set out on his quest for work. It was only through the good graces of his bosses in Cleveland that he was able to survive at all through those first few months.

'The nicest thing they did was when I left,' he said. 'I had already been to New York and wanted to get back there because of some possibilities, but I needed to draw unemployment to live.

'But to get unemployment insurance, I couldn't quit. So I told them, "You have to fire me." They said, "You've done a lot for us. You're fired." It was a very nice thing they did for me.'

For months, Tom doggedly made the rounds of auditions for countless roles in theatre, television and films. Tom had his Equity union card, allowing him to work as an actor, but, having fallen pregnant, Susan didn't get the chance to win her card, which effectively barred her from getting any work.

Through 1979, they eked out a living, managing to pay their $285-a-month rent thanks mainly to unemployment checks and the occasional cash-in-hand job. Things got so bad at one point that Tom's sister, Sandra, cashed in some coke bottles to get $20 to send to her beleaguered brother.

Said Tom: 'I got $25 once for doing a play at the City Court Building — after rehearsing for four weekends.'

'We were young and impetuous. It was a fervent time, 'Tom told *Première* magazine. 'It was also real hairy. It was just the greatest thing that our son was healthy because if he had got sick — if we'd had to take him to a clinic — that just would have been hell. We didn't have the money.'

But he added: 'It made us have a certain amount of stick-to-itiveness. If I hadn't been married and had a family — well, then I could have done anything I wanted to. As it was, it was like, 'Okay, here it is: here's your living situation, here's the amount of time we're going to have to invest in it — and let's not complain!

We have nowhere else to go and we couldn't if we wanted to.'

On the same theme, Tom told *Playboy*: 'It was a war of survival, really. I was a kid who had never been in such a big city before. I was on unemployment and trying to act. This went on for two years.'

Desperately needing work to pay the bills, the situation became so dire that Tom would take all of his money from the bank, about £60 ($100), and drive from city to city looking for work outside Manhattan, going for acting jobs that nobody else wanted. 'Sometimes I'd wake up at night,' he said, 'and I would go into the bathroom, look at myself in the mirror and think, 'What's happened to me? My career is over before it's begun."

By now, Susan was also looking for work using her stage name Samantha Lewes. Irish actress Bairbra Dowling had been in *The Cherry Orchard* back in Sacramento with Tom and had also been a member of the Cleveland company, where her father, Vincent, was the boss. Bairbra then went to live in the same area of Hell's Kitchen in New York to join the audition queues with Tom. 'We were all in the Clinton area. We were on 43rd and I think Tom and Samantha were on 45th. They were pretty awful apartments. All I can remember about Tom's was that it was pretty dark.

'There was a whole group of us and ours was kind of the most admired apartment. But our only furniture was a foam mattress. My sister and I would baby-sit for Tom and Samantha. We called ourselves the spinster aunts.

'We were all unemployed and looking for work. At that time, everyone had high hopes for the future. The world was ahead of us, even though money was short.

'Tom and Samantha were the only ones in the group who had a child, so it was tough for them. They weren't going out gallivanting like we were.

'But we would have Sunday brunches together and dinner parties and that kind of thing. After he got the part of *Bosom Buddies* he would come and visit, but we lost touch over the years, although strangely enough his daughter now goes to the same school as my daughter, so I see him there occasionally.

'He was so fun and great to be around, He was always so positive and lively.'

But even then, Tom would remain slightly apart, as if he cherished the sense of loneliness he had always carried with him as a form of protection. It was a shield that even his closest friends were aware of.

Bairbra, for instance, remembered: 'He was private. I don't think any of us really got to know him.'

After slogging around hundreds of auditions, Tom developed a defence mechanism — by appearing not to care too much whatever the outcome. He would appear so nonchalant and casual, and would try so hard *not* to be seen to be trying too hard that he would wreck his own chances. 'People hate you when you do that,' he said.

The pressures were beginning to get to Tom and, for a while at least, he couldn't see a way out of the depressing spiral he had become caught in. He would admit to *Evening Outlook* many years later: 'I have periods when the black dog follows me around and I can't shake him off, no matter how hard I try. I am a pessimist, pure and simple. I guess it is based on experience, on a certain amount of wisdom you acquire by the school of hard knocks. You always expect everything to stink to high heaven. That way you don't get disappointed.'

But just as his father had before him, Tom kept moving. He returned to Cleveland in the summer of 1979 to play a small role in *Othello* and portrayed the playwright Harold Pinter in another play. But he didn't feel he was being offered enough roles and went back to New York, where he finally landed a $800 (£500) part for three days work as a murderer in the independent slasher film *He Knows You're Alone*.

The breakthrough, small as it was, came while he was acting in a very off-Broadway comic stage production of Machiavelli's *The Mandrake*. 'One of the girls in the production knew a manager who was looking for someone,' said Tom. 'I went up and had a marathon meeting with him. He said, "I am going to send you out and get some feedback," which he did. I met a variety of agents and he called me up the next day and we solidified our business relationship. Then I finished my last season at the Great Lakes, which I had signed for previously. After I got back, there was this motion picture epic called *He Knows You're Alone*. It was one of those hack-and-slash movies they made out on Staten Island for about 40 bucks.'

Tom was eighth down the bill. 'It may have been bad, but it was the first job I had wearing regular pants, as opposed to sword belts, leather jerkins and sandals,' he said.

A poor relative of teen horror flicks like *Halloween* and *Friday the 13th*, the film included the obligatory multiple murders and a *Psycho*-style shower scene. The main storyline twist seemed to be that the killer had a penchant for killing pretty young girls as they were having sex.

Tom, as Elliot, bypassed all the gore and nudity, playing a student who escorts a couple of girls to a carnival and lectures them about the dangers of the human mind. He didn't hold his breath waiting for glowing reviews for his first movie. Kevin Thomas, in the *Los Angeles Times*, was fairly typical when he wrote: 'Standard, grisly rampaging killer fare ... That people should pay money to see such films is ridiculous when you think about it.'

The manager who helped Tom get the small part was his new manager Simon Maslow, who did the rounds of agents and executives trying to get work for his keen young client.

But not everyone shared his belief in the Californian actor without the sunshine tan, muscles or looks. Johnnie Planco, then a rising agent at William Morris, remembers meeting Tom in the late seventies. He told *People*: 'Tom came in. He had long hair like an Afro and his skin wasn't in great shape. His teeth were not great. I was not impressed. When he came in, I couldn't get him to talk.'

At Maslow's urging, Planco gave Tom a second chance. 'And Tom was more charming,' he recalled. 'But I still said, "I don't think so," since he's starting from ground zero.'

Although Planco would later represent Tom for William Morris, the first agency to sign him up was the J. Michael Bloom Agency in Los Angeles, which also helped launch the careers of Sigourney Weaver, Alec Baldwin, Macauley Culkin, Kathleen Turner and Wesley Snipes. Even then, the agency initially thought of Tom as a character actor, rather than a leading man.

On 4 January 1980, when Colin was two, Tom and Susan wed at the Church of the Holy Apostles.

While his part in the low-budget film marked a minor

breakthrough in his career, the first sign that all was not well at home came when he started dabbling secretly in drugs.

There was no shortage of any kind of drug imaginable in Manhattan in the late '70s and early '80s, particularly in the entertainment world. Many clubs, and even some bars, would have people snorting openly on tables. Showbiz parties were awash with cocaine. It was the peak of the Studio 54 era where even out-of-work actors were expected to pep up their lives with some kind of stimulant.

Tom had been around drugs in the theatre since college days, but always said no. Even in New York, he showed no obvious interest, particularly as he was all too aware that smoking pot 'just made me the stupidest human being in the world'.

But unbeknownst even to his closest friends, Tom was dulling his unhappiness and frustration with the use of both marijuana and cocaine. It was, he admits, the most serious kind of drug taking.

'The nature of the drugs I did was a closet kind of thing,' he confessed in 1994. 'It was surreptitious.'

But the perils of his situation soon dawned on Tom. He continued: 'I realised rather early on that I couldn't do that. I thought, I can't be a responsible parent and do this. This has got to stop. This is not good ... You can't hide behind the conviviality of it all. It put not just me, but all the people I loved in a degree of danger. So it became pretty easy to say, "No more."'

Then, just as it seemed the rounds of auditions were leading in an ever-decreasing circle of failure, a scout for the American ABC television network saw something he liked in the cocky young actor's everyman charm. In June 1980, he invited Tom to the dreaded Los Angeles to try out for roles in a number of new projects the station had in pre-production, including the pilot for the proposed series *Bosom Buddies*, a situation comedy about two philandering advertising copywriters who dress in drag in order to live in a low-rent hotel for women.

Tom caught the eye of Joyce Selznick, niece of legendary studio boss David Selznick, and the show's producers decided to take a chance on him, pairing him up with another young actor, Peter Scolari, and the first episode was screened in the United States in November 1980.

With his wife and child in tow, Tom switched coasts with the prospect of settling down for his first steady job.

At 23, he was suddenly earning close to $9,000 (£5,500) an episode. 'There was no reason to hire me,' said Tom, 'I made more money in two weeks than I had my whole career.'

But it was almost over before it began. For just as Tom arrived in Los Angeles, the Screen Actor's Guild and the American Federation of Television and Radio Artists called their members out on strike. As the dispute lingered on with the actor's unions holding firm on their pay demands, it seemed likely that the network would pull the plug on *Bosom Buddies*.

Tom was philosophical in public, joking that it allowed him more time to settle in with his young family. Privately, he was crestfallen that he had come so far, only to be knocked back once again by bad timing and the cruel hand of fate.

Fortunately, the two sides settled before *Bosom Buddies* was jeopardised and Tom went back to work.

The wacky premise for the show was explained by the spoken introduction that played over the opening credits. Tom was Kip and Scolari played his friend, Henry.

> *Henry*: When we first moved to New York we had a great apartment that was dirt cheap.
> *Kip*: And we found out why it was so cheap.
> *Henry*: Our friend Amy said there was a great apartment in her building.
> *Kip*: Dirt cheap — but it's a hotel for women. OK. We made one adjustment.
> *Henry*: Now these other ladies know us as Buffy and Hildegarde.
> *Kip*: But they also know us as Kip and Henry, Buffy and Hildy's brothers.
> *Henry*: This experience is gonna make a great book.
> *Kip*: See? It's all perfectly normal.'

It wasn't exactly Shakespeare, but it was a regular, high-profile job at a very opportune time.

Working for the first time on TV was another valuable lesson for Tom. He said: 'Bosom Buddies was great because it made us very fast. The whole thing was delivering the goods as best you could. If you couldn't deliver them good, you had to deliver them bad, as long as you delivered them. It's flying by the seat of your pants. You ask as many questions as you can, but eventually it's "Never mind, just do it." You can't be lazy. It became our whole life. We did so much of it in such a short time, it all blends. We were always working under some weird time frame. I can never remember now whether we were on that show for seven weeks or seven years. it was a dense, dense time.'

Scolari, who later went on to star in American TV hit shows such as Newhart and the small screen version of Honey, I Shrunk the Kids, hit it off with Tom right away. 'Tom and I hooked up pretty quickly,' he said. 'We were very close in age and experience. We went out that first day and talked about our fathers and our lives. For the next two years we were virtually inseparable.

'We drove to work together every day because we lived within a half mile of each other and his wife needed his car. So I would pick Tom up and we would talk all the way to work and all the way home. And we became — we've often said this — closer friends than the characters we portrayed.'

As his fame grew, Tom's co-stars would often speak of his thoughtfulness and sensitivity in sometimes difficult situations. Scolari remembers a classic Hanks gesture.

He said: 'I went through one very difficult week of being asked to wear bikini briefs for this sequence where he would rip off this towel that I was wearing coming out of the shower, and then make fun of me. And Tom, bless his heart, knowing the kind of humiliation that was there for me, because it was kind of a beefcake effect they were playing with me, because at the time I still had an athletic build — Tommy, in front of the whole audience had gone and gotten a pair of the same briefs and came out in them in the next scene, doing some kind of hilarious Tarzan yell.

'At that moment I thought, Well this is a guy that I could live with on this series for the next ten years because he cares and he's willing to make me laugh when he knows how much that whole scene embarrassed me. Of course, for weeks after that he would insist on wearing bikini briefs in any scene that required it.'

Tom added: 'We were always having to do something that embarrassed us. Meanwhile the writers were sitting around laughing uproariously at our horrible predicaments. And we finally realised. This is going out to six million people. At least Peter looked good in his bikini then.'

Actress Donna Dixon, who also starred in the show and went on to marry comedy star Dan Aykroyd, said: 'I was always in awe of Tom's comic timing and physicality. Working with him became play. He could do anything. He is always very positive and supportive, which makes a big difference. There are some great actors out there who have troubled personalities. Tom gives you everything.'

Although it got fairly good ratings, boosted by its position in the TV line-up right after the popular *Mork and Mindy*, which starred Robin Williams, the series was cancelled after just two seasons.

A *TV Guide* review summed up the reaction of the critics: 'Watching these two mince around in frocks is most of the fun in this little pastiche, but the boys are funny about it. Scolari in his Hildegarde disguise is a dithery dear who says "clappy as a ham", when she means "happy as a clam". Hanks in his Buffy getup is more like a female moose in distress and even more preposterous. The idea that anyone could be fooled by their female impersonations requires a prodigious suspension of disbelief, but I'll make the effort if you will.'

The last of 39 shows was aired in 1982, and, although ABC received 35,000 letters of protest, it never resurfaced. But *Bosom Buddies* effectively launched Tom into the big time and has a cult following in the US that still reveres the show today and still puts it among the actor's best comic work.

One of the guest stars, incidentally, was a young actress called Rita Wilson, of whom we will hear more of later.

Although Tom looks back on the series with affection, he is critical of his own behaviour at the time, admitting that his sudden success went to his head.

'When you're one of the guys in a show, something does happen to you; you do get an over inflated sense of your own importance,' he told *Première*.

With embarrassment, he remembers greeting the show's guest stars with jumped-up snobbery. 'It's like you are minister of architecture or something: "How nice to see you, please do as you are told, we hope you are funny, and please keep with us. And you'll be gone on Friday as soon as we are finished."

'You think you know all the answers,' he adds. 'You don't even know the fucking questions.'

It would be Tom's one and only TV sitcom. 'It was like going to an aeroplane factory every day,' he said. 'You go into a big hangar and build a plane and every Friday it has to fly. Unfortunately, sometimes the wings fell off.'

By now living in California's San Fernando Valley, Tom's short-lived TV fame, even if he was wearing a dress for most of it, had helped bring in more offers of work. The cancellation of *Bosom Buddies* coincided with the birth of Tom and Susan's second child, Elizabeth, on 17 May 1982. But there was no need to worry. The family would never again know the poverty of those early days in New York. As Tom had predicted, he would not have to wait tables or work in a bank in the world's movie mecca.

He found fairly steady employment as a supporting player in various episodes of the series *Taxi* (starring Danny DeVito and Marilu Henner), *The Love Boat* and *Family Ties*. He also starred in *Mazes and Monsters*, a made-for-television film about a fantasy game gone wrong that was first screened by the American CBS network on 28 December 1982.

The film centred on the pre-Nintendo game of Dungeons and Dragons, where the players would take on the identities of heroes and villains in a complicated board game adventure. In the early '80s, there were numerous news reports of participants getting carried away with the game, blurring fantasy with reality, sometimes with tragic consequences.

Playing Robbie Wheeling, a student who loses himself — and his mind — in the game, Tom used his own experiences playing Dungeons and Dragons, saying:'I had a perception of the game that people who haven't played it wouldn't have. If you have a particularly vivid imagination, it can be quite scary. The deeper, darker demons we all have inside us can really come to the forefront.'

The role won Tom tempered praise and was a step up from the sitcom silliness of *Bosom Buddies*.

This *Entertainment Weekly* review was fairly typical: 'In this silly made-for-TV drama about fantasy role-playing adventures, Hanks plays a neurotic college kid who "flips into the game" and becomes convinced he really is "Pardieu, the Holy Man". He almost keeps a straight face too.'

But it was a one-off appearance on *Happy Days*, starring Henry Winkler and Ron Howard, which was to have the most fortuitous effect on his future. Tom played a youngster the Fonz had pushed out of a swing during childhood and who had returned as a judo black belt to claim his revenge. The episode had particularly tickled Howard, the show's Richie Cunningham, who found Tom's antics refreshing and hilarious.

It wasn't until two years later that Tom's agent got a call from Howard, then trying to make a break into directing major movies, and with two small pictures to his credit. Howard had remembered Tom from *Happy Days* and from the actor's extracurricular appearances on the show's softball team. He now wondered if Tom was interested in testing for a role in the upcoming film, *Splash*, which he was helming for Disney.

Initially, Tom auditioned for the part of the libidinous Freddie, which later went to the late John Candy. But Howard was captivated by the boy-next-door charm that would become Tom's trademark in a string of subsequent movies and he deemed it ideally suited for his leading man, Allen Bauer, the addled New York produce manager who falls in love with a mermaid.

That is not to say he was the first to be asked. A whole bevy of stars — including the big names of the day, Dudley Moore, Burt Reynolds, Chevy Chase and Michael Keaton — had already turned the part down. According to Howard's partner, Brian Grazer, they were 'looking for someone who had leading-man qualities — he could kiss the girl and drive a story. At the same time we wanted someone who was funny, but not quirky or eccentric in his comedy. And that was really hard to find.'

Grazer added: 'Tom came in wearing these 501 Levi's and construction boots and a T-shirt. He wasn't nervous at all — and here's a guy who had never had a major movie. I thought, 'Why is this guy so calm?' But we read him and we liked him and we hired him right away.'

The plot was pure Disney. As a boy, Allen Bauer had been rescued by a mermaid after falling off a Cape Cod ferry, but had persuaded himself over the years that he must have imagined it. Twenty years later, he is again saved from drowning by the same mermaid, who follows him to Manhattan, where, after dispensing with utensils to eat lobster, shell and all, in a restaurant, she is eventually captured and imprisoned in an oversized fish tank

There is, naturally, a happy ending with Tom and Daryl Hannah swimming off into the sunset together.

It may have been Tom's first major film. But the $80,000 pay cheque, although considerably more than anything he had ever seen before, was still a long way from the big leagues. At this point, Burt Reynolds was in the $5 million league, and Marlon Brando was paid $2 million for a cameo.

And the initial buzz in Hollywood was not particularly hot for the film, a mermaid movie for Disney being directed by Ron 'Richie Cunningham' Howard. But on its release early in 1984, the romantic fantasy became one of the surprise hits of the year, grossing more than $69 million at the US box office and making another newcomer, mermaid Daryl Hannah, an instant superstar. It would also become a huge draw on video and ultimately grossed more than $120 million.

Although his understated role was somewhat overlooked by the critics, Tom was described in *New York* magazine as 'an expert comic' who was also able 'to command the emotional centre of his scenes'.

In *Newsweek*, critic David Ansen said Tom 'seemed disappointingly bland at first glance,' but he soon began to pick up 'sly comic edges' in the actor's performance that reminded him of 'all-American boys with mischief inside'.

Despite his outward cockiness, Hanks later confessed he began filming totally in awe of his co-stars John Candy and Eugene Levy 'because they're very, very funny guys. But my job in *Splash* was not to be particularly funny. That's what Ron kept drilling into me.'

Howard also helped Tom learn another valuable lesson when the actor turned up on the set one day knowing neither the production schedule nor his part in a major scene.

'It took longer to shoot than it should have, and when we were done with the scene, Ron said, "You know, you should have been a little more prepared." He didn't yell at me. He probably knew that if he had yelled, I'd be paste for the rest of the day. He just let me know in no uncertain terms that I was starring in this movie and with that comes huge responsibilities, and one of them is to be ready to go. I've never forgotten that,' said Tom.

Although the critics may not have singled him out for adulation, the film industry certainly took note of his pivotal performance.

Tom emerged from *Splash* with a career momentum that, despite a number of false starts, would eventually carry him right to the top.

He was on his way. Hollywood was a long way from Cleveland — and certainly paid better than the Bard. Especially when you have just chalked up a bona fide blockbuster. 'Suddenly, here was this tidal wave of people saying very nice things about me and wanting me to be in their movies,' said Tom.

There was only one problem. While his acting career was all coming together, Tom's marriage was falling apart.

7

Playing the Bad Guy

It was perhaps Tom's most unlikely role. The Bad Guy. But this was no film part. It was real life. And the person doing the casting was his wife.

With the success of *Splash*, the actor took on a slew of projects, all offering good money and, invariably, bad scripts. As a result, Tom was spending less and less time at home with his wife and young family. The times he was not working were punctuated by angry rows that had grown in conjunction with his salary.

Susan, under her stage name of Samantha Lewes, was trying to get a foothold as an actress, but with two children to care for and a husband who was away for long stretches at a time on location, it was difficult to get work. While the pressures of the 'year-and-a-half of scary days' in New York had drawn the couple together, it was dawning on the one-time college sweethearts that all the money and success in the world wasn't going to make them any happier together.

'I was so young and determined to establish a beachhead in the entertainment world. I just wish I had been as good a father the first time as I am now,' Tom said in 1998. 'Fatherhood passed me in a blur because I was so busy working and trying to pay the rent.'

Ten years earlier, he had told *Gentleman's Quarterly*: 'I don't think you can have children at an early age and enjoy them the way they are enjoyed on fucking TV commercials. It was the same for my father.'

Still haunted by his own fractured childhood and his fear of following in his parent's much-married footsteps, Tom was determined to try and make the marriage work. After moving to California, Tom took a hiatus from his burgeoning film career to set up a one-woman showcase for Susan, building all the sets, doing the publicity and helping with rehearsals.

Splash was the number one movie in America, and friends fully expected Tom to bathe in his success and try and capitalise on his good fortune. But Hollywood's newest leading man could be found backstage at Los Angeles' Gene Dynarski Theater, manhandling scenery and sticking together the props. Susan was both producing and acting in *Passing Game* by writer Steve Tesich, and Tom was eager to help make the project a success.

He explained to *Drama-Logue* magazine in 1984: 'The reason I got involved was because of the impetus of my wife, Samantha [Susan's stage name]. We had always been desirous to get into the producing aspect of theatre, so this has been a learning by doing situation. We are already talking about two other projects we want to get evolving.

'Sam has a supporting role in this and she swears she will never produce anything and be in it again. She says the pressures are just too great on both sides.

'Listen, it's been an experience for both of us. I have been either driving a truck or pounding nails or sweeping up sawdust. I don't know if I can actually answer the question of why we are doing this. I don't know if I actually know. I think it goes back to the time that we were studying theatre and we all thought it would be great if we could have our own space and do the plays we wanted to do with our friends in them.'

For all their work together, the theatre partnership never really got off the ground. There were already too many holes in their marriage and by the beginning of 1985, they both realised the charade was over.

The couple's new £1 million home on Addison Street in North Hollywood was filled with angry voices. Like his father before him, Tom felt a strong urge to pack up and move on, to try again. He had an advantage over Amos that in acting he had chosen a career where escape from reality was a prerequisite for success. In throwing himself headlong into his work, he was able to either feed off his frustrations, or at least to hide from them for a little while.

The cracks, however, continued to widen. It was an unhappy period for everyone in the family. There was never any question that both parents loved their children with all their hearts. Like so many young couples who commit to each other, for whatever reason, before they are truly ready, it was just too much, too soon.

After a doomed attempt to patch up the marriage in the summer, Susan filed for divorce in October 1985.

And then things began to get ugly. It was a long, drawn-out, bitter divorce battle with both sides wrangling over money, custody of the children and even taking out restraining orders against each other at one point.

It is not a time in his life Tom likes to talk about to anybody, let alone in interviews, and he has long since made his peace with Susan and their two children. But the bulky divorce file, number D152300, lodged at Los Angeles Superior Court offers a fascinating insight into the other, more testy, side of America's favourite Mr Nice Guy.

It would be almost four years before the Hankses were officially divorced. The dispute became so bitter at one stage that Susan asked for a restraining order against Tom and told the court in written evidence: 'My husband has repeatedly verbally abused and humiliated me during the past 90 days in my home. This caused me to suffer great emotional distress.'

There was never any suggestion of physical violence, but feelings ran so high that an order was made barring both of them from molesting, attacking, striking, threatening or otherwise disturbing the peace of the other. It may have been legalese, but it illustrates just how much their relationship had deteriorated.

They couldn't even agree on the date of the split. A trial brief filed in February, 1987, by Tom's Los Angeles lawyers, describes both how the marriage finally ended and how the two parties differed over the date.

The divorce document tells how the couple split and lived apart after Susan asked Tom to leave and demanded that he told Colin that the marriage was over in February, 1985. After living with a friend for a few days, Tom moved into the Sheraton

Universal Premier Hotel in Studio City, Los Angeles.

They 'never resumed the marital relationship' despite two attempts that summer to patch up their differences.

The first, explains the brief, was when Tom and Susan stayed together in a New York hotel room for five days. The second was when Tom moved back into the family home in Los Angeles for less than a week.

Any remaining thoughts of a reconciliation were dashed after Susan went to Chicago with the children and the couple had a 'bitter argument'.

The reason for the date dispute was that Tom had made two movies that year, a fact that would affect Susan's divorce pay-off. If the marriage was officially deemed over in February, it would mean the considerable fees Tom received for the two films wouldn't necessarily be involved in the final settlement.

Susan's lawyer hit back, claiming in a written declaration that the actor 'apparently is attempting to substitute over-cleverness and misinformation for the candour and professional disclosure properly required to remove surprise and encourage settlement.'

As the case dragged on, both sides fired broadsides at one another. In a court declaration, Susan complained that Tom 'refused to grant me any additional time to complete my trial preparation.'

She continued:

> 'One of the things Tom now seeks is to take my deposition, in Los Angeles, for a second time in this proceeding, ostensibly for the limited purpose of inquiring about my recent return to the theatre, which Tom knows is the very reason why I am not now available for further deposition.
>
> 'As I expressly told Tom, I presently am living in Sacramento where I am in continuous rehearsal for a lead role in a series of theatrical productions of the Sacramento Theater Company.
>
> 'The shows now in rehearsal are essentially two person works with no understudies. My absence would, in effect, shut down rehearsals.
>
> 'Moreover, there is no need to depose me now. Tom

knows as much as I do about my theatrical return. In addition, my counsel already has offered to provide to Tom under oath by written interrogatories whatever information he requires about my present employment and living arrangements.

'I reasonably believe that Tom's attempt now to depose me is designed to harass and upset me at a time when I should be focusing all of my energies on my job, in an effort to return to the theatrical world and, in addition, to divert my lawyer's time and energies from proper preparation for trial on my behalf.

'I respectfully request that the court grant a protection order to prevent Tom from moving forward with his eleventh discovery.'

Tom in turn claimed his wife was delaying the trial 'merely to harass me and try to squeeze an unfair settlement out of me'.

When Susan tried to put off the divorce hearing for four months, Tom complained in a declaration:

'I am a highly compensated actor. The entertainment industry requires actors at my level to make commitments for work in films and television far in the advance of the anticipated starting date.

'Petitioner and I were informed in early October that our trial would proceed on January 13, 1987. My present schedule is such that I am available for trial in January and February. I committed myself to begin a major film project in March. My involvement in this project is expected to last for two months. In addition, I have another work commitment that should end in May or June. Additional obligations past June are likely.

'If this court grants petitioner's motion for a continuance, then petitioner has effectively prevented me from earning money and making further work commitments. A trial after June will be at the expense of a work opportunity. Petitioner can then trade my unavailability for work against her seeking an unfair settlement. This is not just a theoretical concern. This dissolution has been a cloud on my career. I agreed to settle this case twice — each time more favourably for the petitioner. Each time, petitioner's counsel argued that it was cheaper for me to pay petitioner more money rather than let this mater interfere with my work. Apparently, petitioner believes that this is such a good tactic that she is utilising the tactic once again.'

'Our lives must go on. Petitioner must be restrained from using court delays to harass me and to seek an economic advantage.

'Petitioner knows that any continuance will restrict my ability to pursue my career and earn a living. Nonetheless, after nearly two years of separation, over $80,000 worth of attorney's bills incurred by the petitioner's first attorney, depositions, document productions, answers to interrogatories and two settlements, petitioner now wants to continue the trial.'

Things really began to get ugly when it was time to try and divide Tom's by now considerable assets. Susan felt that her husband was trying to cut her out of some of his film fortune and bully her into accepting his demands.

In written evidence, Susan said:

'Respondent is a motion picture actor who has earned in excess of $2,000,000.00 during the current calendar year. There is at present in excess of $800,000 in cash and negotiable securities such as certificates of deposit in respondent's possession and in our corporation, Radioland Pictures Inc.

'My husband has stated to me during the past sixty days that if I did not accede to certain demands of his I would receive no community property or support.

'The above comprises a substantial portion of our community estate. If my husband is not restrained regarding the disposition of said assets and if I am not given possession of one-half thereof, it is my belief my interest herein will be dissipated and lost.

'I am informed and believe that respondent is planning to deposit or cause to be deposited approximately $150,000.00 of community property in a retirement plan for the benefit of respondent only. I have not been consulted in this regard. If said proceeds or any portion there are deposited immediate access to said funds at the time of trial herein will effectively be denied me and I may then be required to accept an interest in the said plan which would, in my opinion, be detrimental to my financial needs.'

The other major bone of contention was custody of the two children. By January 1987, the warring couple were communicating through their lawyers. A flurry of letters underlined the animosity.

The letters revolved around Susan's decision to move to Sacramento with the children, where she had found work with the Sacramento Theater Company. It was a move Tom claimed he only learned of after going to pick up the children from school in Los Angeles and discovering they weren't there.

Susan's decision to relocate to the other side of the state did not sit well with Tom, who instructed his lawyers to complain that he hadn't been consulted and to tell her he would be prepared to care for the children while their mother worked in Sacramento.

Susan said that at the beginning of 1987 Tom was already earning $1,750,000 'for a single motion picture appearance'. She insisted Tom should pay her enough support 'for a sufficient time to allow her to return and establish herself in the entertainment community which she left during the marriage to raise the parties' children and devote her energies to furthering Tom's career. Tom, of all people, knows that this is something which generally cannot be accomplished in a few months, or even a few years. Indeed, even Tom who is somewhat of an overnight success, struggled for many years before he was able to earn a reasonable living wage as an actor.'

The final paragraph underlines how bad relations between the couple had become.

'Permanent restraining orders prohibiting Tom from harassing or disturbing Susan's peace should here be issued, along with orders prohibiting each party from in any way disparaging the other in front of the minor children.'

Despite all Tom's fears that his marriage would follow the pattern set by his parents, the final settlement resulted inevitably in the children's time being divided between their parents, just as his own had been. He admitted to *Playboy*: 'We married young. We had a child. That was the last thing either of us needed, and yet there was the fact of the matter ...

'It was a college relationship. I was going off to work in the theatre, but when my son was born, we decided to give it a shot and marry.

'Look, I was doing just a version of what my parents had done and what all of our parents had done. We tried. I was married for five years.'

Tom remained, however, fiercely protective of his children, particularly as his fame grew. 'You see these gossamer little creatures being born, and then you see them learn,' he told *GQ*. 'We all learn through disappointment. You think this guy at school is your best friend, and then he sticks a pencil in your neck one day and you can't figure out why, and you start to notice all the cruelty that goes down.

'I take my kids to Disneyland and we're standing in line, and some people come up to us, people from Oklahoma, "Hey, y'all, when yer in Oklahoma, come on and stay with us, we got a spare room, putcha up nice." And then they touch my kids. They touch my kids. Fuck it! That's beyond the realm. I'm waiting to see *Dumbo* and these people are touching my kids. What am I supposed to say, 'Don't touch my kids'? I have to protect them. Maybe I go overboard because I am not there all the time. They're innocent. I have to give them a fighting chance, have to make things as normal as possible.'

In the end, Tom and Susan settled things as best they could. It wasn't ideal, but Tom tried to see Colin and Elizabeth as much as possible.

Tom Hanks in perhaps his most impressive role to date, as Captain Miller in
Saving Private Ryan.

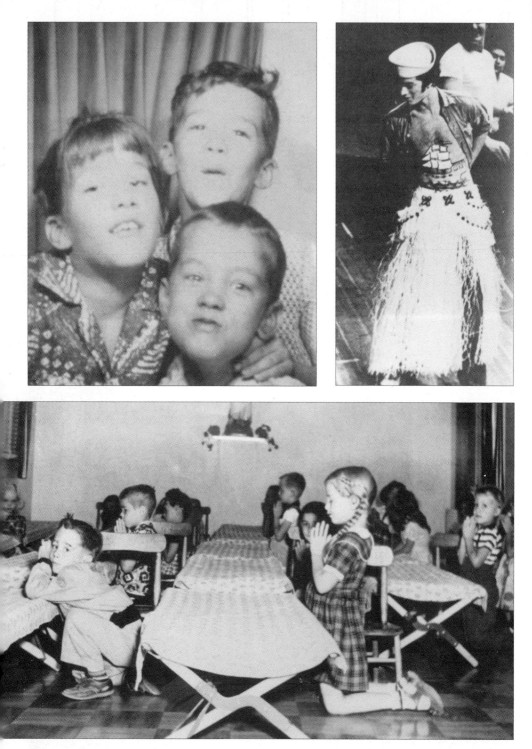

Top left: Tom aged five, with his brother Larry and sister Sandra.

Top right: The dizzy heights of *South Pacific* at high school, aged seventeen.

Bottom: A prayerful moment for a cute Tom at the Holy Child Catholic Day Care Center, Reno.

Top: Rita Wilson, aged eighteen. She was to be Tom's second wife.
Bottom: Tom aged sixteen in the high-school soccer team line-up (middle row, centre).

Not *Richard III*, as Tom said – but good fun nonetheless. Tom plays a goofy bridegroom in the frantic comedy *Bachelor Party*.

Top: Big – a massive success for Tom, leading to his first Academy Award nomination.

Bottom: The Burbs, with '80s heart-throb Corey Feldman, followed a year later.

Top: Tom stars as the scrupulously clean small-town cop, and Hooch is his slavering co-star in *Turner and Hooch*.

Bottom: Although Tom only plays a small part in it, this was his film – he wrote, produced and directed *That Thing You Do!*

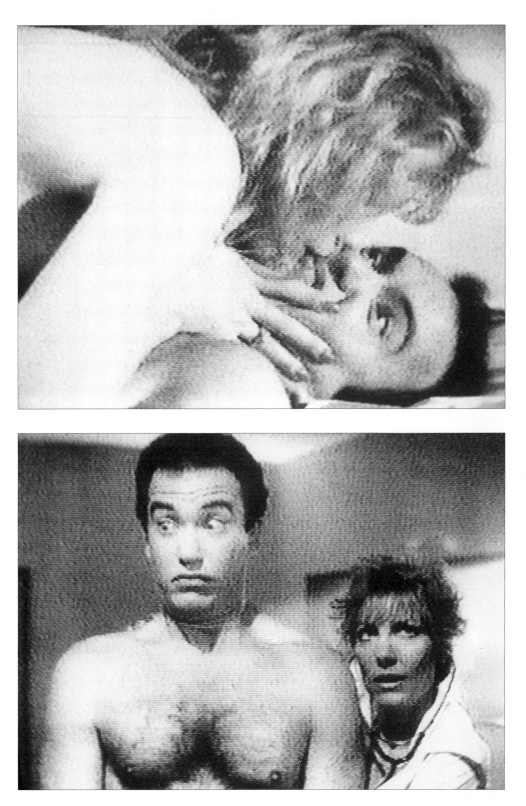

Tom's brother Jim does some acting of his own – as a Forrest Gump-style character in soft-porn flick *Bufford's Beach Bunnies*.

A thoughtful moment for Tom at the première of *Philadelphia*, his first Oscar-winning performance.

He was granted the right to have the children on alternate weekends, between close of school on the Friday to 6.00pm on the Sunday evening, with the proviso they could stay until school on Monday as long as he gave Susan enough notice. He was allowed to see them a number of weekdays a month after school and for five consecutive weeks in the summer holidays. In odd-numbered years, they spent Christmas with their father and on even-numbered years he had them for Easter. He also had them for his birthday, Father's Day and the Fourth of July celebrations.

When the court battle was finally over, Tom agreed to fork out about £8,000 a month to his wife plus more than £600 for each of the children. Tom took the two family Volkswagens, a 1986 Jetta and a 1983 Vanogon, while Susan drove off with the 1980 Volvo Turbo Sedan. Susan was to stay in the house on Addison with the children.

The settlement, when it came, ended one of the most painful chapters of Tom's life. In time, the deep rift driven between Tom and Susan would heal. Like divorced couples around the world, they learned to make their new relationship work for the good of their children.

Tom had little to draw on from his own upbringing in attempting to help his own children best deal with the break-up. His father, after all, had never discussed his divorces with his children and had never offered any explanations.

In 1994, Tom told *Vanity Fair*: 'I explained it to my son the best I knew how, but it was a hideous process. It was a nightmare. It was terrible ... oh terrible.

'Their mother and I don't talk a lot any more, but we're very respectful of each other. I wouldn't say we're friends, or even friendly. But we are very respectful of each other's place and position. All that other stuff that can go along with it? It has not existed. I see my kids at my leisure and at their request and my request.

'There was certainly a period of discomfort and trouble. But once the legal stuff got worked out, it's been quite, well, I wouldn't say pleasant, but it's been easy. And their mother has been a wonderful parent.'

Although he was in the public eye as a famous actor, Tom

refused to accept that his divorce was any worse than anyone else's.

'My work didn't ruin my marriage,' he said to the *Los Angeles Times*. 'You can't put all the blame on the film business. It's just as hard working at a bank and staying happily married as it is in the movies. For a long period of time you go through this period of swearing that you will never make the same mistakes as your parents. But then you realise that they didn't really make mistakes. They just did what had to be done. That's just the way it works out sometimes.'

In the same vein, Tom told *Cosmopolitan*: 'I had some personal problems. Big deal. Everybody has them. We are not talking about a nuclear holocaust. I was a little bit crazy. What I tried to do was turn it to my advantage for my work.

'In some ways I have been like a classic absentee father. My work has taken me away a lot — and certainly being separated, even more so. I think my marriage broke up for any of the reasons that any other marriage breaks up. Lack of communication plays a huge part, and the basic nature of the relationship.'

He added: 'In hindsight, I realise this was an absolutely hideous time for my parents, which is something I was not hip to until I started going through the same sort of things myself.

'My divorce really answered so many questions about how I grew up the way I did.'

Tom told the *Independent on Sunday* that going through the divorce was 'the worst period of time I had'. It was, he said: 'For all the reasons anybody has — a sense of complete failure and a sense of wasted time, a fear of what the future was going to be like. But mostly a sense that somehow, no matter what I would do to combat it, my offspring were going to feel abandoned. That's a bad thing. Because I remember feeling the same thing.'

'I have learned to accept personal failure without being completely demoralised by it for long periods of time,' he said to *Moviegoer*, with just a hint of desperation. 'You can't let that bad dog follow you around for the rest of your life. And you can't believe the hype in either direction. Otherwise, it's peptic-ulcer time and you start to beat the kids.'

Despite all the legal trials and tribulations, Tom's career still seemed virtually unstoppable. And his shattered personal life was about to make a dramatic turn.

For even as he was fighting to save his first marriage, he had already met the great love of his life. She was beautiful, very grounded, and, like Susan, she was an actress.

Rita Wilson would become Mrs Hanks number two.

8
Tom Makes It Big

With sweat pouring down his bristled face, the American passenger searched for the right answers as he was plied with searching questions by his Israeli captors. What was his business in Israel? How long was his stay? Did he have any links to Palestinian groups? What knowledge did he have about Britain's then Prime Minister Margaret Thatcher?

The gun-wielding airport police clearly suspected the suspicious-looking traveller could be a terrorist and decided not to take any chances. They detained him for more than two hours until Mrs Thatcher, who was flying in that afternoon on a state visit, had left the airport with her entourage.

Only then was the very relieved American allowed grudgingly on his way from Tel Aviv.

It could be a yet another scene out of a Tom Hanks blockbuster, with everyone's favourite hero in a sticky situation. But this wasn't play-acting. It was very real.

Tom was in Israel in 1986 to shoot the low-budget drama *Every Time We Say Goodbye*, a lukewarm love story written and directed by Moshe Mizrahi. It was an attempt to give a dramatic new edge to Tom's hitherto zany image, in a role he accepted after *Splash* came out.

Tom plays David, a Protestant minister's son from Montana, who falls for a beautiful Sephardic Jew named Sarah in the treacly boy-meets-girl story. The lovebirds don't exactly thrill Sarah's very traditional family, who yell and carry on in true Romeo-and-Juliet fashion.

The script took David and Sarah to many of Israel's most historic sights as they wrestled manfully with their cultural differences and Tom was thrilled by what he saw. But it had not been an altogether happy trip. Far away from home and his children, he was visited for a fortnight on location by his father and stepmother and while they were watching a shoot one day, Frances's handbag, with hundreds of dollars in cash, travellers' cheques and credit cards, was stolen along with Tom's Levi jacket.

The problem was quickly rectified, but it threw a slight pall over the stay. That wasn't helped when Tom left for the airport after filming had wrapped on the drama, which co-starred Cristina Marsillach.

Mrs Thatcher's arrival coincided with the tired actor's departure and an over-zealous security guard became convinced Tom posed a security threat. Despite his protestations that he was a movie star appearing in an Israeli-made film, he was detained for two hours, powerless to do anything about it.

In his memoirs, Tom's father wrote: 'He was only released after Mrs Thatcher had left the airport ... perhaps Tom did look rather like a terrorist.'

Some of the sights, however, literally took Tom's breath away. He remembered going out with the rest of the cast into the desert 'which was only a stone's thrown away and we lit a fire in the middle of nowhere. We lay back and we watched the satellites go over us, reflecting the sun off them, from horizon to horizon. And you can map out the Zodiac. There's Cancer. There's Leo. You can see them so clearly out there. Beautiful. Stunning.'

He added: 'I wouldn't want to rush through a place like Jerusalem. It's a city that you want to roam. And in Tel Aviv I wanted to see how people decorate their apartments, what their political views are, and since there wasn't as many camels as I had expected, what kind of cars do they drive. You don't have to be religious to understand the worldwide importance of Israel. This is essentially where all Western societies find their base. And the history here is the greatest ever told. As an American and a gentile, I envy the rich Jewish heritage.'

Though backed by the major studio Tri-Star, the film surprised nobody by bombing at the box office, although Tom still claims it was 'probably the most visually beautiful movie I've made,' and took the part 'without hesitation'.

While his personal life was still in tumult, Tom had also reached a crossroads in his career. With the unexpected success of *Splash*, Tom may not yet have been quite a household name, but he was certainly a very marketable star.

Unable to turn down a number of lucrative offers, he made a string of largely forgettable films to capitalise on his new standing in Hollywood. He said later, only half-joking, that he made the quick-fire films 'to get out of the house.'

But question marks were beginning to be raised in the fickle film capital over those choices. The films were rolling one after another, but the hits seemed to be drying up.

First there was *Bachelor Party*, released on the cusp of *Splash*'s success in 1984, which, while doing little for his prestige, still brought in a healthy worldwide profit of more than $49 million (£30 million) and boosted Tom's profile among studio executives always on the lookout for a potential cash cow.

Naughty rather than sexy, he played Rick Gassko in the rowdy comedy from the *Police Academy* team of Pat Proft and Neal Israel. Tom was 28, still fresh from television and still at work on *Splash* when Proft approached him.

'It was an insane movie that needed somebody who had a sane centre, but was funnier than anyone around him. That's what Tom could bring to it,' Proft told the *Minneapolis Star Tribune*. 'Plus, he's one of those guys you like when you meet him.'

It took some convincing for the studio executives to agree to a leading man who, still prior to *Splash*'s release, was a completely unproven quantity. 'They didn't know who he was,' said Proft.

Bachelor Party, in fact, began shooting with TV's *Mad About You* star Paul Reiser in the lead as a bridegroom reluctantly being dragged out by his pals for one final fling.

'He was hysterically funny, but the mix wasn't correct. So the studio said, "Why don't you get the guy you want?"'

Proft said Tom was an instant success on the set. 'He didn't have to think for a night and decide what the character would do. He was ready. We had a dumb party where we wanted him to dance, so he jumped up on a piano and did the Swim, the Pony and all these things. It was hilarious. The camera angles were atrocious because we were falling around helpless with laughter.'

It was never going to grab the attention of Academy Award judges, but Tom's performance swayed a few critics. *Variety* said the 'main reason to see the pic is for Hanks' performance ... he's all over the place, practically spilling off the screen with an over-abundance of energy.'

Tom defended his decision to do the film to *Rolling Stone* magazine, saying: 'Doing *Bachelor Party* is not like doing *Richard III* or *Henry IV, Part II*, but that doesn't diminish the joy of scoring off something that somebody else has written. In fact, at times, it can be more difficult just walking down a hall and talking to somebody and making that interesting.

'That's what I find to be the biggest challenge in making movies. Doing Shakespeare and *Bachelor Party* is not that different, actually. The cerebral processes are the same. The demands are certainly different. The overall appreciation is going to be different. Doing Shakespeare, doing classical theatre, is a luxury.

'This is what I do. I'm an actor. An actor has to act. What else am I supposed to do — sit around the house?'

Irrespective of its dramatic merits, *Bachelor Party* had one powerful effect on Tom's career. It proved that his audience-pulling power in *Splash* was not a fluke.

But then came *The Man With One Red Shoe*, in which Tom, as the movie bible, *Première*, put it, 'seemed to be under a court order not to be funny.' Even the film's star marks it down as his worst film. 'A dog,' is the way he describes it.

Tom plays a symphony violinist and eccentric composer mistaken for a spy in a failed Hollywood rehash of the French farce, *The Tall Blond Man With One Black Shoe*. The spoof, with the bemused Georgetown musician's mysterious rivals trailing him and the requisite bed scene with the beautiful spy, played by Lori Singer, struck a sour note with audiences, who stayed away in droves. The film couldn't even get a big-screen release outside the United States, relegated direct to video for the rest of the world's consumption.

What Tom did demonstrate, however, was his enthusiasm for preparing properly for a part. He spent months learning to play the violin to ensure he looked suitably authentic as a musician in the film. He also says he learned that violinists were invariably bad dressers, a discovery he tried to put over in his choice of wardrobe.

He was slightly less hard on himself in the looks department as he set out to publicise the film. 'I used to be a kind of geeky-looking guy,' he said. 'But I have outgrown my geekiness. Now I feel bad about the way I look only about every other day!'

The other film he made in 1985 was *Volunteers*, another box office flop memorable chiefly to Tom because it was the second time he worked with actress Rita Wilson, who was his girlfriend in the movie and would become his wife in real life.

He played snooty Lawrence Bourne III in the comedy about a self-centred young playboy who, unable to pay his gambling debts, flees to Thailand as a Peace Corps volunteer. The mixed reviews nevertheless noticed, for the first time, the star's stylish similarities to Cary Grant, a recurring comparison through the rest of his career.

In *Newsweek*, film critic David Ansen wrote: 'It's Hanks who gives the movie its seductively sardonic spirit. His character requires both the outsider smirk of a Bill Murray and the debonair inside moves of a Cary Grant, and Hanks has both. His brainy self-interest cuts through the cant.'

Tom worked on his role as a snobbish boor by going to master Hollywood dialogue coach Bob Easton. He would tape the sessions and play them repeatedly on his car stereo. Director Nicholas Meyer said directing Tom was 'like driving a Maserati — you touch it and the whole thing roars off.'

The film opened just one week after the première of *The Man With One Red Shoe*, and fared rather better, raking in $20.2 million in the US. But it didn't provide the jump-start to his career that Tom was hoping for.

Now working at a frantic rate, primarily to offset his domestic unrest, Tom had three films released in 1986. As well as *Every Time We Say Goodbye*, there was *The Money Pit* and *Nothing in Common*, none of which did particularly sterling business.

More Cary Grant comparisons inevitably followed *The Money Pit*, which was a remake of the 1948 comedy *Mr Blandings Builds His Dream House*, which starred Cary Grant and Myrna Loy. Shelley Long, from the TV series *Cheers*, was Tom's co-star in this story of an ill-fated couple who buy a mansion, only to watch it fall apart around them. The critics savaged the Hanks version as 'a miserable rip-off' but it still took more than $37 million in the US.

The Money Pit was a pet project for Steven Spielberg with his own production company, Amblin. He liked the slapstick idea and promoted it to his studio bosses at Universal as their major comedy release for Christmas 1985, although it actually came out in 1986. It was directed by Richard Benjamin, who had won critical acclaim for *My Favorite Year*, and the producers were Frank Marshall and Kathleen Kennedy, who worked with Spielberg on *ET* and the Indiana Jones adventures.

It was the first time Tom worked with Steven Spielberg. He had also reached another milestone in his career — he was commanding a fee of $1 million per film.

Tom confessed to the *Los Angeles Times* in 1993: 'I've made far too many movies. But when *Splash* came out and I started getting offered things, I didn't really know how you could say no, so I worked every chance I got. In retrospect, I can see that was a mistake because I ploughed through several mediocre movies. I don't regret making those choices because those were the only choices I had, but I did seem to get offered an awful lot of goofy, silly roles.'

Like many of Tom's early films, *Nothing in Common* boasted a worthy performance by its star — even if the movie itself came in for some criticism. But unlike the others, there was nothing goofy or silly about it. Through his portrayal of a selfish yuppie who is transformed into a sensitive, caring son when his father falls seriously ill, Tom attracted more attention to his all-round dramatic skills.

He may not have troubled the superstars of the day such as Sylvester Stallone or Mel Gibson. Yet, coming at that stage of his life, it was a very important film for Tom. Until then he had been, as he put it, 'purely a gun for hire', not involved at all in

developing either a script or a character. When director Garry
Marshall came to him with the story of a young man's
reconciliation with his dying father, Tom had a very personal
reason for taking the part — and injecting his own ideas into the
finished product.

'That really completely altered the way I approached making
movies,' Tom told *Première*. 'As a result, that was the first movie
where I thought I knew what I was doing, and it turned out that I
pretty much did know what I was doing.

'I'm still ludicrously more proud of this movie than I should
be, because it didn't do all that great, but still ...'

Co-star Sela Ward, who played Tom's girlfriend, said Tom was
a little shy during the love scenes. 'We were doing a montage shot
were we're running by this lake and he was supposed to fall down
and kiss me. The first time we did it, he bit my lip so hard that
blood was pouring out. Oh, wow, it hurt. We were laughing
hysterically. I said, "You're smooth, Tom."'

The reason for Tom's utter involvement in the film was that, in
part at least, the storyline mirrored his own father's situation.
Weeks before shooting started, Amos had almost died when his
long-term kidney problems took a serious turn for the worse.

Tom's raw emotions were compounded by the fact that his
father in the film was played by veteran TV star Jackie Gleason,
who was himself very ill and died shortly afterwards. 'I think
pretty much everybody knew he was not going to be with us much
longer, although we were all surprised he went as soon as he did,'
said Tom later.

And to add to the outside pressures, Tom's marriage was
falling apart while he was making the film. Not that he let that
harm his performance. Said director Garry Marshall: 'Tom is one of
the few young actors who doesn't believe that the set should
revolve around his private life.'

On the contrary, for the first time Tom really took the subject
matter to heart, using the performance as a forum for his own
feelings rather than an escape from them.

He invited his entire family to an early screening, telling his
father: 'You're in this all over the place, pop. Sorry about that.'

As the closing credits rolled, everyone was in tears. 'Oh yeah, the whole thing was pretty touching,' said Tom. 'I even joked about it. The father in the story had diabetes, so I said, "I pulled for the kidney thing, dad, but they just wouldn't go for it."'

His sister, Sandra, added: 'That was a really hard film for us to watch. Just because it hit real close to home, the illness aspect. We'd all just gone through that. We'd spent lots of time, Tom included, standing next to the bed with dad out like a light with us just yakking up a storm to him. God, we did that for weeks. I mean, they were saying he was going to die.'

The illness had come at a particularly bad time. Throughout his life, Amos had dreamed of being his own boss. Always a hard worker, he wanted to enjoy some of the fruits of his own labour but neither had the time nor the money to set up on his own while he was bringing up his children.

It was only after Tom had left home for good that he felt able to take the gamble and buy his own restaurant. With Frances, he went back to Hawaii, where he had first become interested in the catering trade while working at the Royal Hawaiian Hotel after World War II, and found the perfect site in Kona, the capital of the Big Island.

Amos and Frances put all their life savings into renovating the restaurant and planning the grand opening. Invites had gone out to all of their children and the menus were printed.

But just two weeks before the launch, Amos fell seriously ill from a kidney disease that would plague him for the rest of his life and ultimately cause his death. Toxic chemicals he had breathed in while painting a boat many years earlier had caused irreparable harm.

He had to sell up the restaurant and return to California after being told by worried doctors that the burden of running his own business would be too onerous.

He would have three kidney transplants — one donated by his sister, Mary, and two from cadavers — but all were unsuccessful and he remained on dialysis for the rest of his days.

Just before Tom filmed *Nothing in Common*, Amos sank into a coma and doctors gave him little chance of recovery. His children all spent long days by his bedside, hoping against hope.

In his father's memoirs, Larry describes the scene in the hospital room. 'Tom was washing his face with a warm washcloth, talking to him quietly,' he wrote.

Tom himself said his father's ailment 'wasn't diagnosed for an incredibly long amount of time.'

He recalled Amos's body rejecting the first transplanted kidney. 'And he almost died then, and then he received another transplant which didn't take, and that almost killed him, 'Tom told *Première*. 'There was another time when they were doing this experimental thing of changing fluids just in one area of his abdomen, which kinda went sour on him as well.

'So over the course of seven or eight years, there were, like, four different times I thought I was driving to the hospital to see him for the last time — when I thought, 'Okay, look, we have to resign ourselves to the fact that dad's dead. So let's let him go and move on.'

As the start date for *Nothing in Common* loomed, there seemed to be nothing this time to save Tom's ailing father.

Amos's friend, Arlene Sukolsky, director of the Transpacific Renal Network, recalled: 'He was literally considered to be on his death bed. The doctors had given up. He was just about gone and his doctor said he simply didn't know what else to do.

'Then his Chinese wife asked if they would object to a herbalist coming in to help. They had some traditional Chinese medicine, which they put through a tube directly into his stomach.

'And he came back from the coma. It was incredible.'

The close brush with death had another very positive outcome. It finally healed the rift between Frances and her stepchildren. Together at Amos's bedside through long days and nights, they discovered a newfound respect and understanding of each other.

Amos wrote about Tom, Sandra and Larry's change of heart with a real sense of relief: 'Once feeling little but resentment towards her, they had come to understand something of what was between us, and to appreciate, love and respect her as they might never have done had I never been ill.

'She had once been vehemently disapproving of their ways. Now she could appreciate them and, with me, she was finding it hard to believe that everything had turned out so well.'

He continued: 'Childhood had been a mess for them. Much of the fault was mine, but how would I feel if they were involved in the sick, sordid things so common to their generation?

'Some of them could be in prison, addicted, afflicted, diseased — mentally and physically destroyed.'

After his father recovered, Tom had it written into all of his contracts that the studio concerned would pay for the provision of dialysis and ensure there were hospitals available nearby should his father want to see some new places and visit him on the set with Frances.

Said Tom at the time: 'His recovery really is miraculous. No lie about it. If you saw my dad now, you'd say, "He's a frail old man." And I'd say, "Well, dad's got no kidneys." He's on the dialysis machine three times a week for five hours, which is a major thing you have to make your peace with. He's got a little piece of cow vein in his forearm — you can see the blood flowing! It really is an amazing thing: "Hey, pop, let's see your waterworks again." Talk about understanding how fragile the human body is ...

'At the same time, it's really weird, because through the good use of various kidney foundations, he's travelled the world. When I go off on location, it's a thing I try to work out: well, can dad come?'

Proud of all his children's accomplishments, Amos spent his remaining years helping fellow dialysis patients coping with the disability. Arlene Sukolsky hired him as a part-time patient advocate and he visited countless kidney patients assuring them that life could go on.

'He had been to the brink of death several times and he would visit dialysis units to offer patients help and support and encouragement. He was a very humerous and charming man,' said Sukolsky. 'After he had been doing this for a year or two, his wife Frances felt this was what Amos was destined to do. He was travelling and helping people right to the very end.

'He didn't talk about Tom as much as you would think. He kept that part of his life separate.'

In 1991, he was nationally honoured by *Nephrology News* and Issues magazine with its Quality of Life award and was named

Patient of the Year for his work with kidney patients.

Amos Hanks died on 31 January 1992, aged 67, and was buried in the family plot in Paskenta, Northern California.

For Tom, his father's illness had helped bring his own life back into perspective. First marriage counselling and then intensive individual therapy also played their part.

'I'd been escaping into my work for months and had worked so much I was dead from the feet up,' he told the *LA Times*. 'I wound up in therapy three times a week for several months. I was sad, confused and emotionally crippled — I guess the house of cards has to fall in before you start to figure things out.

'I remember the guy I saw saying to me, "You have a lot to be sad about, but you're going to be all right," and though I didn't believe him for the longest time, I felt like a world of good had been done after several months had passed.'

With discontent over the divorce rumbling through the early part of the year, 1987 came and went with the spartan release of just one Hanks film, *Dragnet*, with Dan Aykroyd as no-nonsense Joe Friday and Tom as his new, freewheeling police partner in a spoof of the hit TV show.

His provisos to the studios were that he didn't want to end up with the girl at the end and he wanted to work with Aykroyd, since he liked the notion of working with another star in a knockabout comedy where he could have some fun after working on back-to-back dramas. The partnership didn't really gell and although it did reasonable business, the critics marked *Dragnet* down as a bit of a drag.

Vincent Canby in the *New York Times* said the laughs in *Dragnet* are 'as isolated as stoplights in the suburbs'.

But just as the death knell was growing louder for him among Hollywood's chattering classes, Tom really hit it Big in his tenth feature film.

The storyline seemed to be everything silly that he had been trying to avoid in films like *Every Time We Say Goodbye* and *Nothing in Common*. In *Big*, directed by Penny Marshall, Tom portrays a 12-year-old boy trapped in a 35-year-old man's body. That's what happens when young Josh Baskin makes a wish on a mechanical wizard at an amusement part. His request to be taller so he can date a girl in his class backfires when his age increases along with his height.

The predictable plot has Josh's parents wondering who the strange six-foot adult in the house is and why he is claiming to be their son; the man-boy becoming a huge success buying toys for a big store; a love scene with a pretty colleague beguiled by his childish innocence; and, of course, the magical transition back to being a schoolboy just in time for the end of the movie.

Like *Splash*, his other biggest film to date, the unlikely ingredients all came together to make *Big* a huge hit, which took more than $114 million at the US box office alone.

And unlike *Splash*, which made a star out of Daryl Hannah, Tom carried the whole film. It even started a franchise, with *Big* drawing in hundreds of fans a night in a Broadway musical.

Most importantly for Tom, his virtuoso performance in the 1988 summer blockbuster won him a coveted Oscar nomination for Best Actor. He may not have won — Dustin Hoffman's *Rain Main* autistic beat out Tom, Gene Hackman, Edward James Olmos and Max Von Sydow. But while *Splash* established him as a Hollywood star, *Big* established him as a fine actor.

Two other much-vaunted actors, Harrison Ford and Robert De Niro, had already turned the part down before it came to Tom.

His success was all the more remarkable for the fact that *Big* was the fourth and last out of the gate of a spate of similarly themed movies. *Like Father, Like Son*, *18 Again* and *Vice Versa* had all been roundly panned and the critics were sharpening their knives waiting for *Big*'s release.

What they found was a delightfully funny, yet sweet and touching film, an almost Capra-esque parable of how much we lose as adults and how a childlike mentality can instruct the modern corporate world.

American TV celebrity Roger Ebert, film critic for the *Chicago Sun Times*, called *Big* 'potently funny, provocative and romantic.'

He added: 'Tom Hanks brings sheer comic inspiration to his role as a 12-year-old boy trapped in a man's body. Okay, so there have been three so-so movies this year with the same child-man plot ... *Big* is different.

'It is that rare film that can tickle the funny bone and touch the heart.'

Once again, Tom was able to draw from his own life to find inspiration for his part. He was all too painfully aware of the conflicting emotions of growing up too fast and leaving life as a kid behind before you are ready. He also studied his own two children to take his own leap back in time.

'If there's any age that I had gone back and analysed, even before preparing for the movie, it was those junior high years, when you can't figure anything out. You're cranky all the time; the chemicals in your body are out of whack.

'When I was 13, 'he told *Playboy*, 'I was younger than my years. I could still play really well. I can remember things that I loved to do, the way you could have toy soldiers or a plane, and you could sit on the couch for hours and have incredible adventures. And I remember being clueless. I remember adults talking to me and just going, "Yeah, right," but not knowing what they were talking about.'

Explaining his approach to the film, he added: 'The issue was whether Josh wanted to skip all those years of pre-adolescence and jump right into the thick of things? And how he decides that he misses what is important to him, which is his family,' said Tom.

'I remember being 13 and being all elbows and knees,' he said at the lavish première party for the film. 'The girls had already grown up. I started the role with the point of view of a newborn giraffe. They have spindly heads that look geeky when they run.

'The expression on the faces of 13-year-old boys tells their whole story. If they try to act older, it's like a drunk trying to act sober. The key to his character was innocence.'

He told the *Chicago Tribune*: 'If we were to maintain our credibility with the movie, we had to tackle this issue of maturation very seriously. We had to confront head-on our own loss of innocence, of intimacy, that comes with adulthood and the competitive nature of the world.

'As adults, we can all probably pinpoint that single moment or month or year when we became adults, the last time of our youth. When it's gone, it's gone and you wish you could go back sometimes to when you were a kid and you could sleep in the back of the car while dad did the driving. None of us would really want to, unless maybe just for a day.

'But that, to me, is what the film is all about, and it's a tough line to walk, to do a comedy with a capital C, one you hope they laugh at, but find endearing and are enriched by as well.'

On the same theme, Tom told *Newsweek*: 'An image that I always carried around with me was that feeling you get when you're a kid and you're driving home from a vacation and you're snug in the back of the station wagon. You can curl up in a ball and fall asleep without a care in the world, and it's warm and the car is rocking and you hear the whoosh-whoosh of passing things ... those kinds of memories and feelings you carry with you forever. Dredging them up was not all that unpleasant an experience.

'There were other things that were unpleasant — the loneliness of being a kid, the confusion, not being able to understand.'

The back-to-back filming, including another movie, *Punchline*, which was shot before *Big* but held back by the studio, had taken a toll on Tom's health and he ended up with a severe bout of pneumonia. For the first time since his enforced breaks between jobs in New York, Tom decided to take some time off.

But he didn't waste his five months of freedom.

By the time *Big* had wrapped in November, 1987, Tom's divorce to Susan had been finalised. By the time the film opened the following summer, he not only had a new hit movie, he had a new wife.

9

The Perfect Couple

Tom will happily admit he has had sex with just seven women in his life. Sure, he had married young and his opportunities as a shy, slightly goofy teenager had been somewhat limited. But here he was, a fully-fledged 31-year-old Hollywood superstar with a very ex-wife, millions in the bank and his pick of beautiful women with stars in their eyes blinding them to bad haircuts and a thrown-together wardrobe.

Many men in his position would take advantage of their single status and international fame to push up their sex stats. With women literally throwing themselves at him, Tom certainly had plenty of chances to do just that. But there were no lurid headlines, no bimbos selling kiss-and-tell stories.

'Look,' he said to *Interview* magazine's Ingrid Sischy, 'I have bedded seven women in my life. That's a paltry sum. I have talked to guys who are into the high three digits, if not actually four digits. I'm not even off two hands.'

But he added: 'I think I have a degree of sexual confidence that is kept in its proper perspective and that is not flaunted. I know what that comes out of, because for years I had no sexual confidence. For years I was lonely. I don't feel a dope because of that. I don't feel as though I have missed out on anything.'

There was one very good reason why Tom kept such a low profile after the break-up of his first marriage. He had already fallen in love.

It didn't happen the first time they met, when the pretty young Californian actress appeared as a guest on *Bosom Buddies*, playing his partner Peter Scolari's girlfriend.

But when he saw Rita Wilson arrive on the Mexican set of *Volunteers* in 1984, Tom knew she was the one.

He was still very much married at the time and Rita was engaged. But he clearly recalled: 'I knew something was going on — Rita didn't, but I did. I knew it was powerfully strong and I knew it was going to have consequences.

'I think men can look at a woman for the first time and say, "Yes, she's the one. This is it." We can be made into drooling idiots much faster than women.'

The film, directed by Nicholas Meyer, was shot on location miles from anywhere by a river near the Mexican town of Tuxtepec, inland from the Gulf of Mexico. One night, the two stars started talking over coffee. They were still talking at two o'clock the next morning.

Although he didn't act on his feelings until much later, Tom was immediately smitten by the vivacious, bright actress who seemed so self-assured even though it was her first big film.

With fellow *Splash* graduate, the larger-than-life John Candy, also in the cast, the two months of shooting was the ideal antidote to the mounting difficulties in Tom's marriage.

The romantic setting and the lack of diversions soon made the emotional undercurrent between the co-stars palpable on the set. 'Rita glowed with niceness,' said actor Xander Berkely, who was in the cast. "You could tell they were fond of each other.'

But when filming was over the couple went their own separate ways — Tom to his wife and Rita back to her fiancé in Los Angeles. It would be another eight months before they would go out on their first official date, to see director Jonathan Demme's concert film, *Stop Making Sense*, with the Talking Heads pop group, in October 1985, soon after Tom and Susan officially pronounced their marriage dead and buried.

Tom described the events that brought him together with Rita in an interview for *US* magazine.

'There was some magic definitely involved. When they were casting *Volunteers*, I remembered her from *Bosom Buddies* and thought maybe she would be good, but I couldn't remember her name. Then, when she was cast, I thought that was petty wacky.

'I thought she was utterly stone-cold delightful when we met again. What a great gal! Then, when we made *Volunteers*, we became really good friends and made each other laugh.'

He continued: 'I was in a marriage that I don't think was good for anybody who was involved. I was in this treadmill of working. My 20s were rapidly coming to a conclusion and I was looking for something different than what I had. And Rita was there.

'It was very romantic. Yet it was fraught with all sorts of very uncomfortable things that really precluded anything that could honestly go on. I'd be lying to say that I just did not see something in Rita that was the greatest thing in the world. But when the movie finished, we went our ways.

'It was obvious we liked each other. But circumstances dictated that there had to be a degree of distance. We realised that there's a type of person who goes from one movie romance to another until they have been romantically linked with 1,800 different people. But she is not like that. Nor am I.

'That February to October everything went wrong! The first marriage was getting smashed on the rocks. We'd just bought a new home that I only lived in for two weeks, and I was off making a movie again. I had two kids I hadn't been home for. The worst aspect of separating was that I was going to be sentencing my own kids to the same sort of feeling I'd felt at the same age. I felt horribly guilty. Food didn't taste good, life wasn't nice. I didn't sleep. It was a time fraught with unhappiness.

'When we split up it was like moving back to Los Angeles again for the first time. I was living in a bad house with rented furniture. But then I could actually pick up with Rita. The magic was quite palpable before, but you gotta do the right thing.'

Tom and Rita were a match made in heaven. He told *Vanity Fair* that 'my notches fit her crooks.'

He went on, once again tracing his 20-something torment back to his childhood: 'When we met it was just bona fide friendship and delight, which rapidly became a kind of passion. I mean, there was a substantial amount of stuff I had to get through. I was married. I had two kids. I could not just ... well, the thing that drove me to the couch was that all I was doing was repeating this kind of life that my parents had gone through, with an incredible amount of pain. Because my parents broke up when I was five, there began this kind of disconnectedness that hung in there until I was 30. But, I mean, everybody's got something that comes along and chews them up for a bit. My loneliness came out of that.

'There just didn't seem to be a table that I truly felt accepted at unconditionally. Coming across Rita, I found someone who could not understand that, and I got a glimpse of how life could be.

'Los Angeles, before I met Rita, was this hideous place where you ended up, not out of choice, but because they paid you to go there. It was a place where the holidays were always going on somewhere else.'

He believes, quite literally, that Rita rescued him from a lifetime of loneliness.

'You get these chances in America, sometimes, to kind of be saved by people. Rita saved me,' he told CNN talk-show host Larry King. 'I'm going to embarrass her right now, but I have found a level of contentment and peace with my wife that I wish everybody could have. I was kind of a wandering and confused guy, and it took me a long time. We took it slowly as well, but as far as the work is concerned, you know, this is what we do for a living and my wife, it's going to sound hokey to say, "She supports me in everything I do," but I get the feeling that she just thinks I'm the greatest, smartest guy in he world, and maybe that's why she makes me so happy. It's never been a problem that we work in the same business, not for an instant.'

Tom had found the family he had been searching for his whole life. With Rita, the 'disconnectedness' was gone.

The daughter of immigrants — her father, Al, is Bulgarian and her mother, Dorothy, is Greek — Rita is the same age as Tom. But their backgrounds could not be more different. Her parents settled in Los Angeles, changing their name from Ibrahimoff to Wilson, the street where they lived, and they still live in the same house where Rita grew up.

Rita's father escaped from communist Bulgaria right after World War II. He managed to jump onto a train with a friend after it separated him and his fellow prisoners from their guards and made a daring bid for freedom that eventually led him to the United States.

Unlike most actresses who leave their small towns to come to Hollywood and then fight their way through the ranks to become stars, Rita was raised a few blocks from the studios and fell naturally into her career.

The second of three children — her older sister is a teacher and her younger brother is a chef — she earned quickly how to make people laugh by doing impressions of children in the neighbourhood.

At the age of 10, she appeared on a popular American TV show, *Art Linkletter's House Party*, and won some luggage, a Parker pen, a lunch out and a limo ride. Coming from a secure, happy home, she never really had any doubt that she would one day be an actress.

Her school, Hollywood High, boasts a galaxy of stars as alumni, from Judy Garland and Mickey Rooney in the 1930s, to James Garner in the '40s, Ricky Nelson in the '50s, Linda Evans and Stefanie Powers, who both graduated in 1960, and Rita in the Class of 1974. Other famous pupils at the school one block south of Hollywood Boulevard included Lana Turner, Beatrice Potter, John Ritter, Carol Burnett and pop star Brandy.

A popular, pretty teenager, she was a cheerleader for the school's football team. As the daughter of immigrants, she developed an innate sense of how best to fit in. The pretty pom-pom outfits were, to her eye, a much more preferable option to the 'black capes and floppy hats' worn by the would-be thespians in the drama group.

On her first day at Hollywood High, at 14, she was approached by a fashion scout, who persuaded her to send a portfolio of her pictures to the respected Nina Blanchard Model Agency in Los Angeles. Weeks after she was signed as a teen model, she was chosen for a bathing suit layout in the prestigious *Harper's Bazaar* magazine.

Nina Blanchard, who also helped launch the early modelling careers of such stars as Melanie Griffith and Rene Russo, said: 'Rita was still in school and I remember some pictures came through the mail. 'I get about 1,000 a week, but once in a while there is a face you are interested in. But I only signed about nine or ten people from mail-ins in all those years. And Rita was one.

'Then, after a very short time, she was modelling for *Harper's Bazaar.*'

Old schoolfriend Debbie Fuqua-Cuen said even then that her classmate had that special something. '*Teen* magazine came in and did make-overs and I remember Rita getting very involved. She had the look.'

Although the modelling was increasingly lucrative, Rita's first love was still acting and she again struck lucky when she went along with a friend to an audition for *The Brady Bunch* TV show in LA. She decided to try out and, to her amazement, won the role of Marcia Brady's cheerleading rival, a part she was well qualified to do.

As well as *Bosom Buddies*, the actress with the Jane Fonda looks played a beauty graduate in an episode of *Happy Days*, where she changed her hair colour and style in every scene. Her first, very forgettable, performance in a movie was the low-budget horror flick *The Day It Came to Earth*, complete with cornball script and tacky special effects.

To finance herself, she also kept up the fashion jobs, working in Milan and Paris after leaving school. 'I can remember at 16 years old saving up all my money to buy a Gucci handbag,' she said. But she soon tired of modelling. 'It was boring, ultimately. There wasn't a lot of room for personality.'

And the kind of acting work she was attracting also began to irritate her. Her roles in *Bosom Buddies*, *The Brady Bunch* and *Happy Days* were examples of the parts she was getting — the pretty girl brought in to spice up the plot without being too memorable or threatening to the sitcom regulars. The routine was to get passed around from show to show without rocking the boat.

'I've forgotten how many times I've played the girl,' she said, soon after completing her first starring role in *Volunteers*. 'Sometimes the girl is a bimbo, a dingbat or bitch whose purpose is to make the hero look heroic and the heroine look good ... The girl is thrown into a script when there's not much going on with the permanent cast. But she's never a threat to the cast members or the formula of the show, whether it's *Hill Street Blues* or *Cheers*.

'I wanted to play less limited roles and the only way to do that was to break cleanly from the rut of playing the girl.'

Rita's way of breaking free was to leave Hollywood completely and enrol in the London Academy of Music and Dramatic Arts. Her modelling had allowed her to save enough money to pay for her digs and for her studies in the classics.

'At LAMDA they really are demanding and you soon discover if you are willing to pay the price. You either get better, change your priorities or drop out,' she said. Rita chose to stay for the full one-year course, appearing in *The Oresteia*, *A Midsummer Night's Dream* and *'Tis Pity She's a Whore*, all at London's MacOwan Theatre.

'They force you to strip away the fantasies you have about your talent and yourself. They take you down to zero so you can make a realistic appraisal of yourself and see what needs improvement. You attend classes from 9 to 5 every day, learning fencing, dancing, singing, elocution, dialects and, of course, rehearsing plays.

'I soaked up all I could at LAMDA and I have retained it. Now when I walk in front of the cameras I am able to create a character and not worry about anything else. Whatever else, I'm not the girl any more.'

After her year in London, Rita studied Greek tragedy in Paris to further hone her talents. Just to get in to Jacques Le Coq's prestigious school she needed at least five years acting experience to even be considered.

When she returned to Los Angeles in November 1985, Rita fired her old agents and signed up with a new manager, telling them she knew exactly what she wanted: the female lead in a major movie opposite a star in a foreign location. Within weeks, she was signed up to star opposite Tom Hanks in the jungles of Mexico.

Again, luck played a part in snagging the prized part. She had auditioned as leading lady but was turned down by casting agents. Then the director spotted a photograph of her at a mutual friend's house and demanded to meet her. He cast her himself and soon she was in a first-class seat on her way to Mexico.

While Tom was instantly smitten with Rita almost as soon as they met up in Mexico, it took a little longer for Rita before the penny dropped. She had got engaged just before leaving to make the film and knew Tom had both a wife and two children.

'We started working on the movie and we became friends. He was really fun. I really liked him. But it was a long, long process before we fell in love.'

She added: 'If Tom and I had met in Los Angeles, our relationship might not have worked out. I can imagine some friend saying, "Rita, I want you to meet this guy. He's married, he has two kids and he's an actor." I would have said, "I don't think so."

'But that situation in Tuxtepec threw us together and we became friends first. There was nothing else to do.'

Rita told writer Candace Bushnell: 'It wasn't like, "Ohmigod. I have to have this man," and I didn't pursue him. The relationship just grew out of a friendship, which was shocking to me because I didn't think that was how love worked.

'When did I know? Probably the first time he kissed me. I was just like, wow-ooooow. Okay!'

The decision to break up with her fiancé was, she says, one of the big turning points in her life. It wasn't an easy choice at the time.

'He was a really sweet guy, a lovely person, but I wasn't completely convinced that I should be spending the rest of my life with him. And I broke up with him not knowing if I was making the hugest mistake of my life. That was terrifying.'

The break-up came after returning from Mexico, but while Tom was still struggling with the guilt and trauma of his first, failing marriage.

'I was very down and low about how I had gotten into this position and why I was with a person I wasn't really in love with. Because then you question your judgment. You think, What have I done? How did I get into this position? That leads to a lot of introspection. You look at that and hope you don't repeat those same mistakes ... Then I met Tom.

'It was a bittersweet parting. You don't know if you are saying goodbye to the person you should be with. You just know you are unhappy in the relationship and you should do something about it.'

She added later: 'I didn't know what being in love was until I met Tom, because I had never experienced it.'

When they finally started dating in Los Angeles, Rita soon arranged for Tom to meet her parents. Although the normally cool actor was uncharacteristically nervous, the evening went well. Rita even noticed that some of her boyfriend's mannerisms, such as the way he stood or drove a car, mirrored those of her father.

But they were bemused by his appearance. Because he was so keen to create a good impression, he had worn two shirts, one over the other. 'My parents thought that was the strangest thing they had ever seen,' said Rita.

As the romance progressed over the ensuing two years, Tom felt reborn. After living in the San Fernando Valley for eight years, he moved in with Rita in the trendy Westwood suburb of LA. 'It's a new world,' he remarked soon after the move. 'It's the Los Angeles you see in movies and TV. It's beautiful girls driving convertibles and people jogging. It's like Starsky and Hutch will drive by at any time.'

Suddenly he was happy enough not to wonder too much about tomorrow. 'I don't know what is going to happen and I don't care,' he said in an interview with the *Orange County Register* about the same time. 'I have no goals. I think goals are something that are being forced on the American people by the powers that be.'

More tellingly, he added: 'I've been off since November, 1987, when we finished *Big*. I no longer miss working when I'm not working. Some people say when you're an actor if you are not working you are not living. I'm content to putter around and be interested in something else.

'Right now I am just enjoying a wonderful life.'

The cobalt-eyed actress brought out the gallantry in Tom. He took his then new girlfriend to the Oscar ball in 1986 only to find screen legend Bette Davis was sitting in her designated seat. Arlene Dahl, who was at the same table, urged Tom to go over and tell Davis to get out of the chair. Worried about upsetting the elderly icon, he finally went over and, in true Hanks style, said: 'Miss Davis, you're sitting in my girlfriend's seat, but if anyone can sit in her chair, you can.' The old lady stared at Tom blankly for several moments before saying loudly: 'I can't hear a word you're saying.'

For months, he drove around his determinedly unfashionable Dodge Caravan with a greetings card on the dashboard, which read: 'I love you always, Rita,' with a little hand-drawn heart.

With his divorce now official, Colin and Elizabeth had quickly taken to Rita. As with Tom, she integrated them into her close-knit family and at the same time helped Tom feel more comfortable with himself as a parent.

Tom had never stopped looking for a faith to embrace since his adolescent experiences at the First Covenant Church in Oakland, but the pressures of his career and fatherhood had left him little time for religion.

Now he started to go with Rita and her parents to St Sophia, the Greek Orthodox Cathedral in Los Angeles. The ritualistic side appealed to his sense of the dramatic; and the deeply ingrained sense of belief struck a strong chord with a man who had investigated and questioned the philosophies of religion at some length.

While the couple were holidaying on the Caribbean island of St Barts with *Robocop* star Peter Weller they met up with *The Graduate* director Mike Nichols and his wife, American TV news doyen Diane Sawyer. They all shared a table for a New Year's Eve party and Tom waited until the last few seconds of 1987 to do what he had known he would do almost from the moment he met Rita — he asked her to marry him. Ever the romantics, they would return to the same isle for their honeymoon five months later, this time without their celebrity friends.

The stag party was classic Hanks. There were no strippers, no lewd behaviour. But it did sound like a lot of fun. With six friends, Tom hired a boat to sail the 26-mile journey across from the California coast to the picture-postcard island of Catalina. He boasted proudly afterwards: 'We didn't shower or shave in 72 hours. It was a manly thing — we got very, very stanky.' The crew drank beer, smoked cigars and told a lot old stories. Oh, and they played at being pirates.

His first marriage may have been due to unforeseen circumstances. But the second time around, Tom was not going to let anything go to chance.

When Tom and Rita emerged to wild applause from St Sophia's

into the sunshine on the last Saturday in April, someone in the crowd shouted out: 'Now you are really and truly well-married at last!'

During the Greek Orthodox ceremony, the same golden crowns once used by Rita's parents were held over their heads. Tom's father was there, as were his childen — Elizabeth was then five and Colin was ten.

'In the Greek Orthodox service,' Tom explained afterwards, 'you don't say anything. You don't sit there and say, "I, Edward G Schwartz, think you're the neatest thing since sliced cheese, and I swear to God from here on in I'm going to do exactly what you tell me." You walk around a table three times, and that's it. The first time you're not married, the second time you're not married, the third time — that's it, you're married.'

More than 150 people dined and danced at Rex's, the luxuriously expensive downtown art deco cafe. Among the glamorous guests were Peter Scolari and almost all of the old *Bosom Buddies* gang; Roger and Luisa Moore; actors John Lovitz, Jon Candy, Bob Sagett and actress Holland Taylor; Dan Aykroyd with his wife, Donna Dixon; director Penny Marshall and actress Kathleen Turner.

Just in case anyone failed to get their wedding picture snapped with the happy couple, a life-sized cardboard cut-out was on display for guests to pose alongside.

Still dancing at 1.00am, the newlyweds finally left for the Bel-Air Hotel before flying back to St. Barts in the morning. 'It was the way it was supposed to be — romantic,' Tom said on his return timed to help promote the release of *Big*. 'On our honeymoon we ran around with almost nothing on and sometimes with nothing on.'

He saw the marriage as 'a cleansing separation between an old life and a new life,' and made absolutely no secret of which he preferred. Success had not made him happy, Rita had.

Tom told *US* magazine: 'You can have the nicest house in the world, but it can still be the shittiest place to live. There's no substitute for that great love that exists that says no matter what is wrong with you, you are welcome at this table.'

He later said that it was only after his second marriage that he conquered the rootlessness he felt and the need to move on every six months or whenever things got tough to deal with. With Rita, he finally became 'comfortable with the idea of home. Everything made sense for the first time, but that was a long time coming.'

Although Rita had not been married before, she had a very strong sense of 'what it should look like. We never go to bed mad and we never let things slide. It's always right out in the open.

'When we got married, we both knew we would be married forever. There's a great amount of serenity and peace in our relationship, so now if we hit rough spots it's not the end of the world,' she said.

Although determined to continue her acting career, Rita made the choice right from the start to put her family first, even if that had a detrimental effect on the roles she was offered. Every time her husband signs on to do a new movie, Rita packs up and goes with him on location, sometimes for as long as three months at a time. 'Everybody has their needs and requirements, and mine is that my family stays together,' she told *Redbook* women's magazine. 'Have you ever experienced what happens when you haven't been around someone for three or four weeks? It takes a long time to get back into a family rhythm. So why disrupt that?'

She didn't forsake her acting career altogether. She went on to appear in the 1996 Christmas film *Jingle All The Way*, opposite Arnold Schwarzenegger and Sinbad, and was part of an ensemble cast that included Melanie Griffiths, Demi Moore and Rosie O'Donnell in a girl's version of *Stand By Me*, called *Now and Then*.

In 1994, she starred with Steve Martin in *Mixed Nuts*, one of director Nora Ephron's less successful efforts, which also featured a young Adam Sandler, and she had a small but memorable role in Tom's *Sleepless in Seattle*.

Rita would also play the receptionist in the remake of Alfred Hitchcock's *Psycho* and had a substantial part in the 1999 summer hit *Runaway Bride* as Richard Gere's ex-wife in the reteaming of the greying star with *Pretty Woman* Julia Roberts.

There's little doubt that Rita — nicknamed 'Bobcat' by her friends — would have been busier had she concentrated on her once burgeoning acting career. But she has no regrets. And she insists her husband has played no part in holding her back. 'He supports me in everything I do,' she says. 'He is ego-less. People would say to me how hard it must be married to Tom, with all his success. I would look at them in total amazement. There was no guarantee that I would be any more successful if I weren't married to him. It's hard to get a job in this business. It's even harder to get a job in this business if you are a woman. Period.'

She said one of the reasons he married him was because he had stopped her in the street one night before they were married and said: 'You never have to change anything about who you are or what you do to be with me.'

'I started crying when he said it. I was standing on 57th Street and 5th Avenue in New York. This was before he proposed to me, and I thought, "Ohmigod, what a man. What a guy,"' she explained.

With Rita's bubbly, outgoing personality to rely on, Tom allowed his own more sociable side to surface. While he had always been superficially friendly, while still keeping most people at a safe distance, he started to lower his protective shield with an inner circle of pals.

So far had Tom come that every Sunday became Chinese food night, when the couple ordered in a vast array of dishes and friends and family dropped in unannounced to dip in their chopsticks. It was a far cry from the bad old days in Oakland when Tom would steadfastly refuse to eat his stepmother's Chinese fare.

Once a week, there was Date Night USA, when the couple go out alone, for dinner or to the cinema.

Even the arrest in Los Angeles of Tom's former business manager Mick Schneider didn't throw a pall on the actor's newfound happiness. Schneider, accused of bilking Tom of in the region of £150,000, was sentenced to one year's house arrest and ordered to pay back his ex-clients the money he embezzled.

The new family was complete when Tom and Rita had their own children, two boys — Chester, who was born in 1990, and Truman, who arrived on Boxing Day, 1995.

In February 1996, they would be featured by *People* magazine in a special issue devoted to 'The Greatest Love Stories of the Century'. Tom would also, as we shall see, declare his love for his wife to a worldwide television audience of 81 million people.

Even after several years of marriage, Tom was still wooing his wife. Briefly parted from Rita while he was filming in Georgia, he arranged for her to fly down for her birthday. When she arrived, Rita discovered to her delight that her husband had rented Teddy Roosevelt's presidential yacht and he proceeded to lay on a lavish champagne-and-candlelight dinner for two on board.

While sometimes bored with the repetitive nature of interviews, Tom still becomes instantly animated when his wife's name comes up. 'I was really very immature and not very wise before I met Rita,' he says. 'I'm sure I was a difficult person to be in a relationship with. Thank God I had the good sense to woo and wed her.

'We had a lot of fights early on, but they were pretty fabulous fights that worked things out. She taught me and awful lot about being a better man, a better father and even a better actor. You know what? She taught me how to fight too!'

He tried to explain to *Interview* magazine just how much his second marriage meant to him. 'I felt lonely for a really long time. That's why I say my wife saved me, because I didn't feel lonely any more. I did right up to the point where she crossed my path. The union of the two of you is better than the actual sum of the two of you. You don't just add two people; you multiply. That's what I think I have got. And it is not a purely romantic thought; it is just better.

'Rita and I have been through a lot just as a couple and certainly as a husband and wife. It takes a while to pound out a relationship, but I think that process ends up being the great hope. Somehow, it's the great hope that is reflected in a lot of the movies that I do.'

After all the excitement of the marriage and a big hit film, another fascinating project was in the pipeline. Tom was being touted for the much-sought after lead in Brian De Palma's screen version of Tom Wolfe's *The Bonfire of the Vanities*. What could possibly go wrong?

Every big name actor in Hollywood wanted the part. But this time, Tom was top of the list.

How was he to know that *Bonfire* was doomed to go up in smoke?

10

A Vanity Project

It was supposed to be the film that put him right up in Hollywood's A-list. His name had been above the title in a couple of hits, sure. He had even shown that he could act a bit. But Tom was still seen by the public — and the industry — chiefly as a funny guy. *The Bonfire of the Vanities* was the film that could focus his career in a serious way, away from the haphazard choices of such comedians as Chevy Chase and Bill Murray.

The novel by Tom Wolfe had been the must-read book of the late '80s, a morality tale charting the rise and fall of the decade of greed. In America alone, it sold 750,000 in hardback and more than two million paperbacks. The book seemed to cross over into real life in the United States at a time when the tabloid headlines in New York screamed out the unrest of an era of racial strife and corporate collapse.

Simply put, the lead character of *Bonfire*'s Master of the Universe, junk-bond trader Sherman McCoy, had about as much in common with *Big*'s Josh Baskin as Tolstoy has with Dr Seuss.

It is not a role many would have thought suitable for Tom, even though he had proved his name was more than sufficient to open a movie. It may not even have been a role he would have chosen to help make the transition.

But at the Academy Awards the previous year, having lost out for the Best Actor Oscar, producer-turned-studio head Peter Guber had searched out Tom at LA's Dorothy Chandler Pavilion to talk some business. He was going to be making *The Bonfire of the Vanities* and was interested in Tom as Sherman McCoy. Was Tom interested in the part? Rarely at a loss for words, Tom stuttered for a moment. 'Me?' he said, thinking Guber was joking. Quickly realising it was no joke, Tom gathered himself to impress upon Guber just how much he was interested. The part had been the talk of the industry for months, with all the top names of the time being linked with the project. The name of Tom Hanks hadn't featured in the gossip.

Tom heard nothing more after the awards show and assumed he had been passed over. Besides, there was no shortage of other projects. Another movie, *Punchline*, with double-Oscar winner Sally Field, was due to come out and Tom was getting a lot of advance buzz for his starring role as a hard-bitten stand-up comic in New York.

Although it was shot before *Big*, it came out after the family comedy and was expected to benefit from the other's success. Tom's Steven Gold, a failed medical student with a sulfurously burning ambition to make it as a comedian, was probably the actor's riskiest role to date and he remains one of his least redeemable characters.

The caustic comedian is no stand-up guy. His anger and mood swings are always just below the surface and they are on full display as he takes a New Jersey housewife with aspirations to be a comedian under his wing. To play Gold, Tom created a childhood for his fictional alter ego, growing up 'in a cold and lonely house, in this family that didn't get him in any way, shape or form.'

'I felt sorry for the guy,' said Tom. 'He's not a good human being, but he's an excellent stand-up comedian. I always viewed him as being trapped by this ability. It was never going to make him happy.'

It was almost as if Tom had drawn on the pleasant memories of his childhood for Big and the darker corners for *Punchline*. Steven Gold was the man Tom could have been had he not got such tight control over his inner demons.

Sally Field saw how much of himself her co-star was bringing to the screen. She told *Rolling Stone*: 'It would be one thing if he was just this great, goofy guy. But that lasts for about 30 seconds and then you want to meet somebody real. The reason he is a movie star and is going to stay one is that he's much more complicated than that.

'Yes, he's very entertaining and funny and easy to be around. But you know there is somebody else underneath, somebody dark. There's a sad side, a dark side. And that's what makes him so compelling on the screen.'

Punchline was a film Tom wanted badly to do. He asked writer-director David Seltzer back in 1986: 'Well, who do I have to sleep with to get the part?' At the time, he considered the film 'the greatest stakes of anything I've done'.

But when he first got the script, there was one major flaw that worried him — it wasn't very funny. A fan of legendary stand-up comedians Lenny Bruce and Richard Pryor, Tom brought in comedy writer Bary Sobel and an old friend from Sacramento State, Randy Fechter, who had been working in comedy in Off-Broadway productions, to write him some stand-up material.

Then he spent nearly two months trying out his act in some notoriously unforgiving comedy clubs. 'The first time I thought I had five minutes worth of material,' he said. 'I was gone in two. I was really terrible the first 15 times.

'But as time went by, we actually did assemble a pretty good act. It wasn't a bad set.'

He added: 'That kind of power corrupts ... walking into a room of 400 people and taking them wherever you want for 20 minutes. Steven is god of his universe as long as he's got a microphone in his hand. You can't help taking that home with you.'

Seltzer recounts one incident on the film set that underlined his star's no-nonsense professionalism. He explained how Tom didn't want to be seen the morning he was due to shoot a very emotional scene where Gold notices his doctor father in the audience and erupts into a tearful monologue about why he quit medical school.

'He wanted to be called from his trailer when the cameras were literally rolling,' said Seltzer. 'Lord only knows what it was he dredged up, but he came out and just did it, and he did it all day long. I said to him at the end of the day, "Did you have any idea you were gonna walk up there and burst into tears?" And he said,

"I had no idea I wouldn't be able to after three o'clock."'

Seltzer went on: 'I had to do some camera set-ups during that scene and Tom at that point was backstage and I was worried he was losing it. So I said, "How about we get the actors playing your father and brother up here? I'll just have them stare at you in the dark."

'And he said, "What is this, Acting 101? I don't need that crap. Go set the lights, I'm doing my work."'

Ever since that ticking off from Ron Howard on the *Splash* set, Tom had vowed never again to give cause for his professionalism to be questioned, a facet of his acting that made him popular with both cast and crew. If a director wanted to shoot a scene 322 times, he would be prepared to shoot it 323. 'That's my job,' he will say. At the same time, he is adamant about offering his own input into his character. 'I don't write scripts, I write on scripts,' he says.

His old friend Randy Fechter said: 'He's a regular dude who can't stand obsequious behaviour. If anything, he errs to much on not being a star. He could get more of what's coming to him, but he sees other people acting like stars and the last thing he wants is to abuse his position. He's a genuinely sweet person. He could get away with murder.'

The release of *Punchline* was delayed because of a changing of the guard at Columbia Pictures and when it finally came out, in September 1988, it was met with mixed reviews. Much of the criticism was aimed at Sally Field's housewife-turned-comedian and her character's relationship with Tom's corrosive comic. But, once again, Tom earned widespread praise for his portrayal.

Newsweek critic David Ansen glowed: 'You feel for Steven because Hanks understands him so completely and allows us to peer inside this brilliant s.o.b.'s stunted soul. You never catch him wallowing in the part. Steven may grandstand, but Hanks doesn't. His acting has wit, velocity, relaxation, and the extraordinary physical dexterity he demonstrated in Big. This guy may give you the creeps, but he holds you spellbound.'

The comparative commercial failure of the film was offset by the continuing critical praise poured on Tom, who was still just 32, and, although nothing came of it, the role garnered some support for an Oscar nomination.

Proud of the film, Tom told *Playboy* the year after its release that his only mistake may have been that he allowed himself to get too close to the part.

'The movie didn't do well, which was really disappointing,' he said. 'If I were going to figure out why, I would end up taking a bunch of cheap shots at an awful lot of people who tried real hard, and that's not fair. What can you say? But it's the best work I have ever done. We were talking some real naked truths about the characters and, in a lot of ways, about myself. I was too close.

'The guy in *Punchline* probably has the worst aspects of my worst aspects.

'He is extremely competitive, for one thing. Competitive to a fault. He is unable to balance his daily existence so that real life and what he does for a living have an equal weight. I've certainly had those problems; I think any actor has. The only time you feel alive is when you are working. I've gotten a little more mature since I was like that. But I think that is what really drives actors absolutely stark-raving mad and why they develop ulcers and drug problems.'

All in all, 1988 turned out to be a satisfying year for Tom, culminating in the Best Actor vote at the Los Angeles Film Critics Awards for his combined work in both *Big* and *Punchline*. And with the *Bonfire* project still hanging tantalisingly in the air, there was considerable promise that the next couple of years would add still further to Tom's box-office bankability.

But, although Tom's personal life had never been better with his marriage to Rita and his ever-improving relationship with his children, he was about to take a few steps backwards in his career.

He returned from a long break, refreshed and ready for three upcoming projects; *The Burbs*, with Carrie Fisher; *Turner and Hooch* with Mare Winningham; and *Joe Versus the Volcano*, with Meg Ryan.

All comedies with attractive leading ladies, they did nothing to improve Tom's Hollywood lustre. In *Turner and Hooch*, the only one of the three that didn't bomb, Tom shared top billing with a dog.

Having made 12 films in six years, Tom still hadn't learned the art of saying no. He confessed: 'Part of it is the insecurity factor — every time, you feel like you are never going to get another chance again. They're going to catch on, and that'll be it. Even when you're working a lot, you think, How many of these do I get? It's like they give you only so many dollars in your wallet and once those dollars are spent, you're broke.'

That would be fine but for the fact that even then, the actor was probably set for life. He was getting more than one million dollars for each movie and his fee was rising all the time. Even in January, 1988, he confided to *GQ*: 'Actually, I'm pretty well set. I could get by without working again.'

What was more surprising was that, after *Nothing in Common*, *Big* and *Punchline*, the roles he took were not particularly challenging. He was, inevitably, the best thing about all three movies. But that didn't mean an awful lot.

It must have been all the more frustrating to Tom that two films he turned down, *Dead Poets Society* and *Field of Dreams*, went on to become massive commercial and critical hits, for Robin Williams and Kevin Costner respectively.

Tom was also lined up to star with Michelle Pfeiffer in the film *When a Man Loves a Woman*, about a female alcoholic and her relationship with her heavy-drinking husband. He even worked on the script with top Hollywood writer Ron Bass. But first Pfeiffer dropped out and then her replacement, Debra Winger, also found she couldn't commit to the film and Tom handed the project back to the studio.

When the film was finally released in 1994 starring Meg Ryan and Andy Garcia, it was hailed as one of the actress's best and most serious roles.

The Burbs, a black comedy of suburban paranoia was directed by Joe Dante. Tom liked his earlier films, *Gremlins* and *Innerspace*, because 'you see a world that is so completely pleasing on the surface yet deep down, something horrible's going on.' In *The Burbs*, filmed during a Hollywood writer's strike, Tom plays a hopelessly dull executive who spends his holiday investigating weird goings on with his nitwit neighbours. Based largely on *Big's* success, the film opened to record weekend box office before sinking without trace when word got out that it was a stinker. *Time* magazine said: 'Hanks throws himself into this anti-audience movie with such suave energy that he seems determined to torpedo his hard-won rep as Hollywood's most comfortable new star.'

A V A N I T Y   P R O J E C T

Turner and Hooch, released the same year, was a much bigger hit, even if its storyline was hardly original. Tom plays a small-town cop who teams up with a drooling junkyard dog that's the sole witness to a grisly murder. It was the first in a multi-film deal Tom had signed with Disney, providing him with his own office and the chance to bring some of his own ideas to the screen.

It didn't start out well, with director Henry Winkler, formerly The Fonz, who Tom knew from his stints on *Happy Days*, leaving the set after 12 days complaining of 'creative differences' with his leading man. He was replaced by Roger Spottiswoode.

The differences between Tom and Winkler really showed as the actor had very definite views about his role — and was prepared to use his star power to ensure his vision of the movie wasn't disregarded.

Turner and Hooch wasn't exactly *Lassie Come Home*. It wasn't even *Beethoven* — any hopes of a sequel or a canine merchandising payday were killed off along with the dog at the end of the movie.

But a note sent from Tom to executive producer Daniel Petrie illustrates the kind of thought he puts into his craft. It read: 'My intention is to shape Hooch into a more unique character whom we have not seen before in a movie, who will constantly surprise the audience just when they think they have him pegged, and who is sexy and attractive in his own peculiar way. My story, from my point of view, is of a man who has developed a very particular mode of living, without realising he has closed himself off from a great deal of the joy that is found in everyday life. Hooch disrupts his life in the way some girlfriends do; he makes Turner crazy, costs him money, and gets him into trouble. But when he is gone, there is nothing Turner wouldn't do to get him back.'

How such an ugly dog can be described as 'sexy' is incomprehensible, but Tom gets to play a couple of scenes in his black briefs, which is about as much as you are going to see of his less-than-stellar body in a Hanks film. Mare Winningham is his love interest, a veterinarian who helps him to calm down.

If his next film, *Joe Versus the Volcano*, is memorable for anything it is for Tom's first screen romance with Meg Ryan. Although it wasn't a hit first time out, the chemistry between the two stars would go on to provide the basis for arguably the finest light-comedy pairing since Tracy and Hepburn.

Playing an office-bound hypochondriac who sets off on an unlikely adventure in the South Pacific after being given six months left to live because of a rare disorder called a 'brain cloud', Tom was attracted to the offbeat story and the prospect of working with Ryan.

In one of her stranger films, Ryan gets to play three different women.

John Patrick Shanley, who got an Oscar for his screenplay for Cher's tour de force, *Moonstruck*, was given a big $49 million (£30 million) budget, and expectations for the film were high. But Warner Bros didn't get much return on their investment. Tom's father didn't even get to visit his son on location in the sunny South Pacific because, despite the production outlay, the island scenes were shot on the Hollywood sound stage where the Yellow Brick Road was once constructed for *The Wizard of Oz*.

Both stars got reasonable reviews, but the film was generally felt to be too much of a mish-mash to work. While saying Tom gave a 'carefully thought-out performance,' the *New York Times* said: 'Not since *Howard the Duck* has there been a big budget comedy with feet as flat as this.' The Oscar drums that had been beating loudly over Tom's career a year or so back had now fallen silent.

In the meantime, however, Tom had finally been contacted over the role all of Hollywood was still coveting — Sherman McCoy.

Director Brian De Palma had called offering Tom the job, saying he saw him combining the comedic and dramatic aspects of the novel in a manner reminiscent of Peter Sellers in Stanley Kubrick's *Dr Strangelove*.

The choice of maverick genius director Brian de Palma for the *Bonfire of the Vanities* astonished Hollywood, as everybody from Steven Spielberg to Martin Scorsese to Mike Nichols had been considered at one time or another. De Palma was considered a stylish thriller maker in the Hitchcock genre rather than the man to take charge of a big budget comedy. But he was still hot from 1997's hit screen version of *The Untouchables* and was given free rein by Warner Bros.

The casting also astonished the movie capital, where William Hurt was considered the favourite and the names of Michael Douglas, Steve Martin and even Tom Cruise had been among those hotly tipped.

Tom admitted he was 'intimidated' by the project, but the challenge — and the $5 million (£3 million) salary — was irresistible. The problem, and even he would probably admit it now, is that the critics of the controversial casting were right — Tom was not Sherman McCoy.

The Ivy League, Park Avenue world of blue-blood McCoy was not something Tom could relate to. In all his best roles, Tom had found something of himself to bring to the screen, giving his performances a vulnerable credibility that audiences recognised. His gypsy childhood offered him nothing to draw on this time.

'All I could do,' he admitted, in preparation for his role, 'is to try to get a sense of the space that Sherman McCoy existed, which is as alien to me as Odessa, Texas, or the planet Mars.' The best he could do was to visit the most elite private schools in Manhattan. He went to Yale. He paced a Wall Street trading floor.

Tom was seen as too young, too middle-class, too goofy to play the WASPy bond trader. Tom's pug nose didn't have the definition of McCoy's Yale proboscis depicted by Wolfe in his seminal novel of the '80s. He was derided as looking like 'Dennis the Menace in worsted wool pinstripes.'

Before the film opened, Tom acknowledged he was never the obvious choice for the part. 'If there was any challenge in this, beyond the simple one that goes into doing what I do in the first place, it was that of the 2.4 million people who read the book, there were 2.4 million casting suggestions for Sherman McCoy — and I wasn't on any of those lists!' he said.

His research, incidentally, didn't include talking to Tom Wolfe. 'I didn't know what to say. "Here I am! Boy, you write really good books. Did you like Punchline at all?"'

The attraction of *Bonfire* was, essentially, its high profile. Few movies had been so eagerly awaited or so heavily hyped — or failed so miserably.

'It's not a matter of pressure that was put on me,' Tom told the *Orange County Register*. 'It's just that all the attention, the scrutiny on the choice of me and why I did what I do and why they put me in it in the first place. I don't have a Yale chin and da-duh-da-duh-da-duh. It is going to have that kind of focus on it. It's much different than if you were just making up a story that you were going to tell people for the first time.'

He put it even more succinctly: 'The idea of me playing Sherman McCoy is a huge, massive crapshoot.'

Tom was not the only questionable casting call, however. In *The Bonfire of the Vanities*, McCoy takes a terrible fall when he and his mistress are heading home to the posh Upper East Side of Manhattan one night and take a wrong turn into a run-down neighbourhood in the Bronx, which, to these denizens of a world of wealth and privilege, looks like hell itself. When they are approached by two black men, their racial paranoia sends them into a panic, resulting in a hit-and-run accident that leaves one of the strangers in a coma.

A drunken reporter latches onto the story in a bid to revive his fading career. And McCoy, who had once proclaimed himself Master of the Universe, sees his world fall around him like a pack of cards as he becomes a pawn in New York's political power games and a poster boy for the ills of society.

The character of drunken hack Peter Fallow was actually Australian in the book and the first actor in the running was Monty Python's John Cleese. But De Palma thought an Englishman narrating the story would alienate an American audience, and decided that Bruce Willis would bring some big box-office starpower to the part.

This casting choice, and that of Melanie Griffith as McCoy's mistress, dumbfounded fans of the book as much as Tom's casting.

It was actually Tom who was responsible for getting Griffith the job. According to writer Julie Salamon, whose book *The Devil's Candy* gives a fascinating insiders account of the making of the movie nicknamed 'The Bombfire of the Vanities', Tom had a lock on the role from the moment studio boss Peter Guber paid Wolfe £1/2 million for the rights for Warner Bros.

De Palma at first wanted Steve Martin. The studio wanted Tom Cruise. But Guber would call the director and the executives and chant: 'Tom Hanks, Tom Hanks, Tom Hanks, Tom Hanks ...'

In his contract, Tom had it stipulated that he would have a say in his leading lady. Although Melanie Griffith was always in the running, De Palma was excited about Uma Thurman, particularly after she auditioned with Tom. But Salamon said Tom thought acting with Thurman would not work.

As nice a guy as he was, Tom certainly was not above pulling rank. And he preferred Griffith. Salamon said Thurman flew in for a screen test with Tom. 'She was marvellous, or maybe she just seemed to be because she was so very beautiful,' wrote Salamon. 'But there were dissenters, and in this case the only dissenter who mattered was Hanks. The studio had indeed asked for his opinion and he had given it.

Ever the survivor, Tom came out of Salamon's book reasonably well, certainly compared with his co-stars, who are portrayed as insecure and professionally limited in comparison. Tom's icy wit was largely lost on both Griffith and Willis.

On one occasion, Griffith, who was married at the time to *Miami Vice* star Don Johnson, 'tottered' over to Tom, who that weekend had gone to his first Lamaze birthing class with Rita, who was expecting their first child that August, and sat on his lap. Salamon wrote: 'Griffith crawled onto his lap and asked him if he was nervous about their love scenes.

'"Not at all, no," he said, pulling his head back stiffly. "You know, Melanie,' he said in a bantering tone, 'I saw your husband on television. He was on a large boat looking very small." Griffith looked at him uncertainly.'

Halfway through shooting the film, Griffith shocked her colleagues by turning up with newly inserted breast implants. Fortunately, the sex scenes had not yet been shot so her breasts didn't seem to magically grow during the film.

Willis, fresh from his action man exploits in the first *Die Hard* film, was equally nonplussed by Tom's humour.

Wrote Salamon: 'In between takes, Willis and Hanks sat on their canvas chairs and watched themselves on playback on the video monitor. Hanks looked bored as Willis droned on about how much his work on *Moonlighting* improved his ability to play to the camera. Suddenly Hanks leaned forward until his face was just inches from the video monitor.

'He examined the close-up on Willis, whose image was wearing the wise-guy smirk that had become a subject of much mocking commentary among the *Bonfire* cast and crew over the past few weeks. "Big, shit-eating grin I see there on the monitor," said Hanks jovially. Willis showed no sign of registering the comment. Hanks peered at the monitor again. "Yup," he said. "There it is."

'Just then the Willis entourage converged around their boss. Hanks kept staring at the monitor.'

Willis's entourage, incidentally, included two bodyguards. Tom's only 'hanger-on' was his pregnant wife, who would pop onto the set periodically and made a fleeting appearance in the opening of the film, escorting an inebriated Willis to a society function.

Tom would later tell *Vogue* that Salamon 'did an amazing job. It was pretty fair and accurate. Of course, that doesn't mean I didn't want to throw myself off a bridge after I read it. Some people will assume that all that madness and indecision and overspending is how an unsuccessful movie gets made. But that's how every movie gets made. If *Bonfire* had been a stellar success, people would have looked at the book as some sort of blueprint of how chaotic making a great movie can be. The odds are always that you'll make an atrocious movie. The fact that you often don't is what makes you a hall-of-famer.'

The filming itself caused controversy with demonstrations in both the Bronx and New Jersey, where production was interrupted by real New Yorkers, who didn't see themselves as being on the edge of moral and political breakdown as depicted by Wolfe's book.

There was also a considerable furore over the casting of the judge in the film. This began with De Palma auditioning a real-life Bronx judge, Burton Bennett Roberts. It was decided he wasn't likeable enough so the job trickled first to Walter Matthau, who agreed to do it but named his price too high at $1 million for a little over a week's work: then to Alan Arkin, before he, too, dropped out. In the end, the job of feisty Jewish judge Myron Kovitsky went to black actor Morgan Freeman, thus comlicating the role the judge plays in the climactic, racially driven trial. The shoot was further distracted because Freeman was contracted to do a Shaklespeare play *The Taming of the Shrew* immediately after *Bonfire*.

When shooting was over, Tom predicted the film would

disappoint a lot of people 'because many will have a certain idea how the movie will look.' He was right. The film was a commercial and critical disaster.

Vincent Canby, in the *New York Times*, called it a 'gross, unfunny movie,' although he adds: 'Mr Hanks comes off best as the bewildered victim. He's nobody's idea of a prototypical Yale man, which is the way he's described in the novel, but he's a good comic actor ...

'In one brief love scene, Miss Griffith's body appears to be so perfect as to be surgically reconstructed. Perhaps not, but *The Bonfire of the Vanities* is so wildly uneven that everything in it seems open to question.'

In its first 45 days of release in the US, the $50 million (£30 million) film took just over $15.7 million (£10 million) at the box office and was voted the worst film of the year in a poll of newspaper, magazine and TV film critics.

On 13 February 1991, the Oscar nominations were announced. *Bonfire* didn't get a mention.

Much later, Tom told *Time* magazine that ultimately, his Sherman McCoy was 'a pussy'.

'It comes down to that,' he said. 'In the nature of how Brian wanted to make that movie, McCoy couldn't be anything other than a pussy. Therefore, there was no mystery to it. He was a pussy from the beginning, and he was a pussy all the way through. He was just a big, fat pussy.'

He told the *Chicago Tribune*: 'The disappointment of a flop movie only stings for a few weeks, just like the Oscar euphoria only lasts a few weeks. I remember coming out of the shower, having forced myself not to think about '*Bonfire*,' having told myself all the usual stuff about everybody having a major flop, and feeling pretty much OK. But the television was on, and one of those morning shows came on, and the blistering review of '*Bonfire*' was the first thing on the show, and I went 'AAAUUUGGGHH!!'

'But by the time the movie came out, most of us knew '*Bonfire*' was not a good movie. When everyone looked at it, Brian De Palma said, "Hmmm. It might not be happening."

'Our mistake was that we made big changes in a novel that had entered the national consciousness and failed to pay attention to the minute details that made the novel so great on the page.'

Nearly a decade after the film's critical and box-office nosedive, De Palma remained unrepentant about his spurned vision for the movie. 'Again it's an example of people not seeing what's on the screen,' he told the *Irish Times*. 'They bring these preconceptions of what they think the movie should be and then criticise it harshly because of that.

'In Europe, the film was better received because not so many people there had read the book. It was very much a book of it's time. That happens. Some things tend to be very fashionable for a time, but they don't have the quality that makes them endure over the decades.'

What did the book's author, Tom Wolfe, have to say? In fact, he refused to join the throng criticising the film and the casting. 'I think it's bad manners in the Southern sense to harp and be critical of it,' he said. 'After all, I did cash the cheque.'

Tom's attempt to kick-start his roller-coaster career had failed, so he decided to take a longer break to recharge his batteries. Rita had given birth to their son and Tom was looking forward to playing dad for a while. Besides, he explained, Hollywood would wait. 'It's not like they stop kissing your ass right away. I think you really have to go a lot of years before you stop getting your ass kissed.'

11

A Serious Star

It seemed the whole world was settling down to watch the 1994 Academy Awards on television. Tom was walking nervously into the Dorothy Chandler Pavilion, his wife on his arm, with a very real chance of winning a Best Actor Oscar.

If he was rightly considered an outsider when he won his first Academy Award nomination for his man-boy role in *Big*, Tom was the hot favourite this time for his memorable, bold performance as a lawyer dying of AIDS in the landmark film *Philadelphia*.

After one more flop, 1992's *Radio Flyer*, Tom was back on a winning streak. His next two films, *A League of Their Own* in 1992, with Geena Davis and Madonna, and *Sleepless in Seattle*, with Meg Ryan in 1993, had both been big hit comedies.

But *Philadelphia*, with its ground-breaking plot and serious message, was everything that *The Bonfire of the Vanities* was not. It was a thought-provoking, spellbinding drama with brave casting of actors who outgrew the shackles of their celluloid CVs to put in some magnificent performances.

More importantly, it was the darling of the critics and a big box-office success.

Even alongside such established serious actors as Denzel Washington and Jason Robards, as well as Latin heart-throb Antonio Banderas, Tom's star shone the brightest.

So it was no great surprise when Tom Hanks's name was read out ahead of fellow nominees Daniel Day-Lewis, Anthony Hopkins,

Liam Neeson and Laurence Fishbourne as the winner of the Oscar for Best Actor.

*   *   *

The road to *Philadelphia* had begun more than three years earlier when Tom took a conscientious decision to take a firmer hold on his career. After the *Bonfire* débâcle, where he even found himself being critiqued by a coffee shop waitress because he didn't have a 'Yale chin', Tom took his self-imposed sabbatical very seriously.

'It was the best thing for everybody,' he told *Vogue*. 'I needed a break from the industry. And the industry needed a little less of me for a while. How many times can you see somebody on yet another magazine cover? Plus with me it's always the same story. I'm an average guy, down-to-earth, kinda quirky, blah, blah, blah.'

He thought, simply, that he had been working too much. 'What had happened was, the kind of glamorous fun of making movies had just completely dissipated for me,' he told *Entertainment Weekly*. 'And I just felt as though I was no longer the hammer, but I was the anvil instead. I was very, very, very, very tired.'

Tom ended up staying away from Hollywood for 18 months, a risky recess for a star whose golden touch seemed to have deserted him of late.

He had now bought a beach house in Malibu, close to Steven Spielberg on the strip of beach hugging the Pacific Coast Highway that has become known as the stars' colony, and he fired his agent and allowed the scripts to build up as he played with his newly-born son.

The house had been owned by director John Frankenheimer and cost Tom and Rita more than $3 million (£1.8 million). Right on the sand, the two-storey 1928 home has two bedrooms downstairs and one upstairs in about 1,800 square feet. The master suite opens out onto a balcony overlooking the Pacific Ocean. There is also a separate maid's room and a two-bedroomed guest apartment with a kitchen.

The new oceanside home gave Tom the perfect excuse to take up a new hobby to mark up alongside 'hanging around the house, chatting on the phone and watching my stomach grow'. He bought a surfboard and found privacy and solace riding Malibu's famous rolling waves.

Only Tom's most fervent fans will remember his part in the ill-fated *Radio Flyer*, which nose-dived on its release in 1992. It was one of those movie projects that seem to crop up once or twice every few years in Hollywood: an idea that everyone gets very excited about and throws obscene amounts of money at — and then, just as quickly, loses interest in and condemns for its sky-high budget.

Director Richard Donner's film tries to show how a boy escapes the daily misery of domestic beatings by building a fantastic flying machine from household odds and ends. But the mix of the child abuse theme underlying the plot and the whimsical fantasy of the story was an impossible sell.

It didn't help that the only famous name involved — Tom's — was unbilled and, although his narration runs through the film, he only appears briefly at the beginning and the end.

Sandwiched between the higher profile failure of *The Bonfire of the Vanities* and the start of his successful run of hit movies, *Radio Flyer* had virtually no effect on his career.

The same can certainly not be said of *A League of Their Own*. Tom's fully-fledged return to the screen in 1992 was as brave as it was unexpected. It was with Penny Marshall, the director he had made *Big* with a few years earlier.

But in *A League of Their Own*, Tom had little more than a supporting role. The film about women's baseball starred Madonna, Geena Davis, Lori Petty and Rosie O'Donnell in equally prominent parts. What's more, Tom piled on 30 pounds to play Jimmy Dugan, the broken-down, bloated, alcoholic ex-big-league baseball star who was reduced to coaching an all-girls professional team formed as a promotional gimmick during World War II.

Tom called it the start of the 'modern era' of Hanks movie making. What he couldn't have known at the time was that it was also the start of the most lucrative and consistently successful winning streaks in contemporary Hollywood history.

The actor was 36 at the time. The part he wanted to play in *A League of Their Own* was supposed to be fat, 50 and over the hill. It fitted right into Tom's new criteria, as long as he could barter down the age.

He had recently signed with Creative Artists, the most powerful talent agency in Hollywood. He told the *Observer*'s Lynn Barber that he instructed his new agent: 'I'm not going to play pussies any more.'

'What are pussies?' he continued. 'Those kind of guys that don't have a girlfriend, who can't commit, who run around trying to make sense of their lives and have some kind of Peter Pan syndrome.'

So he told his agent: 'If it's a story about a lawyer who loses his job and breaks up with his girlfriend, just throw it out. I'm looking to play men who are my age and are going through something bigger.'

'And that was actually a pretty big moment of clarity for me. Now I'll probably have to make some kind of decision like that again in another couple of years, but at that point, I decided that I was not going to take on a job unless it was a test of my range, and my abilities and my emotional horizon.'

At one point, he had asked Ron Howard how he could avoid the fate of Elliott Gould, whose poor choice in material eventually torpedoed his career. As a £3 million-a-film actor, he realised he had enough 'fuck-you' money to say no to studios dangling big fees for mediocre, type-casted comedies.

One of the first suggestions made by Tom's new, powerful CAA agent, Ron Meyer, was to go after the part of the coach in *A League of Their Own*. He had actually been offered the role several times already, but had rejected it as too small for a star of his stature. Now he went back and begged to be given the chance to take what was a supporting role.

Even though Tom was effectively taking a step back to do the baseball movie, Penny Marshall was not convinced at first that Tom would fit in. She told him: 'I don't want you to play cute. We don't need cute.' But cute was the last thing on Tom's mind. That wasn't part of his plan.

Another attraction was his love of baseball. While Madonna was moaning about the boredom of being on location in small-town Evansville, Indiana, Tom was enjoying every minute. When he wasn't on set, he was happy playing ball with the crew and Rita, as ever, had come to join him, renting a house in five acres of land for the whole family.

Tom's Jimmy Dugan, the big leaguer who overcomes his booze-tinged humiliation of coaching a girl's team to take pride in his players, was a delight, as was the 1992 film, which was a surprise hit, earning $107.5 million (£66,264,000) at the US box office.

Tom told *Entertainment Weekly*: '*A League of Their Own* did an awful lot for me, and this is strictly from the crass business point of view.

'I had any number of people saying, "What the hell are you doing? It's not even your movie, you're just a guy passing through. Do you love Penny Marshall so much that you want to spend the summer and listen to her whine? Look what you could be doing!"'

But he had no idea what alternatives he had. 'I could have done *Popo Goes to the Big Town* and *Oops, I Tripped on a Lawn Chair*. Things like that. I was looking for something to do different and I think the message got out that he'll do anything. Which is a good thing. He'll get fat. He doesn't have to be the cute guy. He will cut his hair in an unattractive manner. He will be disgusting and sit there. He doesn't have to be the king of every scene that he is in. Well, that's a marvellous message to put out there.'

If his next film, the romantic comedy *Sleepless in Seattle*, wasn't exactly a stretch for Tom, then it certainly displayed the deft versatility that was to become his lasting trademark.

Sleepless not only called for his funny and his dramatic skills — Tom in fact turned it down originally, but changed his mind after a script rewrite. It also gave him the chance for the first time to play a role he had been practising for some time offscreen — that of a father and family man. He didn't have to dig through buried memories for motivation. It was right there at home.

Sleepless, which paired him up once more with Meg Ryan, scored with a public tiring of death and devastation on the big screen. Director Nora Ephron shamelessly romanced her audience.

Once upon a time, it provided the essential formula for every great Hollywood love story — the notion that each one of us has a perfect mate waiting for us out there in the tangle of humanity and that we know it the moment fate brings us together.

With *Sleepless in Seattle*, released opposite Steven Spielberg's *Jurassic Park* in 1993, romance came back into fashion. And while *Jurassic Park* broke box office records, its closest rival was the sleeping dinosaur weepie that eventually topped $126 million (£78 million) in the US.

The film made no attempt to disguise its debt to the golden days of Hollywood. From the opening moments using Jimmy Durante's rendition of *Casablanca*'s 'As Time Goes By' to set the tone, to the closing scene at the top of the Empire State Building, it owed little to subtlety and everything to sentiment.

Star-crossed would-be lovers Tom and Meg don't meet until the closing minutes and even then they don't kiss. At that moment, when we would expect the music to rise and the cameras to close in for a lip-smacking close-up, we have to settle for a deep, mutually-longing stare and the slightest touch of hands.

The grand finale is consciously reminiscent of the sublimely soppy 1957 weepie *An Affair to Remember*. Throughout the film there are film clips and references to the Cary Grant and Deborah Kerr classic to underscore the romantic theme.

And, although her husband gets top billing, Rita — playing his sister — almost steals the show with a sobbing, three-minute monologue describing the maudlin 'chick movie' plot of the '50s tearjerker.

The *Sleepless* story is simple. Sam, played by Tom, is a widowed architect living with his son in Seattle who describes his feelings about perfect love over the phone to a national talk show psychiatrist. Annie — Meg Ryan — is a newspaper reporter listening on her car radio in Baltimore who becomes smitten by his sentiments.

That Sam and Annie are destined to meet and fall in love is never in doubt.

What writer and director Ephron, the ex-wife of Watergate journalist Carl Bernstein, succeeds in doing is to keep the audience's interest in the budding romance until their eventual dramatic meeting in the final frame.

After taking more than $18 million (£11 million) on its opening weekend, the film was credited with reviving the date movie in Hollywood.

Although it was a comedy, and a fairly soppy one at that, *Sleepless* was still a far cry from *Big*. Tom was very much an adult dealing with adult issues: the loss of a wife, bringing up a child alone, dealing with loneliness.

'He is one of the few actors around that can do tender and irritable and angry all at the same time,' said Ephron.

Tom identified strongly with the theme of finding love the second time around. After a miserable first marriage, his life with Rita was ample proof it wasn't a fantasy.

'That whole concept of the second chance is a powerful one to me,' he told *Vogue*. 'There's something wonderful about the notion that if you hang on long enough, it will all come around. If you just continue to breath in and out, eat and pay your rent, things will eventually get better.

'You know, I'm 36, and like us all, I've been through a bunch. It's petty pantywaist stuff, nothing terrible. The relative aspect of the human condition being what it is, I've gotten my ass kicked a number of times by life. I mean, I've had any number of reasons to have sleepless nights myself, so that helped make *Sleepless in Seattle* a pretty real story to me.'

At a time when many movies were focusing on how far they could push the special effects rather than push the acting envelope, Tom instinctively understood the attraction of the old-fashioned love story.

'It's a simple movie told within its confines and largely free of artifice,' he said. 'And I think audiences just responded to that. In order to enjoy most blockbuster hits these days, you've got to believe that dinosaurs can be genetically mutated, or that a guy in a bat-suit can drive through a city rounding up penguins.

'Here, the only thing you have to believe is that two people can still fall in love. When you look at Hollywood movies these days, that's a fairly original concept. And the strength of the whole thing is that you have a sense of these two people together until the end — well, what better way to end the movie?'

Sleepless made two hits in a row. Now *Philadelphia* was about to give him the critical respect — and the Oscar — that would elevate his career onto an altogether new level.

Curiously, Tom had not always shared the general angst over the direction of his career. He always felt that the right roles were out there for him — and that in time they would land up on his desk. Now was that time.

He had met director Jonathan Demme in New York while doing publicity for *A League of Their Own*. The script for *Philadelphia* hadn't even been written then but Demme, whose previous film, *The Silence of the Lambs*, enraged members of the gay and lesbian community because of its depiction of a crazed transvestite serial killer, asked Tom if he was interested in being in the film.

'I probably would have run across the street just to watch him get into a car,' Tom told *Vogue*. 'We had one of those meetings where I just try not to sound like a dope. He told me about the idea for the movie and asked if would take a read of it when the script was done.

'And when I got it — well, all the adjectives won't do it justice. I want to say it's powerful, but it's more than just powerful. I thought it was a very real approach to what is going on. It's not one of those exploitative TV movie things that they always say is ripped right out of today's headlines — but the fact is, it is a story ripped right out of today's headlines.'

When Daniel Day Lewis, Demme's first choice for the role, turned it down because he was taking a six-month break, Tom jumped at the chance.

Although such prominent stars as Richard Gere, Al Pacino, William Hurt and Michael Caine have all played gay characters without jeopardising their careers — in some cases considerably enhancing them — the notion persists in conservative Hollywood that it can be a risky departure, leaving the question lingering, Is he really ...?

It wasn't a question that was ever really going to dog the twice-married father-of-four. But he was still asked all the time before the film came out. Why take the risk? What about your image? This time around there were no jokes, no Meg Ryan.

To Tom, that was never a factor. In fact, his cheerful, non-threatening image made him the perfect actor to dispel people's irrational fears about AIDS. Harking back again to his peripatetic childhood, he saw the constant moves and changes as a lesson that helped him early on to appreciate idiosyncrasy and diversity.

It also taught him that the easy path was not always the most satisfying. So when Demme offered him the choice of playing Andrew Beckett, the popular homosexual lawyer who gets fired when his bosses discover he has AIDS; or the cynical, ambitious Joe Miller, a family man who takes on Beckett's case without altogether losing his fear of gays, Tom was more intrigued by Beckett, even though he knew Miller was the more obvious choice.

He told CNN's Larry King: 'I felt from the very beginning that I had an awful lot in common with the character of Andrew Beckett. I thought that he was like me in so many aspects of my past and so many aspects of the way I look at life now. The fact that he was a gay man who was suffering from a terminal disease was, you know, in there, but I didn't see that as a massive obstacle.'

He added: 'I learned in making the film how much I have in common, how much we all have in common — but me specifically — with an awful lot of men out there who are supposed to be so different from us. We are so used to drawing the lines between the two poles, heterosexual and homosexual, and to find out that the men that I talked to had much the same sort of upbringing as I did, had the same sort of feelings of confusion when they were young. They had a lot of the same sort of adolescence. Came from a lot of the same sort of families, both for good and for bad.'

To learn how to emulate their lives, Tom interviewed AIDS patients who told him first-hand about growing up gay and living with the disease. Doctors taught him what happens to the body.

'To say the movie taught me a lot is really quite an understatement. I thought I was as hip and enlightened a man as you would find on average on the street. But this is the thing I think this movie and this script gave me when I read it was that I have never been very, very close to someone who has died of AIDS. I've known people, people in my family. I've lost a cousin. I wasn't very close and I haven't really witnessed it. What I thought this movie would give people who had never had it was the sense of a loss of someone that they loved and cared for to AIDS,' he said.

There was one particular encounter with an AIDS patient that made up Tom's mind to sign on for the project.

He explained: 'I went to see one man who was dying. We talked for hours and he was giving me tips on how I would look, act and feel at various stages of the illness. He told me that when he was first diagnosed, he went to the window and thought, "Clouds, this is the last time I am going to see you." I thought about that when I did one scene in the film and it brought tears to my eyes.

'When it was time to leave him I gave him a hug. His body was like it was on fire. AIDS was eating him up. As I hugged him, I knew I had to make the film.'

Tom didn't just have to prepare his mind for the part, he had to work on his body too, losing more than 30 pounds and having his hair thinned. He also read a lot of gay literature, including the memoirs of writer Paul Monette, author of *Borrowed Time*.

Co-star Denzel Washington would sneak sweets into Tom's pocket so he could 'smell the wrappers' and get a brief respite from his rice cake diet.

Inevitably, Beckett's character started to spill over into Tom's real life. 'You have to understand that I was always tired and hungry while I was making the movie,' he told the *San Francisco Chronicle*. 'We were also working with a lot of people who have AIDS. And every day I was coming out of the shower and seeing this emaciated body of mine. I was constantly bombarded with all these unsought images that you take home with you — about mortality and our society.

'I'm not a big Method actor. I don't immerse myself totally in a character. But I do end up being affected by all the stuff I do, and I found myself on this one crying over the most amazing and silly things.'

The intensity of the shoot meant Tom spent a lot of time thinking about the impact of the disease. He explained to the *Los Angeles Times*: 'Having thought about AIDS a good deal for quite a while now, I've come to think of it as a test of us as a civilisation, among other things. Is man more enlightened than he was during the Black Plague in Elizabethan England? I don't know. I do know there are still a lot of people who think this disease is about hedonism and is therefore deserved. All I can say is, that's not a very Christian response to suffering.'

But he wasn't always so politically correct with his interviewees. He told *Vanity Fair*: 'This woman reporter once asked me why there is this difference between the perception of gay men and gay women. I told her that I thought it is probably because most straight men think that gay men are forever lost, but that a gay woman can be cured with just one good big one right down the middle. She kind of looked at me like … I wanted to go, "Look, you asked me the question, sweetie."'

The film opened in December 1993 with some gay activist groups claiming Tom's lawyer wasn't intimate enough with his boyfriend, played by Antonio Banderas.

Larry Kramer, a leading light in the gay movement, lashed out at *Philadelphia* in the *Washington Post*, saying the film didn't portray gay life realistically, claiming it was unheard of for a family such as Beckett's to accept his homosexuality without prejudice. He also challenged the film's premise, since the passage of the Americans with Disabilities Act made it illegal to fire a person with AIDS, and he wondered why here were no gay love scenes, which would be standard in straight romantic movies.

Tom went on CNN's *Larry King Show* to promote — and defend — the film. He refuted Kramer's criticisms, but added: 'I think he has an awful lot of integrity and, out of the research I had done for the movie, I thought that if there was one bona fide hero from the beginning of the AIDS dilemma, it was Larry Kramer. At the same time, I signed autographs for a man downstairs who has an AIDS discrimination suit pending against his employers. I've received letters from the family members of men who died, who loved their sons or brothers just as much.

'There's one guy in the movie who plays my brother-in-law, who's pretty darned uncomfortable being in the same room with me there, but it's a very passive thing. How many times have we seen a door slammed in someone's face, especially in something like this? "No son of mine is going to bring this into my house!" We would have been dealing with some other brand of potboiler melodrama had we gone that way.'

Tom said a love scene between Beckett and his lover was

discussed. 'There's a dancing scene, and we do kiss very briefly, and the fact that Antonio Banderas plays my lover, he's amazing. We're lovers who have been together for nine years. We're very secure in the relationship. But about the actual kissing scene, that we have both received heat for, there was a discussion — if it's the obligatory scene, or if we have that scene where everybody's saying, "OK, here's the two straight guys. They're going to kiss, and they are going to get credit for finally kissing."

'If we do that then the organic-ness of the moment is going to be lost somehow, because you are going to take it right away. There were other ways to show that these two gay men loved each other and would love each other for the rest of their lives, and that's what we found when they had the opportunity.'

In spite of the harping of some activists, the critics applauded the film — and raved about the performance of its star.

'Hanks makes it all hang together in a performance that triumphantly mixes determination, humour, perseverance, grit, energy and remarkable clear headedness. Whatever else might nag about the film's treatment of a difficult subject, Hanks constantly connects on the most human level,' wrote Todd McCarthy in *Variety*.

People's Leah Rozen spoke for many when she said: 'Above all, credit for the movie's success belongs to Hanks, who makes sure he plays a character, not a saint. He is flat-out terrific, giving a deeply-felt, carefully nuanced performance that deserves an Oscar.'

The publicity plus the involvement of two trusted stars like Tom and Denzel Washington combined to shock the industry by pulling in a mainstream, as well as a gay, audience. The box office topped $77 million (£47 million) — not a blockbuster but more than anyone in the project had dared to hope for.

As the Oscar talk grew following the film's success, Tom declared: 'Let me tell you, I'll go to the Academy Awards to be a seat filler during the commercials. It's an honour to go. I'll park cars. I'll buff the plexiglass of that podium if they need somebody to do that. If I get nominated, I'll get to be able to go to my grave as a two-time Academy Award nominee, and that would make me very, very happy.' He wasn't to know he would soon become as close as the Oscars could get to a sure bet.

Tom had put 'the full force of my damned likeability behind the film' and it worked. He was even invited with Rita to spend the night at the White House after a special screening for President Clinton.

'What can I say? It was wild,' he told the *Los Angeles Times*. 'During the screening Clinton got up and walked out after a scene where Antonio Banderas and I are dancing together in military uniforms at a costume party, but I don't think he left because he objected to the scene. He said he thought the film was very nice and would be effective.'

Tom and Rita hardly slept they were so excited at staying in 'the most exclusive bed and breakfast in America'. But in the morning, Tom bumped into the President in the kitchen. 'I was looking for breakfast and there was the President in his running shorts, carrying the *New York Times* and a mug of coffee. I said, 'Good morning, Mr President,' then we sat around for an hour and a half talking about everything under the sun.'

The success of *Philadelphia* meant he had finally left behind his zany image for good. He steeped himself in the part of a top corporate lawyer who is fired from a blue-chip firm when the partners discover he is dying from AIDS.

With a shaved head and make-up used to mask cancerous Kaposi's Sarcoma lesions on his face. There was no doubting his commitment both to the film and the cause.

*   *   *

So this, then, was the magic moment. The evening when all Tom had put into *Philadelphia* might be rewarded. The audience roared its approval as Tom was called to the stage. Clutching the golden statuette, a very emotional Tom went on to give one of the great, albeit rather rambling, acceptance speeches in Oscar history. Tears streaming down his face and sporting an AIDS red ribbon in his lapel, he paid a moving tribute to two gay men who had inspired his now Oscar-winning performance.

Following is the speech in full, with the first sentence alluding to Bruce Springsteen's 'Streets of Philadelphia' theme song, which also won an Oscar, and a nominated Neil Young tune.

'Here's what I know: I could not be standing here without the undying love that was just sung about by not Bruce, but Neil Young. And I have that in a lover that is so close to fine, we should all be able to experience such heaven right here on earth. I know also, that I should not be doing this ... I should not be here. But I am because of the union of such film makers as Ed Saxon, Ron Nyswaner, Kristi Zea, Tak Fujimoto, Jonathan Demme — who seems to have these things attached to his limbs for every actor who works with him of late. And a cast that includes Antonio Banderas who, second to my lover, is the only person I would trade for. And a cast that includes many other people, but the actor who really put his film image at risk, and shone because of his integrity, Denzel Washington — whom I must really share this with.'

His voice shaking with emotion, Tom went on: 'I would not be here if it weren't for two very important men in my life. Two that I haven't spoken to in a while but I had the pleasure of the other night: Mr Rawley Farnsworth, who was my high school drama teacher, who taught me to act well the part, there all the glory lies; and one of my classmates under Mr Farnsworth, Mr John Gilkerson. I mention their names because they are two of the finest gay Americans, two wonderful men that I had the good fortune to be associated with, to fall under their inspiration at such a young age. I wish my babies could have the same sort of teacher, the same sort of friends. And there lies my dilemma here tonight. I know that my work in this case is magnified by the fact that the streets of heaven are too crowded with angels. We know their names. They number a thousand for each of the red ribbons we wear here tonight. They finally rest in the warm embrace of the gracious creator of us all. A healing embrace that cools their fevers, that clears their skin, and allows their eyes to see the simple, self-evident common sense truth that is made manifest by the benevolent creator of us all, and was written down on paper by wise men, tolerant men, in the city of Philadelphia two hundred years ago. God bless you all, God have mercy on us all, and God bless America.'

Speaking from her home on the outskirts of Oakland, where Tom and John had attended Skyline High School together in the early '70s, Mrs Gilkerson said they had once been very close friends.

'John was there for Tom during a very difficult time in his life when his parents were divorcing. John was never too busy to be a friend and was a great listener. When they were kids, John used to throw a lot of parties and Tom often came around to our house.

'He was the life and soul of the party — he showed the kind of wit that would later make him famous.

'But they drifted apart and did not stay in touch over the years. Maybe in his speech, Tom Hanks felt some regrets over the fact he was not there for John when he contracted AIDS.'

John Gilkerson died in 1989, aged 34, within a year of being diagnosed with the AIDS virus — never having heard again from Tom as the actor soared to fame and fortune in hit films such as *Splash* and *Big*.

A well-known ballet set and costume designer, John won an Emmy award for a TV puppet show. He collaborated on three ballets with eccentric rock star Frank Zappa and some of his stage designs are still used around the world.

Many of Tom's old friends, particularly actors he worked with in his early years, talk admiringly of his loyalty. Some even say he has helped them find work on his film projects. So his behaviour towards his old school friend — who helped him really belong for the first time in his life — is all the more curious.

Trudi Stillwell, a high school classmate of both men, said Tom had cold-shouldered his Skyline pals.

'I called Tom's publicist to get word to him immediately after John had died, but I never heard back. I had been in touch prior to that too when John was helping me to organise a reunion of our high-school drama class.

'I got the name of his publicist and I wrote several letters, but got no response. I got a number for Tom's agent and an old, old address. I called and wrote to his agent but I never heard from anybody. I suspect Tom probably would have known John had AIDS. But as far as I know he never wrote to him or called him. I know Tom had not been in touch with John since high school.

'John died a month before the reunion. It was very difficult for everybody. Some chose not to attend. We dedicated the reunion to John.

'Tom dropped out of sight from all of us right after high school. He didn't make any effort to stay in touch. I have a feeling that Tom mentioned John in his speech because he feels a bit guilty that he was not more in touch when John was dying.

'John lived life to the fullest right up until the end. He was a very fine, decent — and private — person.'

Added Trudi, a film projectionist: 'John had a strong influence on all of us. We all expected John to be in the famous position Tom is in today. I am just glad that Tom realised, after the fact, that John and Rawley Farnsworth had such an impression on his life.'

Ballet-company founder Ron Guidi, another of John's close friends who helped nurse him to the end, was also amazed at Tom's Oscar speech. 'I was so surprised when Tom Hanks mentioned John. I was very touched by his Oscar speech, but it sounded as though he thought John was still alive. I am sure someone must have kept him in contact with John's condition.

'It didn't take long for him to die. He was gone within a year. He refused to take medication. From the waist up he was like a skeleton — towards the end we had to carry him around. He got so thin that it hurt him to sit down.'

The other person from the past Tom saluted in his speech, high school drama teacher Rawley Farnsworth, was also effectively 'outed' by his old pupil. Farnsworth had never told any of his students during a long and distinguished career that he was gay and hadn't heard from Tom for nearly 18 years, following his career on the screen, along with everyone else.

Three days before Oscar night, he got a call at his San Francisco flat. 'I don't know if you remember me,' the caller said, 'but I'm an old student of yours. I've got a ticket to the Academy Awards and, if I win, I would like to use your name in regard to the content of *Philadelphia*.'

The student was, of course, Tom Hanks, and, although he didn't actually explain he was going to say his mentor was gay, Farnsworth said: 'I'd be thrilled.'

Farnsworth described sitting in front of the television on Oscar night. 'My friend and I had a couple of drinks and were planning to have dinner. It turned out that we never had dinner.'

Tom had told Farnsworth on the phone to 'just remember, when I'm looking into the camera, I'll be looking right at you.' After the speech, Farnsworth turned to his friend, dazed, and said: 'Did he say what I thought he said?'

The bemused teacher, now retired, said later: 'I would have had second thoughts about being outed as a gay if I had still been teaching. If I was still in professional life, I don't know how I would have reacted.

'Tom obviously feels strongly and wanted to get a message across. Now I am retired I don't really mind that my name was used. I actually thought Tom's speech was absolutely terrific. He had something he wanted to get off his chest and he did it in a very beautiful way that inspired people.

'When Tom Hanks phoned me three nights before the Oscars to ask permission to use my name, it was the first time I'd heard from him since 1977. I believe, like most straight men, Tom had stereotypical images of gay people and how they acted.

'But he said he had found inspiration in his association with John and I. Through us, he understood that not all gays are stereotypes.'

Farnsworth, a teacher for 30 years, added: 'I was never aware that he knew I was gay. Evidently, he did. Ours was a teacher-student relationship and I didn't discuss it with him and I haven't discussed it since. I was very discreet with all of my students. My lifestyle is my own business, and not theirs.

'Tom seemed to know what had happened to John Gilkerson when we talked. I had stayed in touch with John and saw him for lunch six months before he died. It was very sad. He had lesions around his face which he used make-up to cover up, but I saw one behind his ear. He had a terrible cough and was going through physical deterioration.'

Although he admitted to being 'a little paranoid' after the speech, particularly when he was besieged with calls from the media, Farnsworth has used his 15 minutes of fame to help promote gay causes, even though he has never been an activist. The white-haired, slightly-deaf teacher became something of a celebrity. He was commended on the Congressional Record in

Washington, constantly sought out as a spokesman for gay rights and was the recipient of a number of awards himself — one presented by Tom — recognising his role as a mentor and role model.

After the furore died down, he said: 'Tom wrote me a beautiful letter saying he hoped he hadn't brought the press down on my head. Some months later we had dinner together and I wondered if it was all to do with his ego, but after studying him, I saw no signs of it at all.'

In an ironic footnote to the story, Tom's 'outing' of his drama teacher was itself turned into a hit Hollywood film. Producer Scott Rudin watched the 1994 Oscars at home with theatre director friend Lori Steinberg and was struck by the drama of Tom praising his 'great gay teacher'. Rudin recalls Steinberg adding, 'whose job I just lost'. Thinking instantly that the story would make a great basis for a film, Rudin took the idea to Paramount Pictures, and the studio green-lighted a budget of more than £20 million.

Giving Farnsworth's alter ego a fiancé and a classroom was Hollywood's way of injecting drama into the movie, which vied for controversy by having Tom Selleck, as a gay TV reporter, kiss the teacher, played by Kevin Kline, full on the mouth.

The film, *In and Out*, also starred Matt Dillon as the old pupil who names his drama teacher as a big influence — and a homosexual — in his speech after collecting the Best Actor Oscar. On its opening weekend in 1997, the film took over $20 million (£12 million), the second-highest September opening after *The First Wives Club*, which headlined Goldie Hawn, Bette Midler and Diane Keaton.

But Rawley Farnsworth, while stunned and awed by Tom's dramatic range in the powerful *Philadelphia*, was unimpressed with *In and Out*. He offered his services to Paramount, but was told, 'thanks but no thanks'.

He was especially critical of the film's climactic ending, where the townspeople revolt against a homophobic school board to announce, one by one, that, if Sir is gay, then so are they. Says Farnsworth: 'The ending is just stupid. People don't behave like that.'

Talking about his famous speech to the *New York Daily News* in

1998, Tom denied outing his teacher. 'I didn't out him. He was thrust into the public eye, which he kind of liked, which he deserved, which was kind of great. And I've gone back and been at some things where he has been honoured. He's a very sweet guy. I get a letter from him now and then.

'I hadn't seen him or spoken to him in many, many years. But Mr Farnsworth made acting in the theatre the most fun in the world for me. And I knew then that he was gay. So when I referred to him at the Oscars, the nature of the world had changed so much that he had no problem. I don't know what it would have been like in 1974 if a teacher were to say, "I'm gay." It could have been an ugly and much different circumstance. But one whole aspect of *Philadelphia* was: What's to be afraid of? And if I hadn't had this gay teacher in high school, I wouldn't have been up there getting an Academy Award, so think it was even more important to say I wished my kids had the same sort of influence that I'd had from a human being like I had from my gay drama teacher in high school.

'And then they made a movie out of it and I got the best reviews of my career for a movie I am not even in. And not a dime in residuals — but that's okay, I'm not making a fuss.'

Chief among critics of the now famous Academy Awards speech was news review magazine *The New Republic*, which said one of the premier 'wince-making' moments of the Oscars was Tom's 'belaboured and incoherent attempt to immortalise those dead from AIDS'.

Tom's friend, Steven Spielberg, said he thought it was 'incredible'. The director, who won an Oscar the same year for *Schindler's List*, believed the speech 'in a sense communicated more about what *Philadelphia* was saying and reached more people than the movie itself will.'

Tom told *Vanity Fair*: 'I knew that I was going to have to say something to somebody, win or lose. So when the time came, I wanted to be armed somehow so that what I'd say would be germane to the work that I had done and the movie that I was connected with. I was also aware that there was going to be this big audience for what I was going to say.'

* * *

Unintentional furore aside, the Oscar-winning actor had come a long way. But the journey was far from over. He was about to become a box-office phenomenon ... and an exceedingly rich man.

12

Life Is a Box of Chocolates

It was exactly one year later and Tom was back in the Dorothy Chandler Pavilion with Rita again by his side and his stomach full of the same butterflies. Surely he couldn't be the first actor since Spencer Tracy in 1937 and 1938 to win back-to-back Best Actor Oscars. John Travolta's thrilling comeback performance in Quentin Tarantino's *Pulp Fiction* was the sentimental favourite and the 1995 nominees included the venerable Paul Newman, Morgan Freeman and Nigel Hawthorne

Tom's unique role in the offbeat *Forrest Gump* had helped the film become an unlikely triumph. Against all the odds, it was on its way to being one of the highest-grossing movies of all time. But the film breaks every mould of movie making. There's no quest, no bad guy. The hero is an idiot. And besides, Tom Hanks got his Oscar the previous year.

After his first nomination in 1988, Tom had spoken of his good fortune, telling the *Los Angeles Times*: 'I remember going through the phalanx of TV cameras at the 1988 Academy Awards and somebody said, "It is going to be hard to live this year down, isn't it?" I said there that I knew a year like I had comes once every 15 years if you are lucky, once every 10 years if you are amazingly lucky and once every five years if you are a phenomenon. And I am not laying any claim to being that.

'I just knew that it had been wild and it would probably fall apart somewhere down the line. I said that I would feel bad about it for a while when it happened, but that in the end I'd be okay.'

Well, even under his own classification, on that cool Californian evening in March, 1995, he became a phenomenon twice over.

For Tom would once again dumbfound the critics. A thunderous ovation greeted him as he accepted his second successive Best Actor Academy Award. This time, he didn't need anyone's permission for the tribute he planned to give from the podium. It was a love letter to his wife. It was also another memorable speech.

'Thank you. I'm standing here in lieu of my fellow nominees who are just as deserving, if not more so, of this moment. I'm standing here because of an army of people who, over the course of a back-breaking schedule that was set by Bob Zemeckis, worked much harder than I did and had much more at risk if our efforts were not successful. I am empowered to stand here thanks to the ensemble of actors, men and women, who I shared the screen with, who, in ways they will never understand, made me a better actor.

'And I'm standing here because the woman I share my life with has taught me, and demonstrates for me every day, just what love is.

'Man, I feel as though I am standing on magic legs, in a special effects process shot that is too unbelievable to imagine and far too costly to make a reality. But here is my mark, and this is where I am supposed to look and believe me, the power and the pleasure and the emotion of this moment is a constant speed of light. It will never be diminished nor will my appreciation and the meaning between two simple words that I can only offer you here: Thank you. God bless you — in this room, and God bless you all around the world.'

The award, in such a contrasting role to that in *Philadelphia*, would cement his name in Hollywood lore forever and guarantee him just about any project he fancied in the future. It also earned him a fortune. For although it had a troubled history, Tom so believed in the project that he agreed to forego his upfront salary, which would have probably been in the region of £8-10 million. Instead, he was given a percentage of *Forrest Gump*'s gross, meaning his financial benefits would live or die with the success or otherwise of the film.

At last count, Forrest Gump had taken close to $356.8 million (£219,934,000) in the United States alone and more than $600 million (£369,845,000) around the world. Tom's personal share was estimated at up to $60 million.

The great irony, however, was that Paramount was still claiming one year after its release that the fourth-highest grossing movie ever was $60 million (£36,984,000) in the red.

It was one of the most striking examples yet of creative Hollywood accounting — and a slap in the face to Gump writer Winston Groom, a former Washington journalist, who got a comparative pittance for allowing his novel to be put on the big screen. He was paid $300,000 (£184,922) for the book's rights and given a three per cent cut of the net profits.

The good news for Groom was that the movie turned out to be a great success and turned him from an obscure author into a household name. The bad news was that while some of the participants in the project — like Tom Hanks — were going to become incredibly rich incredibly fast, he was going to have to wait for any additional money to dribble in.

Groom's problem was that instead of signing a royalty deal linked to gross profits, his deal depended on net proceeds and, as he found out to his cost, that is controlled by the vagaries of the studio money men.

By December of 1994, Paramount had collected about $191 million from domestic and international Forrest Gump ticket sales after cinema owners had already taken their 50 per cent cut, according to a Paramount accounting document quoted by the Associated Press news agency in a June 1995 article.

Paramount then took $50 million in production costs, added a distribution and marketing fee of about $74 million, $62 million in distribution expenses, payments to the film's star and director of close to $62 million and $6 million in interest.

The result: a loss of more than $60 million.

If there was a negative net profit, then Groom's percentage deal wasn't worth a bean, leaving cruel studio insiders to dabble with one of the film's stock aphorisms in reference to the unfortunate writer: 'Simple is as simple does.'

As you can see from the balance sheet above, Tom and director Bob Zemeckis were far wiser in the ways of filmtown. They did indeed take a gamble on the film being a success, but they stood to profit handsomely if their hunch about *Gump* was proved right. For they negotiated contracts which guaranteed each of them an estimated eight per cent of the film's gross receipts — that's *receipts*, not *profits*. The deal gave them a cut of the very first dollars that came in from cinemas, video stores and soundtrack sales.

There was little sympathy for the writer in Hollywood. Paramount advanced Groom another $250,000 against a projected net profit after he hired a lawyer to claim a fairer share. But the general feeling was that A-list guys like Tom and Zemeckis deserved the cash for making the project happen. As an untried writer who wasn't on any list before the movie, he should be happy for his success.

It certainly wasn't the first time Hollywood's 'net profits' accounting has caused jaws to drop. In 1992, Warner Bros maintained that the hugely successful *Batman* movie lost more than $20 million.

One thing about *Forrest Gump* that pretty much everyone was in agreement about was that it was successful primarily because of its star.

'There is no one else like Tom working today,' said Gump co-producer Wendy Finerman. 'He has such a likeability. As an actor, and as a human being, he's a dream.'

What's more, while such popular stars as Julie Andrews and Dudley Moore once won the same kind of warm acclaim, their careers dipped after their hit films because of their limited range. Tom had shown he wasn't confined by any such handicap.

Finerman, who toiled for nine years to bring Groom's little-known novel to the screen, found a great ally in Tom. He told her that if she could get together a good enough screenplay he would take the part. They had both been working on a project called *The Postman* which was later, much altered, a major box office flop for Kevin Costner. When that fell through, they persevered with *Gump*.

Warner Bros spent a considerable sum developing the project, commisioning first Groom and then two further writers to write screenplays. But because executives didn't think it was ever going to work, the studio wrote off the cash and passed on the project, allowing Paramount to resurrect it and put it on the fast track. Tom signed up immediately, as he had promised Finerman he would do.

It was another risky role and the tinseltown soothsayers were again predicting Tom was taking a wrong turn. The word was that the film about a low-IQ Southern simpleton would make the Academy-Award winner look stupid.

But Tom saw in the plot the same thing that his audience would. He was a baby-boomer. He had grown up with JFK, Elvis, The Beatles and Vietnam. With his slow-witted grace and honest to God truthfullness, Forrest was taking the audience back through 30 years of their own history, and making them laugh and cry along the way.

Said Finerman: 'The childlike innocence of *Forrest Gump* is what we all once had. It's an emotional journey. You laugh and cry. It does what movies are supposed to do — make you feel alive.'

Gump was an implausible hero, an opinion-free dimwit who naively fumbled his way to successive triumphs as football star, a Vietnam soldier and a shrimp-fishing mogul. But he tapped the sentiments and captured the hearts of filmgoers.

He always seems to turn up in the right place at the right time to become celebrated, wealthy or offer a pearl of wisdom — 'stupid is as stupid does' and the lasting 'life is like a box of chocolates — you never know what you are going to get', for instance.

Director Robert Zemeckis, who made *Back to the Future* and *Who Framed Roger Rabbit?*, used the latest technology to splice Gump into footage of the famous, from Kennedy to Elvis. His influence on events extends from helping to capture the Watergate burglars to collaborating with John Lennon.

The film is a celebration of innocence and Gump's invincible goodness found a resonance in a world where the weak and trusting are customarily abused by the strong and the crooked.

Nevertheless, the scale of its success remains a mystery even to its creators. 'You figure it out,' said Tom. 'There's no bad guys or suitcases full of money. Nobody is trying to solve a mystery or save the life of a cow.

'But you don't have any problem believing that he has met three presidents or that he played ping pong in China or won a medal in the army.'

The fact the unlikely character is so believable is primarily due to the actor who played him. Tom took six months researching his part, finding ways to make it real. He spent a lot of time at a school for the mentally retarded in Los Angeles, but, as he had done with all his most successful films, he also looked inside himself for inspiration.

The font of loneliness he had carried from his childhood right through to his early 30s was again the source he immersed himself in.

Tom told *Interview* magazine: 'It's about a guy with a limited IQ who operates at the speed of his own common sense. He lives an amazing life and sees amazing things, but the purity of how he sees the world was what I thought was amazing about the screenplay, and what he goes through to get to the point where we are all at. All the great stories are about our battle against loneliness: *Hamlet* is about that; so is *The Importance of Being Earnest*. That's what I always end up being drawn toward.'

Journeying through such uncharted territory, however, Tom still admitted he was 'scared every minute' of filming, never quite knowing how it was all going to turn out.

In fact, *Forrest Gump* was seen as anything but a sure thing before its release. The book was supposedly too wide-ranging, quirky and uncommercial, and Tom was perceived as making a major career blunder in taking the bizarre lead role.

The key to the character was when he found Gump's voice. Said Tom: 'We had none when we started. Then Jessica Drake, my voice coach, and I heard Michael Humphreys, who played the young Forrest Gump. He was from Mississippi up by Tennessee and he had this great vocal cadence with very particular characteristics, with hard "Gs" in the middle of things. Like he said, "sing-ging'. I listened to Michael a lot, she made linguistic templates and then I read the entire script to her. It took the better part of three weeks and by the end I was doing it without having to think about it.'

He needn't have worried what the public would make of the

movie. When *Forrest Gump* opened on the Fourth of July weekend in 1994, it took more than $25 million in just three days. It was a considerable success for a non-action film with such a quirky plot and the phenomenon would only grow from there.

Having lost so much weight for *Philadelphia*, Tom, who has always had to watch his waist, felt he was looking his very best for *Forrest Gump*, even if he had to put up with the bizarre haircuts. 'I was in incredibly good shape then,' he told the *Observer*. 'My God, I was my butt in that movie! When Forrest is running across the football field, I just say look at that, my legs! Actually, I hurt myself in the course of doing that, I pulled a muscle in my quadriceps and I had to get a massage therapy, because I had to keep running for the rest of the movie, so I was being worked on by a lady and she muttered, "My God, You have the legs of a 16-year-old!"'

Tom's reply was a suitably Gumpian: 'Thank you ma'am.'

By now a regular on the annual Hollywood 'power lists' , Tom followed such screen luminaries as Bette Davis and Cary Grant in November 1994 as a recipient of the Louella Parsons Award, granted by the Hollywood Women's Press Club for the star who 'represents the best image of the entertainment industry to the world.' The award also recognised 'the social consciousness of his films,' adding that Tom's work 'is proof that responsible film-makers can also win at the box office.'

And the acclaim kept coming. In 1995, the *Hollywood Reporter* named Tom one of the five most powerful stars in Hollywood together with Arnold Schwarzenegger, Mel Gibson, Harrison Ford and Tom Cruise. The following year, *Screen International* made him the top player, ahead of Cruise, Ford, Schwarzenegger and Brad Pitt.

Harvard University even made him their Man of the Year. He dressed up in drag to accept the Ivy League college's Hasty Pudding Award, sashaying across the stage in high heels, a satin dress and a long auburn wig to tell the cheering tuxedo-clad crowd in his best *Bosom Buddies* voice: 'Not bad for a guy who didn't even make it through Sacramento State University.'

An interesting sidebar to the *Forrest Gump* success story involves Tom's youngest brother, Jim, who is also an actor.

Jim, four years Tom's junior, was drafted in as his famous

brother's stand-in for the film. 'Tom had other doubles, but they couldn't do the run,' Jim told *People* magazine in 1995. 'That's a stupid Hanks thing.'

There has never been much doubt who has taken all the prizes in the unsaid sibling rivalry between the brothers, who grew up separately — Tom with his father and Jim, the 'baby' of the family, with his mother.

Despite various commercials and small movie roles, Jim has never broken through into the big time. But there is a connection between Tom's comic masterpiece in *Gump* and a character his lookalike brother played in a sex comedy film.

Hollywood producers who hired Jim in the soft-porn romp *Buford's Beach Bunnies* were stunned over the striking similarities.

In the tacky B-movie, made three years before *Forrest Gump*, Jim plays lovable buffoon Jeeter Buford ... with some of the same physical mannerisms that Tom used later to turn his character into a cult hero worldwide.

By astonishing coincidence, some of Jim's scenes are even similar to his brother's in *Forrest Gump*.

The largely forgotten *Buford's Beach Bunnies*, made in 1992, now gathers dust in the comedy section of some video shops. The low-budget film is hardly a classic. But it bears watching alongside one of the biggest movies in history.

As Jeeter Buford, the sexually repressed son of a burger bar king, Jim:

* Invents the now famous jerky run associated with Forrest Gump.

* Sits straight with his knees together and hands folded in his lap — the familiar Forrest Gump look which became a trademark of Tom's portrayal.

* Panics and freezes when a topless girl tries to seduce him — as does Tom in a scene when he meets up with his old Vietnam war pal at a New Year's Eve party.

* Is dominated by his father who wants to help his dimwitted son get over his mental problems — in Gump's case, it is his mother, played by Sally Field, who is his mainstay in life.

* Demonstrates shy politeness to women, calling them 'ma'am' — as does Gump.
* Gets pushed around by bullies. At the start of *Forrest Gump*, Tom is shown as a crippled child in leg calipers being chased by stone-throwing little thugs.
* Keeps the flames of passion going for a girl he marries at the end. The main theme running through *Forrest Gump* is his love for his troubled childhood sweetheart Jenny — whom he eventually weds.
* In the Jim Hanks movie, the 'ghosts' of Humphrey Bogart, Marilyn Monroe and Clint Eastwood appear in front of Jeeter. Computer trickery in *Gump* allows Tom to be seen apparently meeting President Kennedy and John Lennon.

Director Mark Pirro, who went on to make a schlock horror movie called *Nudist Colony of the Dead*, said: 'When Jim first auditioned for the Buford role, he didn't tell me that he was Tom's brother.

'I kept saying he should get a job as a Tom Hanks lookalike. It was only afterwards that he told me he was his brother. I guess he didn't want me to know. He was pretty sensitive about it.

'We spent a couple of days filming at Venice Beach and a big crowd started gathering. Jim said to me, "They all think I'm Tom. I hate it when this happens."'

Michael Wojciechowski, who was director of photography on *Buford's Beach Bunnies*, commented: 'Jim's character and Forrest Gump are definitely very similar — the naïve, wide-eyed wanderer through life. Jim did the movie two years before *Forrest Gump*.

'I would have thought Tom saw his brother's film. Our movie was shot in three weeks on a very low budget. It only cost around $300,000.'

Film distributor Edmund Fernando added: 'There are some similarities.'

Jim has never commented on the parallels, although he told the *Los Angeles Times*: 'The casting director said you should go in and not tell them your real name. So he took my headshot and cut my name off and I used my middle name. I went in as Jim Matthews.'

Asked about his brother, Jim explained to *People*: 'Since I moved to Los Angeles, we have slowly built a relationship. It's strange. He sounds and looks a lot like me, but our backgrounds are very different.'

Unlike his sister and brothers, Jim grew up in the same area of Red Bluff, Northern California, attending the local Mercy High School and seeing his siblings only when they visited at weekends and during the holidays. The shy brother didn't share Tom's drive to be an actor as a young man and moved to Sacramento with his girlfriend Karen Praxel, where he found work waiting tables.

The couple married in 1986, with the whole family — including Rita — in attendance and Karen decided to try and give it a go as an actress in Hollywood. Soon after they moved, Karen found a job as a receptionist for an agent. The agent then managed to coax Jim into showbusiness.

He admitted his first auditions were 'horrific'. But he went on to make a modest living with advertising voice-overs and parts in small films. Jim and Karen moved into a home in trendy Venice Beach, Los Angeles and, in 1992, they had a son, Gage.

A commercial for the Volvo 960 in 1996 led to an outcry among Hanks fans who were incensed that their double-Oscar-winning hero was peddling cars on the small screen. The pitchman, of course, was Jim. Little brother also helped sell Jack in the Box fast food, Hyundai cars and fresh packaged salads.

The part in *Buford's Beach Bunnies* came after a few acting lessons and was followed by a role in a film called *Night Skies*, in which he was blown to smithereens, and a part in a pulp fiction sci-fi film *Xtro: Watch the Skies*, playing a wisecracking Marine. He also starred in an ill-fated series with original *Batman* TV actor Adam West called *The Clinic*. But reviews for the soap opera spoof were not very kind. The *Indianapolis Star* said:'A curiosity here is Jim Hanks, Tom's brother, in a small, bizarre role. With the same high forehead and haircut, laugh and a very similar voice, Jim looks and sounds eerily like his sibling. But who got the family acting ability is evident from his performance — and his presence in a loser like *The Clinic*.'

He was supposed to team up with an actress with another famous name, Alison Eastwood, daughter of Clint, for another series called *High Hopes*, about staff working at the Universal Studios theme park in Los Angeles. Jim was going to play a father-figure entertainment director, but the show never got off the ground.

Comparisons with Tom have inevitably haunted his acting career. 'Some people are really great about it. Some aren't,' Jim told the *Los Angeles Times*. 'I auditioned for something recently and heard back later that because the casting director could not get over the fact that I looked so much like Tom, she didn't even hear me. She did not HEAR my audition.'

Novelist and director T.L. Lankford wasn't distracted by Jim's amazing similarity to his big brother. He cast him in *Dark Red*, a low-budget thriller, but even then he lost out on a bigger part because of one of Tom's hit films.

'At first, I wanted to cast him as one of the leads, a character who has suffered brain damage,' said Lankford. 'But when he read it, I realised it was far too close to Forrest Gump, and neither of us wanted to exploit Tom's name or that character.'

The director felt awkward asking Jim to play a policeman, a much more limited role. But Jim told him: 'At this point, a job's a job.'

However, Jim has turned down potentially lucrative projects because they were obviously aimed at cashing in on Tom's success. He was approached about doing a made-for-TV remake of *Splash*, and later a network wanted him to play the lead in a television series based on *Big*.

'I was contacted five different times,' he said in 1995. 'Then somebody from one of the studios called me at home on a Saturday morning pleading me to come in and read it. I said no.'

When he told Tom, his brother told him: 'You're right. You're absolutely right. It would be the most stupid thing you could possibly do.'

That didn't stop Jim from moving in on Tom's turf when Disney made a CD-ROM based on the hit *Toy Story* movie, which the actor made after winning his Oscars. Jim stepped in for Tom as the voice of the cowboy, Woody, on the computer disc.

He has since been featured as the voice of Spike the dog in a 1998 show called *Sunset Beach*.

Jim is the only other member of the Hanks family to try his hand at acting. Although Tom went on to greater fame and fortune, it was his big sister, Sandra, who was the first to hit it big in the entertainment world.

After being brought up by her father, she moved back to live with her mother as a teenager. Having finished her education, she moved to Sacramento and set up her own company supplying newsreel clips to television stations. The business was a huge success and, as she says, 'I actually had a fancy car and a huge house before Tom.'

Sandra — nicknamed 'Pandora' by Tom — has been married three times. She had two daughters, Jennifer and Jaren, with first husband, Stan Combes. After divorcing second husband, Scott Adamson, she met British bobby Mark Benoiton on holiday in the Seychelles. Sixteen years her junior, Benoiton joined the Dorset police after studying agriculture and working on pig farms.

He comes from the Seychelles and met Sandra there while on a visit home. The couple moved out to the paradise island to set up a restaurant after living in a comfortable flat in Bournemouth for a couple of years.

Sandra told *OK!* magazine: 'Mark grew up on a beach in a home with electricity and no television. I've had to show him *Casablanca* and say "This is Ingrid Bergman and Humphrey Bogart," and he had never heard of them.

'But he knows about the sea and the jungle. He can fish for dinner and he can climb a coconut tree. Although our backgrounds are very different, our interests are the same. Jungles and wildlife are my passion, my obsession.

'I love to travel and I don't stay in fancy hotels. I backpack and eat and drink what the locals do. At the moment, I am writing a novel on environmental issues from home.'

Sandra's life in Bournemouth and then the Seychelles could not be more different than Tom's glamorous Hollywood lifestyle.

But, in the 1995 interview, Sandra said the family was still close. When Sandra and Mark got married, Tom couldn't make it to the wedding in the Seychelles because he was filming. But when he asked what gift he could buy, Sandra asked him for cash to help furnish their new Dorset home. The money he sent was 'great,' said Sandra. 'Tom doesn't throw his money around, but over the years his presents have got better. His wealth isn't a thing between us. He has never felt he has something to prove and he doesn't have a chip on his shoulder, which is why there aren't any horrible stories about him.'

Sandra is the only member of the family not living in the United States, but she said: 'As I'm the eldest and the only girl, I get to do all the organising of the family get-togethers. I'd describe the Hanks family together as really goofy — we play basketball in the living room and we're a noisy crowd.

'We're loud, funny and lively. We haven't had a row since we were kids but we love a good debate. Tom and I especially have strong political views.'

Sandra is probably the closest to Tom of the siblings. He credits her with holding the family together when they were children, and even for 'making it all fun'. The two boys always took her lead, he wrote in a touching letter he sent in 1986, which described how important she had been in moulding his personality.

She told *OK!*: 'Despite the tearful speech he made when he won the Oscar for *Philadelphia*, Tom isn't one to walk around with his heart on his sleeve. He doesn't find it that easy to open up and talk. I know I can talk to him when I have a problem.

'We speak on the phone every few weeks, and when he was getting divorced from his first wife and having a tough time emotionally, we spent a lot of time talking. He was very supportive when my first marriage broke up.'

Sandra believes their California upbringing had a lot to do with keeping Tom so down to earth. She has met big names like Steven Spielberg, his wife Kate Capshaw, and Jamie Lee Curtis at Tom's Los Angeles mansion. 'Most of them are nice people,' she said.

But she added: 'Growing up in California teaches you not to be impressed by celebrities. For me, being Tom's sister isn't a factor on a daily basis. It doesn't really affect our lives. I'm impressed with Tom's work and I'm very proud of him. I'm still knocked out by the fact that he has won two Oscars.

'All my brothers have great taste in women and I get on great with Tom's wife, Rita. He introduced her to me when they were still dating.'

She sees all of Tom's films and makes a point of being honest about them. 'I was lukewarm about *Bonfire of the Vanities,* and I wasn't real hot on *Bachelor Party* either, although it made a ton of money. I thought *Splash, Big* and *Philadelphia* were great — especially *Philadelphia.'*

Sandra admitted there was one thing involving Tom that left her green with envy. 'I am stunningly jealous of the fact that Tom has stayed at the White House with the Clintons. To be able to sit down with the President of the United States and ask him what you want — that's what I call cool!

'I asked him, "Did you call the President Bill?"

'But Tom said, "No, you can call anyone Bill. I called him Mr President."'

Their father had been insistent on giving all his children the best education available. But Larry was always the academic of the family, collecting and inventing things even as a young child.

Three years older than Tom, he became a doctor of entomology — that's an insect expert — and has gone on to become one of the leading researchers in his field in the world, first as an insect ecologist at the University of California in Riverside and then as a Professor at the University of Illinois at Urbana-Champaign, where he has specialised in wood-boring insects, in particular the Asian Longhorn Beetle, a 'major tree killer' which recently turned up in Britain.

Larry married girlfriend Jean Mahew in July, 1996.

While very supportive of his younger brother, Larry has remained strictly out of the spotlight, hitting the headlines in *The New York Times* only when he was part of ground-breaking research into insect eating-patterns in 1994.

Although he is the academic of the family, Larry says Tom has followed their father's passion for reading and self-education. 'Tom started off at state college in California, but I don't think that traditional educational institutions really train you for that business. The only way to learn how to act is to actually act. I think that most reputable actors and actresses, like Tom, came through the school of hard knocks.

'But Tom's not uneducated. He reads a lot. He probably reads two entire newspapers a day. He really knows what is going on in the world. That may be why, rather than the fluff, he seems to be going for more important movie projects.'

Tom would always say that Larry was the comic in the family when they were young. But times have changed. 'He was the younger brother, but Tom eventually started telling his own jokes rather than taking mine. He has his own jokes now,' said Larry. 'I don't feel like I am the funny one in the family any more. Everybody seems to have developed their own sense of humour. I think I used to be the funny one because I was older.'

The siblings have always remained in touch, even as they went off in their own directions.

'With Sandra living in the Seychelles now we stay in touch mainly through E-mail as a phone call costs about $100. With Tom, he does a lot of travelling. Right now he's working on a movie in Fiji, an island movie he has to lose a lot of weight for. We also stay in touch through family occasions. Everyone would always converge on my mother's home at Thanksgiving and Christmas. The Hankses tend to marry a lot. My mother was married a number of times and my father was married a number of times and you tend to accumulate a number of people in your life that way. That's the positive side.

'We were young when we had our first stepmother. It's kind of strange but we lost touch with all of them. We still stay in touch with our second stepmother, my father's last wife. Any differences between us are all in the past now.

'We have all seemed to have turned out okay. Nobody has killed anyone.'

Larry has got used to some of the difficult experiences of his early years being replayed through Tom's interviews over the years. He said: 'Tom is pretty careful. Fortunately he doesn't go into any grisly details. He respects everyone's privacy.'

However, the professor has had to put up with fans visiting his office at the university asking for autographs or photographs of his famous brother, or just wanting to talk about him. 'It's just a big waste of time,' he added.

'Tom handles it all pretty well. He doesn't let it get to his head too much.'

Janet, Tom's mother, and his stepmother, Frances, stay in touch with Tom. Now retired from her job as a vice-president of a convalescent hospital chain, Janet still lives in the Red Bluff area with her third husband, Rudolph, who is retired from the construction industry. With Rita's parents, Janet was at the Oscar ceremony in 1995 to celebrate with her famous son.

The one-bedroomed bungalow she lives in is reported to have cost just £20,000. In the drive sits a new £18,000 car, which Tom reportedly bought for her.

Friends say she talks proudly of Tom's achievements and lives with husband 'Rudy' in the modest neighbourhood, a world away from the splendour of her middle son's luxurious Los Angeles mansions. She has no hired help and Rudolph likes to go hunting with his rifle for their dinner.

The night Tom won his first Oscar was, she says, 'one of the happiest moments of my life'.

The family had all gathered at Tom's house the night before the ceremony, one of the rare occasions they were able to get together at the same time, and taken snapshots of everyone.

'When he won the Oscar I cried,' Janet said. 'It was like, despite everything, we were a family again, all of us.'

In a 1998 interview with *New Yorker* magazine, Tom appeared to take a harsher line with his family than in previous interviews. Asked whether he was still in contact with Janet, he said: 'See, the thing is I never lived with my mum. So she's tighter with the other kids in the family. I was the only one who just never lived with her.

'Sometimes we talk really honestly about this. I say, "Mom, you didn't raise me!" There is a brand of peace that had to be made.'

He said his relationship with his sister and brothers was 'not the tightest. We're kind of terse.'

When it was suggested that the movie version would have been that the adversity they lived through would have brought them together, he replied: 'Well, life didn't quite work out that way.'

The article upset and angered Tom's close family and the actor quickly assured them that his comments had been taken out of context.

'It caused quite a stir,' said Larry. 'The story was very disconcerting to us. There was one quote saying that Tom doesn't have particularly good relationships with his siblings. But that's just not true. It said something about being terse, but I talked to Tom for about six hours the last time I was in California. That doesn't fit my idea of terse.

'Actually, I spoke to Tom about it. He was unhappy about the way it looked. My mother wasn't very happy about it either.'

The point is that as much as Tom has always liked to see himself as a free spirit, he has spent much of his life searching for the idealised family he had longed for as a child.

In one sense, he may hold his less than happy childhood memories against all those that shared them — his siblings — and those that crafted them — his parents and step-parents. But the fact that their actions did mean, and continue to mean, so much to him underline just how much family has always meant to Tom Hanks.

In truth, he has never been much of a free spirit. He had children, a wife and all the responsibilities they bring at a young age while he was still trying to make a place for himself in the world.

He is very aware that real life doesn't always end up like it does in the movies. The great tribute to him is that he has never let his family down and has learned enough to know how central that is to his own happiness.

In a business where egos are fed daily by sycophantic praise, Tom's sense of family is the key to his huge success. He has come to know what is important. And that is not sleek, fast sports cars, Gulfstream jets or Harry Winston jewels. To Tom, his wife and children are more important than all the money in the world.

13
Reaching for the Stars

Shooting through the night skies, Tom kept blinking for fear that the most exhilarating feeling in his life was only a dream. Ever since the early *Apollo* missions, Kubrick's *2001: A Space Odyssey* and even *Fireball XL-5*, it had been his dream to fly in space.

As a little boy, he would sometimes fill his swimming trunks with rocks and sit on the bottom of the pool breathing through a garden hose to simulate weightlessness. With his science skills at schools extending little further than lighting the Bunsen Burner, he always knew that his abiding ambition would never realistically be achievable.

But now he was an actor, an extremely successful one at that, and in Hollywood anything is possible — even if it is only make believe.

After two successive Oscars, Tom could choose just about any project he cared to do. By simply attaching his name to a movie, he could ensure that a studio would automatically give it the green light and find however many millions were required to put it on the screen. The fee for the 'best actor' alone was now approaching £15 million per film.

The movie he had decided on was the story of the doomed *Apollo 13* mission, directed by his old friend Ron Howard.

Quite clearly, they wouldn't be shooting the film in space. Hollywood sound stages had been recreating stars of both kinds with varying degrees of success for many years.

But speeding through the pitch black skies over Texas, his hands clamped tightly on the controls of a small plane, this was about as close as he was ever going to get to experiencing what his boyhood heroes like Neil Armstrong, Buzz Aldrin and co. must have felt.

Previously, the closest he had come to copying them was in a comic routine he used to ease the tension, first at one of his very earliest auditions in New York and, many years later, as he walked into the press room at the Golden Globes. Tripping up a small step on purpose, he would regain his composure and say with a smile: 'One small trip for mankind ...'

Now one of his heroes was in the plane seat behind him. Jim Lovell, veteran of two Gemini flights as well as Apollo 8 and Apollo 13 missions, wanted the actor who would portray him on celluloid to get an idea how it really felt to be lost in space.

Tom spent four days with Lovell at his home close to the Houston Space Center in Texas. Never one to take too much notice of 'the suits' as he called studio executives, Tom happily trusted his life to the former Navy pilot.

Lovell explained: 'Tom Hanks came down to my house in Horseshoe Bay to sort of get in the mould of the part. I don't think he's done much small plane flying. I wanted him to get the feeling of what it's like to be a test pilot and an aviator and an astronaut, so I let him fly the plane.

'That evening, I said, "Don't have anything to drink." We had dinner at home, then at 10.00pm I took him to the airfield at Horseshoe Bay.

'We took off and I told him, "Tom, the space capsule is in darkness all of the time. You see the sun, but there's no atmosphere to have nice blue skies. Essentially, you are going to be in the dark, except for stars occasionally."

'To recreate the constricted view from a spacecraft, I installed a triangular cardboard cut-out on his side of the cockpit.

'I took him out West where there are no lights. We flew around and I showed him the constellations and the stars that are used to navigate when we got on the backside of the moon and the sun wasn't there. I let him control the airplane, because it's a little bit like a spacecraft. He liked it a lot.'

In truth, Tom's initial emotion once up in the air was stark terror. He came out in a hot sweat and felt extremely nauseous. But he refused to admit his fears to Lovell and gradually relaxed. Soon, he was overwhelmed with the speed and the darkness and the feeling that this was something he had been waiting his whole life to experience, even if it was not quite the real thing.

With all his success, his love for his wife and his dedication to his children, he would still be among the first to volunteer if there was ever a chance for a civilian to fly into space. Tom told the *New York Daily News*: 'There's no way I'm going to be an astronaut because I don't have the math or anything. But if there was a lottery and they asked who wants to go, and I got picked, I'd be gone. Do it in a minute. Even if they said my job was to clean up the barf if anyone got sick. I'd do it.'

His friend Sally Field added one cautionary note however: 'Rita would kill him.'

As a baby boomer, Hanks reveres his space heroes as others worship film stars. 'They were princes among men,' he said. 'These guys in their gold flight suits with matching jackets — they were real stars. To be an astronaut in Houston in the 1960s. It was like being a Beatle.'

But studio bosses at Universal were less than happy about their own brightest star flying about in the middle of the night. They were terrified of a mishap and feared he was not properly insured. 'I told 'em not to worry,' said Lovell. 'His best insurance is sitting right next to him.'

To Tom and Ron Howard it was important to change the perception of the *Apollo 13* mission as the heroic failure that America wanted to forget.

For four heart-stopping days in April 1970, the world watched as Lovell and his crew struggled in total darkness and sub-zero temperatures to bring their crippled spaceship back to earth.

Despite their miraculous escape, the life-or-death saga 200,000 miles from home exposed the vulnerability of the US *Apollo* programme — and accelerated its nosedive. In a country where failures — however heroic — are poor substitutes for success, the episode was quickly relegated to the archives of space history.

Apollo 13, the Hollywood version, was finally going to give the men — and women — involved the recognition that had long been their due for probably the greatest rescue operation ever launched.

The script was based on Lovell's book, *Lost Moon*, and the former *Apollo 13* commander found a new job in retirement as the film's technical advisor. A quarter of a century after becoming the most famous astronaut NOT to walk on the moon, James Lovell would also finally become a household name, such is the power of Hollywood.

Lovell admits the mission had been neglected over the years 'because we like to forget our failures'. As if to prove his point, he talks about the study in his house, which is littered with awards and trophies from his first three space flights. The only recognition of *Apollo 13* was a letter from Charles Lindbergh.

The bittersweet irony is that it is now the familiar face of Tom Hanks the public will forever associate with the name Jim Lovell, a fact that is not lost on the ex-spaceman. While Tom was staying with him, the two men were drinking in a local bar when Lovell was asked to sign a framed picture hanging above the bar. Lovell said he pointed to Hanks. 'I told them, "Hey, that's the real Jim Lovell, let him go over and sign it." Because after the movie's out, it's not going to be me any more. Tom Hanks is going to be Jim Lovell.' Lovell said he was delighted at the choice of Tom to play him and happily went out of his way to help the actor, who was playing a real person for the first time in his career.

Tomhad been well aware of all the details of the *Apollo 13* story years before he contemplated recreating it, and had told his 'crack team of showbusiness experts' that he would definitely be interested if any of the studios came up with a script to bring the story to the big screen. When he learned Howard and his partner Brian Grazer had paid $600,000 to Lovell for the rights to his book, Tom joked that he held a broken bottle to Howard's neck in a Manhattan restaurant and told him: 'I've got to play Jim Lovell. I was born for that part. Give me the part or else!'

Both producers and star could have been taking a serious risk. Because of *The Right Stuff*'s failure at the box office, it was widely thought that *Apollo 13* would have the same crash landing on its release.

In fact, the film would help imprint the full details of the story onto the American consciousness.

It started with a normal launch from a mostly clear Cape Canaveral. Although it was supposed to be a routine flight, the omens were not good. *Apollo 13* was launched 13 minutes past the 13th hour. Scientists scoffed at such talk. But halfway to the moon, an oxygen tank exploded leaving the three astronauts — Lovell, Fred Haise and Jack Swigert — with little oxygen, almost no heat and a leaking spacecraft.

The explosion turned out to be the beginning of a four-day duel between the wonders of human engineering and the limits of technology.

Lovell recalls looking at Haise hoping the quaking sound he heard was the jolt from a lever his colleague had pulled in jest. The look Haise gave him told him otherwise. 'They were the eyes of someone who was truly frightened — truly, wholly, profoundly frightened,'he said.

At the time, *Newsweek* reported: 'The three astronauts faced a death no man had ever died before — death in space, cold and alone, outward bound into the blackness of the void.'

Battling the unknown, with a moon landing out of the question, the spacemen had just one aim — to avoid spinning out of control in a high-tech coffin.

As they orbited the moon in a cramped lunar module, with lights and heating turned off to conserve energy, they plotted a split-second manoeuvre to make it possible to re-enter the earth's atmosphere.

The cool strategies of the three men and their advisors at Houston mission control managed to guide the stricken craft to a successful splashdown in the Pacific on 17 April 1970.

Swigert, who was portrayed by Kevin Bacon in the film, successfully ran for office in the US Congress after leaving the space programme, but tragically died before taking office.

Haise, played by Bill Paxton, went on to pilot the shuttle prototype *Enterprise* five times and has survived five plane crashes. He went on to be chairman of Grumman Technical Services in Titusville, Florida — the same company that built the lunar module that saved his life.

'It is the ultimate human interest tale,' said Haise, who lives in Brevard County, Florida. 'It has a happy ending. That is definitely the most important thing — a Hollywood ending.'

Although the ensemble film would not add to Tom's Oscar collection ('If I won again there would be suicide jumpers from the roof of the Dorothy Chandler Pavilion'), its success — pulling in more than $30 million on its opening weekend and going on to make over $172 million — once again proved Tom's ability to take an unfashionable subject and turn it into a blockbuster. His track record was such that the public simply trusted his ability to lead a good film into the cinema.

Apollo 13 was also the first time he had the luxury of starring in a film he had a strong personal interest in, with the possible exception of *A League of Their Own*, which although about his beloved baseball, was still about women's baseball.

Tom's interest in space began early. He was at the heart of an era when ten-year-old boys were busy building Airfix kits of lunar modules and putting star charts on their walls alongside the pop posters and football rosettes. It is hard to believe now how quickly space flight sank in popularity. Trains, planes and football may have had their fluctuations in fascination among the young, but Man in Space fell into such a void that *Apollo 13* would reach a whole new generation that had probably thought at first that it was an offshoot from a *Rocky* movie.

He told *Daily News* writer Dennis Hamill: 'When I was a kid I paid a lot of attention to the space programme. The *Gemini* programme was done between 1965 and 1966, so I was aware of that because at school they would march us over from class to the auditorium to watch launches. But I distinctly remember *Apollo 7* going up in November 1968. Then in December we were on Christmas vacation from school, and in my mum's house and *Apollo 8* was all over the television. And here were these guys who were on their way to the moon. And that was a very big deal to me. I couldn't get enough of it. It was very glamorous, the nature of the adventure was, what's the word? It was romantic. Three guys in this little thing, going to the moon. Heroic.'

He continued: 'One of the biggest things I discovered in the course of doing *Apollo 13* and being able to meet all these guys, not just the astronauts, but also the flight directors at NASA, was the particulars of who they are and why they were doing it in the first place.

'The first real astronaut I got to know was Jim Lovell. Jim's a great guy, but he's the last guy you would pick to be that standard kind of Wheaties box vision of an astronaut. Astronauts are supposed to be these great, mythic figures. But they're all kind of short because you couldn't be too tall to be in one of those capsules. The tallest astronaut was like, six feet. They all have these backgrounds as engineers, physicists and rocket scientists. They're all very learned and almost bookish, and they all fly jets and stuff like that. Also, they're married, or divorced, with kids and houses.

'We went into Jim Lovell's house in Houston. And it's a small American house. And you connect to the idea that the kids were sleeping upstairs, and he'd get up at 5.30 in the morning, eat breakfast and drive off to Ellington Air Force field, get in a jet and in an hour-and-a-half he'd be at the Cape and he'd get into a simulator. Stuff like that, the real nuts and bolts of how they got there. It was a steady job. But they were utterly consumed by it. They just loved it. We've all done stuff in our lives where it's not even like working. You realise, gee, all this time has gone by and you didn't even think about it because you loved it so much. And that's how these astronauts lived their lives. They drank a lot of coffee and worked 16-18 hours a day.'

Tom said it was how he visualised it as a boy, sucking on his garden hose in the swimming pool. 'Back in Oakland, it was just the idea of three guys in a tin can, surrounded by the cosmos, drifting slowly into the history books. I dreamed about being one of them constantly.'

With *Apollo 13*, he realised that, although most people knew the outcome, very few knew the fascinating 'nuts and bolts'. People didn't know 'you could take a piece of gaffer tape, a plastic bag and a sock and you could make this thing that could clean the carbon dioxide in the craft.'

Even before signing on for the project, Tom had named his production company Clavius Base, after a crater in which the moon monolith is discovered in *2001: A Space Odyssey*. So strongly does he believe in the importance of the space programme that he even has a theory that the world can be divided into two periods of human history: before and after we landed on the moon.

Right after Neil Armstrong's *Apollo 11*, space travel dropped 'right off the face of consciousness.'

'And that's because,' Tom told Hamill, 'everyone born after World War II grew up thinking that eventually someone was going to land on the moon. And that was going to be a truly evolutionary moment in the history of our species. That once we did that, once we figured out how to put a man on the moon, we would have reached a technological level, after which, truly anything is possible. Now people say, "We figured out a way to put a man on the moon, but I can't get the paper out of my fax machine."

'But prior to the landing on the moon, there was still this great goal, that we were waiting to see become a reality. It was still like, "Man, how do you think they are gonna do it?" We knew there was this great enterprise that was afoot in 1961 which started the clock running. So for all those years, there was a question of who was going to do it first, who is going to win, which propelled things and made it happen much, much faster than it would have.

'But removed from all that, everyone in the world knew that all this technological stuff, both good and bad, from the atomic bomb to mechanical pencils to the telephone to thermos bottles and Saran wrap were all going to be used somehow or other to put a man on the moon. And what was he going to do? Claim it in the name of someone or the other, or stick a flag in it. Or he was going to maybe die getting there. But everyone was waiting for it to happen. And then it happened. Neil Armstrong, "One small step ..." and all that stuff.

'How many times has the world literally stopped to watch something that was not a tragedy unfold on television? Precious few times. It wasn't a funeral. It wasn't cops chasing someone on the street. Instead it was all of us, as a planet, a species, sitting down and watching this truly extraordinary thing happen. Then, when that happened, it was all done.

'But the thing that's not fair about that, or the thing we're missing here, is that we explored the moon only for about three years. I think the last time was in December of 1972. And just getting there, and landing, and walking around was not nearly as important to me as all the stuff that has happened after that.

'All the things we've found out about the different places that we went. I mean, the moon is roughly five times the size of Africa. So what we explored would be equal to going to Paris, landing at the airport, getting in a cab, driving around Paris, and then going back to the airport and flying back home again. But what do we really know?'

None of this was something Tom had just thought of to help promote a film. The subject had consumed him for as long as he could remember. And he would put it to use again in another award-winning project, the 12 hour, £40 million TV series *From the Earth to the Moon*.

But first, Tom had some more down-to-earth things to worry about in the form of a specially designed training aircraft that simulated weightlessness for would-be astronauts and, in this case, for actors pretending to be astronauts. Howard spurned the expected use of computer graphics to send his actors on more than 600 trips on a unique jet plane they very quickly nicknamed the 'vomit comet'.

Tom and fellow 'astronauts' Bill Paxton and Kevin Bacon are shown weightless (or in 1/6th gravity, to be precise) for virtually half of the film.

And if Tom felt nauseous on his night flight with Jim Lovell, he was going to get used to the feeling when shooting began on NASA's KC-135, a stripped-down 707 used to introduce astronauts to the phenomenon before they get to space.

The plane achieves zero gravity the hard way. It flies steeply up to about 36,000 feet and then screams earthward in a prolonged dive. The aircraft's parabolic motion creates enough centrifugal force to counter gravity at the top of the arc, and as it reverses direction, everyone and everything inside is gently released from the earth's gravitational pull.

But it only lasts for 25 seconds. After that everything floating around is flung violently to the padded floor. So every bit of footage had to be shot piecemeal in a lunar capsule built into the plane's zero-gravity compartment.

Bacon didn't want to do it at first, but agreed after Tom, who was thrilled at the idea, and Paxton voted to give it a try. 'I didn't want to be the weanie,' he joked.

For Tom, it was another playground and he proudly boasts that no one actually vomited. But after a few flights, he got confident enough to turn down the motion sickness pills they had all been advised to take. 'I wanted to see if I could handle it because the people who do this all the time don't use drugs. Well, my ... it was bad. I'll tell you, I have never felt that sick.'

He said he came close to being sick when he moved his head too quickly. 'It took three hours for the nausea to die down.'

After that, he toned down the jokes aimed at his old *Forrest Gump* cast-mate Gary Sinise, playing Ken Mattingly, the astronaut who was grounded by flight surgeons the day before his scheduled ride on *Apollo 13*. Sinise had suffered so much with motion sickness that Tom said: 'I thought Gary looked nice in khaki, but not when the colour is his face.'

He added: 'The person I felt sorry for was the photographer Annie Leibowitz, who came up with us to shoot pictures for *Vanity Fair*. She was throwing up all the time. Yet she still took the pictures. She had the camera in one hand and a sick bag in the other. She's a real trouper.'

In the end, the actors spent more time in the 'vomit comet' even than astronauts going into space. Howard told *People* magazine: 'Saying something is better than sex rarely lives up to that claim. Weightlessness doesn't quite, either. But it came awfully close.'

Bob Williams, NASA's test director for the Zero-G Aircraft Programme, wasn't happy when he first learned that Hollywood's finest were about to descend on his operation. He said: 'All we knew about Hollywood folks is what we read and see on TV. We were expecting a bunch of prima donna Hollywood types.

'But I can't tell you how impressed we were with this group. There wasn't an ounce of prima donna in any of them.'

Back down on the ground, the actors likened shooting in the cramped *Apollo 13* capsule fabricated on the Universal back lot as like 'shooting a movie in a Volkswagen Beetle'.

During the last month of filming, Howard even had the

temperature on the sound stage dropped to a near-freezing 34 degrees to simulate the frigid conditions when the crew turned off the heating to conserve energy.

To warm up, the actors huddled in Tom's trailer watching movies. One mini-film festival was devoted to comedian Buster Keaton, because they thought the silent films star looked like Tom.

Throughout the five-and-a-half months of filming, Tom gorged on every detail of the space mission. 'Oh, Hanks,' said Bacon, who watched his co-star devour NASA procedure manuals and physics lessons. 'You could just put him on the shuttle now and he would know how to fly it.'

Said Tom: 'I knew about 20 per cent of what was going on. But I was a pain in the ass.'

In his 21st film, Tom was as comfortable with himself as an actor as any star in Hollywood. He no longer had to wait until scripts were turned down by bigger stars to get the chance to shine. There were no bigger stars.

And while other so-called superstars may have been uncertain of their ground and blind to their limitations, Tom was very sure why he was a 'movie star'.

'I can't do what Gibson and Costner do. But they can't bring to their roles what I can bring. People relate to me as a regular guy. If Costner had played Jim Lovell (as was considered) it would have put a completely different focus on the story. It would have been about him. I am just one of the three guys in the pod. That's how it was.'

Although the two became friends, Tom was also critical of Tom Cruise earlier in his career, perceiving his major A-list rival as losing himself in his stardom. 'Look at Tom Cruise,' he told *Cosmopolitan* in 1987. 'The way he walks, the way he talks. He's losing it as an actor. He's becoming a movie star. He's on the wrong track.'

The success of *Apollo 13* got its star thinking. There was still so much to learn about the space missions, about their effect and their standing in the cultural history of the 20th century. There were so many mind-boggling nuts and bolts an audience would, he was sure, find intriguing.

In dealing with one, specific *Apollo* mission, there was so much that had to be left out. It was a subject Tom had fervent opinions about, as exemplified by his theories about man reaching the moon. But he also had a more personal slant on the '60s that he was hankering to give vent to.

'I remember those as some of the worst years of my life. It was hell,' he told *The New York Times*.

'Our world was very, very polarised. If you had long hair, you were a good guy; if you had short hair, you were a bad guy. We mistrusted just about anything that had to do with the Government.'

To Tom, who was 13 when Neil Armstrong stepped foot on the moon, the space missions were among the few lasting, happy memories he had of the era. But for many, they were mistrusted along with everything else the government of the time was involved in. It was a historical viewpoint Tom had a vested interest in changing. In essence, he wanted to reclaim the '60s for his own generation by giving the space programme a context he felt it had been denied.

The ambitious idea of telling the entire space story, from President Kennedy's dare to beat the Russians right through to the last, half-forgotten flight of *Apollo 17*, was one that perhaps only a double-Oscar-winning star of Tom's magnitude could bring to television.

It took two years of his life and its £40 million budget made it the single most expensive project in television history, but *From the Earth to the Moon* showed just how far Tom had come. Not only did his involvement as a director, writer and star of the series guarantee it a budget, among the first to watch it was President Clinton, at another private White House screening.

Tom had read author Andrew Chaikin's 1994 book *A Man on the Moon: The Voyages of the Apollo Astronauts* while researching *Apollo 13* and had recommended it to his fellow actors. It was on this 584-page tome that he based and pitched his own series to America's Home Box Office cable channel.

Tired of the cops-and-robbers space mentality of *Star Trek* and *Star Wars*, he wanted to get it right.

HBO's director of original programming gave the series the go ahead after meeting Tom. He said: 'The amazing thing about first

Time out at a press conference, during the Venice Film Festival.

Top: The role of a degenerate baseball coach in *A League of their Own* was another of Tom's great acting moments.

Bottom: Sleepless in Seattle was a tear-jerker that broke box office records, and established a friendly partnership with co-star Meg Ryan.

Tom starred as the eponymous hero in *Forrest Gump*, the feel-good tale of an ordinary man in extraordinary circumstances.

Inset: Tom plays second fiddle to Dan Aykroyd in spoof cop-film *Dragnet*.

Top: Tom's sensitive portrayal of a twelve-year-old boy endeared him to millions in *Big*.

Bottom: Never living up to the promise of the novel, *The Bonfire of the Vanities* starred Tom as a broker fallen on hard times.

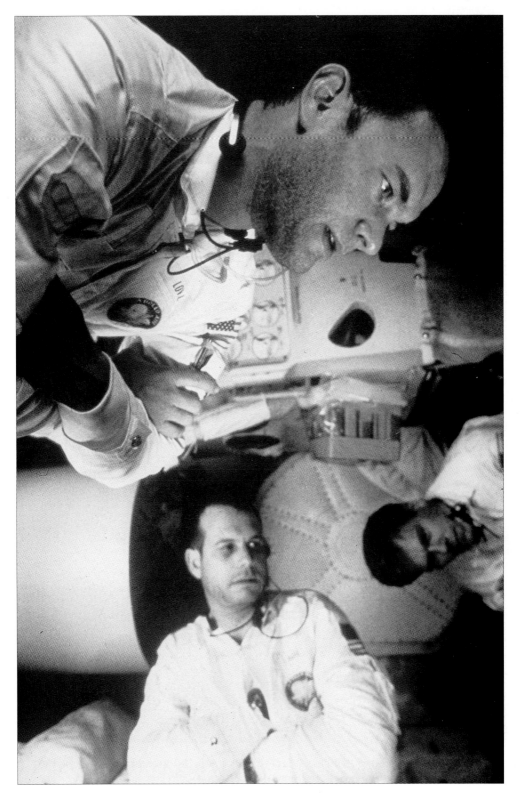

Tom's childhood obsession with space finally found fulfillment with *Apollo 13*, the movie of the ill-fated space mission.

Top: Tom kept his band of 'soldiers' together during the boot-camp programme that director Steven Spielberg insisted they undergo.

Bottom: You've Got Mail was another successful partnership for Tom and Meg Ryan – a light, romantic comedy.

Tom Hanks as Captain Miller, searching for Private Ryan.

Tom Hanks – a man for all seasons – and Hollywood's top earner.

meeting with Tom was he knew exactly what he wanted to do. In that first meeting, he had a handful of index cards that contained an outline of every episode as he saw it. And we got lucky in that Tom wanted to take a break from being a movie star.'

Tom took a pay cut and enlisted the help of his *Apollo 13* cohorts Ron Howard and partner Brian Grazer to get the project off the ground. He was the executive producer, wrote one episode himself and co-wrote three more, directed one, and was in charge of choosing writers, directors and the cast. He only took a small acting part.

Using 500 actors and ten different directors, the series was not so much a series as a collection of filmed short stories, built around the belief that nearly every angle of the *Apollo* missions had its own inherent drama.

Author Chaikin, a space buff who looks upon Tom as a kindred spirit, was employed as a consultant on the series to ensure the details were accurate.

'I remember being on the set with him,' Chaikin said, 'and we walked by the *Gemini* spacecraft that they had created for the series. And I said to Tom, "This is the coolest thing I have seen all day!" And he said, "Yeah, I know. I think I am going to take it home and put it in the garage." He said, "Can you picture that? You know, like I'll put a TV in there. It's gonna be like, honey, I'm going to be in the spacecraft."'

The series, originally broadcast in the US in the April and May of 1998, went on to win an Emmy for best mini-series. And Tom repaid Chaikin by writing a new foreword for his book. In it, Tom wrote: 'The thing that still fuels me in my day-to-day life and what I want to convey to my children, and to the audience, is that if mankind can figure out a way to put 12 men on the moon, then, honestly, we can solve anything. That's why I believe the six *Apollo* landings are six of the seven best stories ever told.'

Like other projects Tom became involved in at this stage of his career, he made a point in using trusted friends to boost the show's cohesion and professionalism. As well as wife Rita, Tom used former co-stars Sally Field, who directed one episode, Peter Scolari, his old *Bosom Buddies* buddy, and Elizabeth Perkins, his leading lady in *Big*, as well as many others in smaller roles.

As much as he liked to consider himself a regular guy whose main hobby was watching his weight, Tom was no longer living an ordinary life, if indeed he ever did. He could count the President of the United States as a friend for goodness sake!

His close coterie now also numbered Hollywood's most powerful players. But, as we shall see, he hadn't forgotten all of his old friends.

14
Friends to Di For

Just for once, there were no autograph hunters, no over-earnest fans. There wasn't even any paparazzi. Tom stood with his best friend Steven Spielberg outside the doors of Westminster Abbey waiting for them to open.

Dressed in black, they chatted with fellow American Tom Cruise, wearing dark glasses, and his Australian actress wife, Nicole Kidman. At any other time, such a gathering would be a focus of considerable attention anywhere outside Hollywood.

But on this breezy September morning in 1997 the thoughts of the world were with someone else. Tom was among the grieving celebrities invited to Princess Diana's state funeral. From Luciano Pavarotti to Diana Ross to Elton John and George Michael, they joined the royals, politicians, charity representatives and close friends at the sombre celebration of Diana's memory.

A sensitive man, easily given to tears, Tom struggled during the service to hold his emotions in check. 'We all sang God Save the Queen, which was not something I do a lot, and then the first thing that happened was that the coffin came in,' he told the *Express*. 'It was electrifying and ... well, you know,' he added, his voice trailing off as he tried to describe one of the most poignant moments of the 20th century.

Just two years earlier, Tom had spent the evening with Diana and was immediately struck both by her offbeat sense of humour and by her grace and intelligence. Their meeting came as Diana was asserting her independence from the Royal Family and beginning to organise her life around some of her pet charities.

The Princess and the movie star had spoken a number of times on the telephone after Diana phoned Tom to congratulate him on *Philadelphia*, a film she was particularly moved by as she had played such a large role in helping AIDS sufferers find acceptance in society. But this was the first time they had met in person.

The British première for *Apollo 13* had been held in Leicester Square the previous night on 6 September 1995, when Tom, Rita and most of the cast and crew left after the film for an informal party at Planet Hollywood.

Now Diana was holding her own, unprecedented mini-première to raise funds for Turning Point, a charity helping drug addicts to kick the habit. Forsaking the usual glitzy West End cinemas, she had taken over a cramped 46-seat theatre in an anonymous corner of Hammersmith, West London, and kept the event secret from all but a few, favoured press photographers.

An uncharacteristically nervous Tom, in dinner jacket and bow tie, with Rita and *Apollo* director Ron Howard, were greeted by a vivacious-looking Diana, wearing a tight black Versace dress, at the nearby United International Pictures office building and they were taken together to the cinema, where the Princess sat down beside the film's star.

When Steven Spielberg had been in a similar position during the Royal première of *Indiana Jones and the Temple of Doom*, he had apparently been told to cough loudly in Diana's ear the exact moment his wife-to-be, actress Kate Capshaw, starring in the film with Harrison Ford, shouted 'shit', so worried were her courtiers about offending royal protocol. But now Diana, unfettered by hangers-on, quickly put Tom at his ease.

When the film finished, with the Princess lavishing praise on Tom's stellar performance, she didn't quietly retire to Kensington Palace as she had been required to do in the past, to sit alone in her quarters while all the stars her own age high-tailed it to the première party. This time, Diana was the host — and she wasn't going to miss out on any of the fun.

The 46 guests were whisked in a fleet of limousines to the Green House restaurant in Mayfair, where another 50 guests in dinner dress were waiting. Once again, Diana took the seat next to Tom. She chatted gaily about films, asking him all about some of her favourites, which included *Forrest Gump* and *Philadelphia*.

After giving a brief speech describing the work of Turning Point, and making a thinly veiled request for support, Diana bade farewell to Tom, Rita, Ron and the *Apollo* executives. As a friend of President Clinton and some of the biggest names on the planet, it was not easy to impress Tom. But that was a night he would remember — and later treasure — as a very personal memory of a remarkable woman.

Tom had been asked by Spielberg to accompany him to the funeral as both were filming in London at the time. The director had known Diana ever since she had first appeared at the British première to his *ET* blockbuster. There was no problem getting an invitation to the funeral because Spielberg had lunched at Chequers with Tony Blair and his family just a few weeks before Diana's death. They had been mulling over the potential of turning the Hertfordshire location of the director's latest movie into a permanent British studio. Number 10 ensured Hollywood's grim-faced ambassadors would be able to pay their respects.

Tom was in England when the Princess was killed in the Paris car crash and had experienced at first hand the unforgettable outpouring of national grief that followed.

So involved did he feel that he later bristled at the feeling in the United States and elsewhere that the stiff upper-lipped Brits had suddenly become hysterical after losing their beloved Queen of Hearts.

He said: 'I saw all the crowds. I saw them every day. And these people were not hysterical. They were simply in mourning, showing their respect for the loss of someone very special.

'It really annoyed me the way it was made to look as if the people of Britain had lost their minds. What I saw was dignity and decency on a grand scale. It filled me with respect for the British.'

He told the *Mail on Sunday*: 'To be an American at the funeral was something else. But I have to tell you, no way in hell does America come to a standstill for any reason like that — I mean, the last time America came to a standstill was to watch the O.J. Simpson trial.

'And after the funeral, we had to listen to all of the incessant analysis of what was going on. 'Why is there such hysteria in the streets? What does it all mean?' And I thought the media are out of their minds. These people are just sad. 'Why are people piling up flowers outside Buckingham Palace?' Because they're sad you morons, that's why.'

When the Westminster Abbey service was over, the Duchess of York asked Tom and Spielberg if they were doing anything that evening. Apparently, they did have a dinner planned, but didn't want to be rude and so accepted an invitation to her home in Sunningdale that evening. Realising the Hollywood contingent were feeling low and slightly lost after leaving the Abbey, the Duchess also invited Tom Cruise and wife, Nicole Kidman, as well as Hong Kong businessman David Tang. It would be, she told them, 'a wake — a celebration of Diana's life'.

Spielberg's driver was so stunned when he phoned the number the Duchess gave his boss to call for directions and Prince Andrew answered that he didn't write them down. According to the *Express*, the embarrassed driver phoned back only to be told by the amused Prince that it was not an unusual occurrence.

Fergie and her estranged husband met Tom and Spielberg at the door — their respective wives had returned to California with the children who were due back at school — and they found Sting, his wife Trudie, and singer Chris de Burgh were already there.

After dinner, de Burgh sang a lament dedicated to Diana and was persuaded to sing a medley of his hits, including one of the Princess's favourite songs, 'Lady in Red'. As he sang, Fergie stood close to tears by the fireplace in the living room, swaying in time to the music. Much of the talk, inevitably, revolved around memories of Diana, much as it did at dining tables around the world.

For Tom, it was a surreal end to a very emotional and unforgettable day.

Tom was in England shooting *Saving Private Ryan*, a World War II film being directed by Spielberg. It was an all-star collaboration both men had resisted up until then, fearing their friendship would in some way be harmed by a working relationship. They needn't have worried. The two men became, if anything, even closer and the film was a commercial and critical *tour de force*, of which more later.

Rita had, of course, spent a year in London as a teenage student, but Tom had always looked upon the city as just another stop in his jet-setting schedule. He'd been to Britain for film premières and publicity tours — the type of visit that often leaves Hollywood's visiting royalty thinking the UK is just a collection of TV studios and posh Park Lane hotels.

When he signed on to do the Spielberg movie, it went without saying that Rita and the kids would go too. The family moved into pop star Sting's Georgian house in Highgate, a short drive from the disused airfield in North London where most of the action would be filmed.

Cruise and Kidman were in town on their mammoth filming of *Eyes Wide Shut* with the capricious Stanley Kubrick, and fellow cast members included Americans Ed Burns, Tom Sizemore and Matt Damon. And Spielberg and his actress wife, Kate Capshaw, were regular visitors and welcome reminders of home.

But the Hanks family wasn't homesick at all. They fell madly in love with London. Said Tom after the trip: 'The Hanks family are big fans of Britain. We lived in Highgate for about two months and loved every minute of it. When I announced that we would be living in London for a while, we were all prepared for it to be hideous. I really don't mean to be rude, but in America there is a certain image of Britain which I now know is simply not true. So, as we were packing, we were all saying, "Oh no — we've got to go to shabby old London." But from the moment we arrived it was clear we were wrong and that the beautiful capital city is in great shape.

'It's going through a tremendous renaissance. It really is one of the world's great cities. Apart from the terrible traffic, every day was a true adventure for me and my family. We had this lovely house in Highgate and after a day at work I didn't want to go to the West End — so we would have a meal at the local Chinese restaurant and go to the pub across the street.

'It was fantastic. And Hampstead Heath was like a treasure trove to us. Every spare moment, we were down there wandering around exploring. We all miss London terribly.'

Tom and his Hollywood friends would later take the brunt of criticism for 'snubbing' a charity ball arranged in Los Angeles to raise money for charities supported by the Princess. Tom and Rita, Spielberg, Tom Cruise and John Travolta, as well as Bruce Willis, Demi Moore and Kim Basinger had all been expected to attend the ball organised by Diana's butler, Paul Burrell.

When none of them turned up, patriotic rock star Rod Stewart blasted them as 'bastards'.

Stewart, who paid £1,200 for tickets for himself and wife, Rachel Hunter, said: 'I think they are bastards for not coming.'

And, in a pointed reference to Tom, Spielberg, Cruise and Kidman, Rod's wife, Rachel Hunter added: 'They went to Diana's funeral because they knew they would get on television, but they can't be bothered to come here. It's disgusting.'

With the exception perhaps of this particular event, Tom appeared to have an almost Gump-like ability to be at the right place at the right time. And it wasn't just his professional life that seemed to dovetail into success. At Rita's urging, his private life was flourishing too. He had his family. Now he had his friends too.

One minute he is appearing on stage in New York as a favour to his friend, comedian Steve Martin. Then he is at Princess Diana's funeral. Back on America's East Coast, he is living it up as a guest at Spielberg's Quelle Barn estate in the fashionable Hamptons on Long Island. And in California again, Tom is one of the most prominent guests at the hush-hush 1998 wedding of Barbra Streisand to beau James Brolin, where, incidentally, he was spotted doing a limbo dance next to the swimming pool.

How many ordinary Joes have spent not one but three nights in the Queen's Bedroom at the White House; sent the most expensive caviar to showbusiness mogul David Geffen as a thank-you for allowing him to use his private jet; leased a luxury 12-seater suite at a cost of more than £160,000 a year to watch basketball and ice hockey games in Los Angeles; and can afford to spend more than £2 million on a house that 'needs a lot of fixing up'?

'I know, I know, I know,' Tom laughed, burying his head in his hands when *Vanity Fair* offered him evidence of his high-flying ways. 'Isn't it wild? Isn't it hilarious? What am I going to do?'

He went on: 'I can tell you exactly when it all began. We're friends with Peter Weller, and Peter Weller took us to St. Barts. We were on the American plan, for crying out loud! 'Oh, wow! This is great! The houses are so beautiful!' When we were there on that trip, we met Mike [director, Mike Nichols] and Diane [TV anchor, Diane Sawyer]. We were all at this table.

'I had just proposed to Rita during the last few seconds of 1987. I'd asked her to marry me, and she said, "You bet!"

'So we've all ended up having this kind of history together. Between St Barts and, say, Carrie Fisher's parties, you meet everybody who's on the creative axis of Western society ... So, yes, there it is. I am actually a boulevardier. I am a member of café society. At the same time, I'm this kid from ...

'Therein lies my charm.'

While Tom has the innate ability to turn on the charm at the push of a button, he can also switch off just as quickly if he is preoccupied. That privacy door he would slide down gave rise to the claim from even some of his closest friends over the years that they never really knew what was going on inside his head.

Tom is one of the very few people in Hollywood who would dare call Steven Spielberg 'chucklehead'. And their friendship has its professional boundaries. Tom wanted desperately to be cast as the camp commandant in Spielberg's *Schindler s List*, but the director went for Ralph Fiennes. Tom still argues he could have done the job well. 'I just know it,' he says. But their mutual respect and a recognition of aspects of themselves in each other provides the basis for their relationship.

In 1994, Spielberg told *Vanity Fair*: 'The nice thing about being with Tom is that when he feels comfortable around you he doesn't feel a responsibility to spearhead the conversation. There's no nervousness. And I think when you can get rid of the nervousness in a friendship between two guys, then it becomes a, well, older kind of relationship.

'Now we just take our kids to school and talk about the quality of the American teaching system.

'I think that the thing Tom and I have in common is that we were both loners and then we met two terrific women. A lot of our friendship can be traced to the fact that our wives are bestest friends. They get us out. I'd rather stay at home and watch television all night; Kate has to drag me out to a restaurant. Tom is he same way. So often, if we are dragged by our wives into a room together, we get along great.

'But, in a sense, I have never seen Tom as a lonely person. I think Tom is just really in touch with himself, and you can't be in touch with yourself if you are always serving others. I think he needs to spend time alone getting familiar with that part of him that he needs as an actor, as an artist.'

He added: 'Tom doesn't fit into the moulds of other American icons. It's too easy to find a couple of people that share the same all-Americanness that you can compare him to. But Tom Hanks will always be remembered as Tom Hanks. He is without peer.'

High praise indeed, but then the two friends do have more in common than just movie making. Like Tom, Spielberg met Kate Capshaw while still married to his first wife, actress Amy Irving. The director's passionate affair with Kate, who he had cast in the 1984 hit *Indiana Jones and the Temple of Doom*, effectively ended his marriage, although there were painful reconciliations between Spielberg and Irving before they divorced.

The Spielbergs' extended family includes his son with Irving and her daughter from an earlier marriage. Having put her career on the back burner to care for the family, Kate stepped up her acting again, much like Rita.

While Tom took up Rita's Greek orthodoxy, the Spielbergs did it the other way around, with Kate converting to Judaism.

Both families own houses on the oceanfront at Malibu and, after Tom and Rita bought the 'fixer-upper' on one acre in the upscale Pacific Pallisades neighbourhood of Los Angeles — his real life 'Money Pit' — in 1996, they are neighbours there too.

Families are at the heart of the friendship. Spielberg told *Time*: 'First, he's a wonderful daddy. In between raising his kids, he does pictures. We're friends because his interpretation of family life is so retro. It's car pools, barbecues, play weekends, talk about the PTA, take videos of the kids. The other thing is that he completely, unerringly loves his wife.'

Once a month, Rita's 'mummy group' — which includes Capshaw, Annette Bening, Goldie Hawn, Sally Field, Jamie Lee

Curtis and Nancy Short, among others — meets up in one house while their husbands and partners meet in another. The wives call themselves 'Girls Night Out Productions'.

'We leave our dinners and we've had five million belly laughs, figured out someone's love life, and got two more kids sleeping through the night,' Capshaw told *Ladies Home Journal* magazine. 'The men come home from their dinners with three-picture deals.'

The superstar support group even takes night calls. When actress and talk-show host Rosie O'Donnell was having problems feeding her newly-adopted child, Rita and her mother rushed over to her home to help. Rita's mother proudly persuaded the baby to drink his first full bottle of milk.

Sally Field, who has worked with Tom on *Punchline, Forrest Gump* and *From the Earth to the Moon,* said her favourite co-star and his wife are a focus of Hollywood's most A-list inner circle.

She told *People*: 'They are both people who appreciate hard work and excellence. They are well read, they are aggressively curious, they drive each other. She is a mimic, really clever. More often than not, Tom's is the loudest laughter. He'll run over, pick her up and run out of the room. We go, "There they go again."'

Tom told *Interview* magazine: 'I got lucky in love first, and now I finally got lucky in friends. I actually think I needed the foundation of a family before I got a group. I had to take that very, very slowly. It goes back to what we were saying about the imbalances of fame. I'm kind of ashamed of how many possibilities probably went by the wayside.

'Our group is the same kind of group that I was in at high school or in the Green Room at Sacramento. Everybody gets an entrance, you know, whether they are actors or not. Everybody has that kind of presence that emboldens the table, and we do stuff like old people do. We have cocktails and dinner parties and stuff like that.

'We go on vacations that are hanging on the edge of disaster all the time, because anything could happen during them! It's got the same bona fide *oomph* that is based partly on the fact that we laugh a bunch and that we have an awful lot in common, partly because we are parents.

'It's also an intellectually powerful kind of atmosphere to be in.

Some of these people are famous or incredibly accomplished, and some of them aren't.'

Tom clearly feels more comfortable with these rarefied relationships. But that doesn't mean he has forgotten his old friends.

As an actor, Tom had always been credited for his subtle negotiating with directors to get his view of the movie across. Even on bad films, he usually took particular care of his own part and consequentially managed to avoid going down with the ship when the project sank without trace at the box office. It was only natural, particularly when you consider his close friendship with the likes of Spielberg, *Gump*'s Bob Zemeckis and *Philadelphia*'s Jonathan Demme, that he would one day want to try his hand at directing.

So while on what he called 'the trophy-run world tour of *Forrest Gump*' in 1995, he began seriously to write a script as an escape from 'too many airplanes and too many hotel rooms and too many journalists and too much free food'.

The script about a pop group of one-hit wonders in the 1960s would provide the basis for Tom's 'vanity project,' *That Thing You Do!*, the first Hanks-directed feature film, which opened in the autumn of 1996.

Although he only rated a few minutes of screen time in the film, he directed, wrote the script, handpicked the cast and even commandeered the soundtrack, writing four songs.

He also found time to give work to two old friends at times in their lives when it meant a great deal to them.

Peter Scolari, Tom's old *Bosom Buddy* had gone on to a solid, if not earth-shattering, TV career in popular American shows like *Newhart*, *Goodtime Girls* and *Baby Makes Five*. But in the mid-90s, he was having trouble finding the kind of work he wanted and was going through a costly divorce.

'I can tell you honestly that if it hadn't been for Tom Hanks, his friendship and his standing behind me in 1996, I would have had to declare bankruptcy,' Scolari told the *Pittsburgh Post-Gazette*. 'He put me to work in *That Thing You Do!* and *From the Earth to the Moon*. He said, "I've never done you a favour. I'm doing myself a favour by putting you in this movie." But he was my friend.'

Scolari was cast as the smarmy host of *The Hollywood Television*

Showcase, the fictional show that helped launch the film's short-lived pop heroes. Tom said on an American TV interview afterwards that he enjoyed the perks of being the boss. 'You know, that's the best gig. The biggest plus about the job is that you really get to hire your pals. And you get to wrangle them on the phone a little bit. With Peter Scolari, I just said, "Look, I need you for a week. We have got to make up a bunch of stuff. So can you just come on down?" [Shooting for the film was on *The Price is Right* set] And I gave him a big trailer and he was able to take part.'

Another old friend Tom called up was his Cleveland Shakespearean cohort Holmes Osborne, the other half of *The Two Gentlemen of Verona*. Osborne had long given up his hopes of stardom, toiling for years making corporate workplace videos, commercials and doing regional theatre in his native Missouri.

At the age of 48, he was finally able to make his debut in a major motion picture — thanks to Tom. As the main character's curmudgeonly father, Osborne makes eight appearances in the film.

The role was the result of a pact the two men had made long ago — that if either of them became a director they would find the other a juicy part.

Osborne had watched from afar as Tom rose to fame and, although he couldn't help but envy his friend's career, they kept in touch with the occasional phone call or letter. On a trip to California in the early '90s, Osborne called Tom. 'I hadn't seen him for years, and I asked if he could help me find some work in films,' he told the *Kansas City Star*.

'Tom said, "No, no, no — I'm an actor. They don't ask an actor who should be in a movie. But if ever I get my own project, you're at the top of the list."

'I didn't doubt for a minute that he meant it. The public thinks of Tom Hanks as a great guy, and one of the reasons for that is that you can count on what he says. What I doubted was that he'd put all that pressure on himself. I mean, why should he direct? He was getting along great just acting.'

When Osborne read that Tom was writing a script about a '60s rock band he wrote and asked him to bear him in mind for a part. A few weeks later, he received the first draft of Tom's screenplay for *That Thing You Do!*

'Tom wanted any ideas I might have. Well, from 1963 to 1966, I played in a garage band called The Trends. I had lots of stories from that era. So I sent Tom a seven-page letter on my experiences. I didn't figure he'd pay much attention, but during the filming all these ideas I'd suggested started popping up.'

One souvenir Osborne later took away with him was a mock pop-concert poster used as a prop. The band being advertised was The Trends.

He was used to driving to auditions and finding his own motel room. But Tom sent a limo to pick him up from his home and take him to the airport for his first-class flight to the film set in Los Angeles.

'Tom was on the set telling everybody they had better look sharp because he's bringing in this guy from Bates City, Missouri.'

For his big scene in the film, Osborne was suddenly asked to improvise by Tom. 'So I did and Tom keeps the cameras going. I'm getting a round of applause from the crew. That's encouraging. Tom's feeding me ideas and laughing. When I get a laugh from Tom Hanks, I feel pretty secure. Truth is, he doesn't laugh much unless it really gets to him. So I'm having warm, bubbly feelings about the entire shoot.'

He added: 'I don't think of Tom as a huge star because he doesn't let me think of him that way. I mean, he drives a pick-up truck. A new pick-up truck, but it's still a pick-up truck.

'Inside, Tom hasn't changed much. In a one-on-one environment he's exactly the same as he was.

'The problem is that because of his fame he has to be guarded in public. During the filming he would always pose for pictures with people who came by the set to watch the movie being made. But he has to be careful. He can't just go anywhere whenever he feels like it.

'I wouldn't say that I've never envied Tom, but I'm not jealous. Yeah, I have some bitterness about struggling for so long. Why couldn't this have happened 20 years ago? But I didn't have the opportunity. As I told Tom in a letter, "If nothing else happens as a result of this, they can't take the experience away." At least this movie is finally giving me credibility with my kids. Shakespeare never did that.'

Following his screen role, Osborne was hoping it would be a springboard to more Hollywood roles. 'Tom Hanks gave me the opportunity to put my work before lots of people. The rest is up to me,' he said.

Tom made it perfectly clear that the hiring of a friend from his salad days in regional theatre was in no way meant to be charity. At the première of the film at the Toronto International Film Festival in Canada, he said: 'For me, working with Holmes again was one of the added bonuses of making this movie. It wasn't a huge part, but I wanted a guy who could do the riffs. I've talked to Holmes periodically over the years and know him pretty well. I never doubted he could do it.'

Interestingly, Vincent Dowling, both men's mentor at the Great Lakes Shakespeare Festival, explained what separated the two actors. He said: 'Both Tom and Holmes are brilliantly talented. But there are a few actors who — when you first meet them — their charm, their humanness, the whole breadth of their personality comes bang over. They can walk into an interview or audition and it's all there from the first moment.

'Tom always had that. Holmes didn't.'

He said Tom has a 'quiet but absolute determination and need to win. While all actors have a need to act, certain actors have a need for fame and success. And that need is what puts a person continually in the right place at the right time.'

Tom couldn't leave out Rita, who had given birth to their second son, Truman (actually Truman Theodore, after two American Presidents), shortly before filming started. She plays a bargirl in a sexy, very revealing, outfit. 'It was Tom's idea of a cruel joke,' she laughed. 'Dressing me up like that just after I'd given birth.'

The roots of *That Thing You Do!*, like many of Tom's projects, has its beginnings in his childhood. Like most of young America in the mid-'60s, Tom was caught up in the British pop invasion, but, ever the contrary child, he spurned the Beatles for a lesser-known London group, the Dave Clark Five.

He explained to the *St Louis Post-Dispatch*: 'I was always toying around with the notion of a band that, about the time they are ready for the biggest success of their careers, they flame out because of the various personalities involved.

'When I was a kid, eight years old, the youngest in a family of teenagers, the British invasion was it. It was a very evocative time for me, very glamorous, and you could see the Dave Clark Five every week, it seemed, on the *Ed Sullivan Show*.

'I was one of the kids convinced that the Dave Clark Five was way better than the Beatles. While we were working on *That Thing You Do!*, Dave Clark paid me a visit and it sent ripples of excitement through me.'

Tom's £20 million film tells the story of The Wonders, a fictional garage band from Erie, Pennsylvania, that reaches the top of the charts in 1964 with a tune called, surprise, surprise, 'That Thing You Do!'. The four naïve musicians go on the road under the wing of their controlling, manipulative manager — played by Tom — and collapse without ever recording a second record.

Again, his personal experience came into play as a reference for the four young men who are totally blindsided by fame. 'It is like being hit by a freight train,' he has said.

Tom asked advice from his director friends. But he said two stood out as being particularly useful. Ron Howard told him:'Look, the greatest movies are made by shooting wide, and then going in tighter, and then going in tighter.'

The aspiring director added: 'And Garry Marshall told me to change my shoes at lunchtime.'

The film, with its pretty much unknown cast — save Liv Tyler, best known at the time for being Aerosmith singer Stephen Tyler's daughter — did good, if not outstanding business and was well received by the critics.

It wasn't another in an ever-growing list of Tom Hanks blockbusters. But then, nobody really expected it to be.

It wasn't all fun either. Directing, as he discovered, could be downright hard work. 'I was working 18-hour days on *That Thing You Do!* and wasn't seeing my kids as much as I wanted,' he said. 'And I got into an elevator and this lady said, "Oh, Tom Hanks! What's it like living at the absolute top of the heap?" And I said, "Lady, life is just one damn thing after another, no matter where you are living."'

He told *Entertainment Weekly*: 'Any movie is going to be some sort of vanity project. There's no getting away from that. I did say, "Jeez, I'd really like to do this. Will you let me?" And they let me put my fat ass in the fire.'

It just shows how you can get by with a little help from your friends. And the critics were gentle with a film that, although without Tom's usual power, was still a pleasant, professionally-made diversion. Said *Variety*: 'The best thing to be said about Hanks' feature debut as a director is that it bears all the elements that have made him into a movie star — boyish charm, natural ease, comic precision and, above all, generosity of spirit.'

If Tom spent little time on screen in *That Thing You Do!*, he hadn't even shown his face on the hit movie that preceded it — and he still helped it gross more than $191 million (£118 million).

He had taken most of the summer in 1995 off, meeting only with director Oliver Stone to discuss, and later reject, the lead role in the high-profile biopic, *Nixon*. The shamed president was eventually played by Anthony Hopkins. He took time out to nix any possibility of a *Forrest Gump II* on the grounds that 'it wouldn't be a good movie'.

More forthright, he added later: 'Stupid is as stupid does makes me sick. I'll be saying "life is like a box of chocolates" again about the same time as Sean Connery says, "I'm Bond, James Bond."'

Toy Story was released by Disney in November 1995 with very little fanfare or advance buzz. Tom had been attracted to the project through his long working relationship with Disney, which was making the film, and because he thought his own kids would like it.

He certainly didn't do it for the money, getting paid the union scale fee for the job, a fraction of his market value in Hollywood. Coming off back-to-back Oscars, he had also hoped to fade into the background for a little while, feeling that he was becoming too overexposed to a fickle public. In fact, his voice-over work as Woody, the toy cowboy, took a little over two years and he had to record most of it separated from co-star Tim Allen, the voice of the spaceman toy Buzz Lightyear, because they kept making each other laugh too much.

Neither Tom nor Disney could have expected the huge success

of *Toy Story*, the first full-length feature film to be completely computer-animated.

The story centres around Andy, a six-year-old boy, whose toys come to life when humans are not around. Woody is the toy's leader and they all live in harmony in Andy's bedroom until the boy gets a new toy for his birthday — Buzz Lightyear, a technologically advanced astronaut that immediately gets all of Andy's attention.

The feud between the two toys provides the platform for a string of adventures that captured the heart of audiences around the world. Much to Tom's amazement, there was even talk of him being nominated again for a Best Actor Oscar, a first for an animated film.

Far from staying out of the spotlight, the film had thrust Tom back onto the entertainment pages with yet another hit movie, which topped many critics lists as the family film of the year.

It had been a fascinating — and challenging — diversion for Tom, and another remarkable string to his bow. But his next blockbuster was most definitely not one for his kids. In fact, he barred his two younger children from watching it.

Having finished his directing and all-round plate spinning act on *That Thing You Do!*, Tom was off to England to head the cast of a World War II movie called *Saving Private Ryan*. The film would unite him for the first time on a project with his friend Steven Spielberg. It would also shock cinema audiences as never before with its graphic scenes depicting the true horror of war.

Little did Tom know when he first discussed the movie with Spielberg, that his role as a wartime leader would cross over into real life for him to head off a threatened mutiny among his fellow actors.

15
Hollywood Boot Camp

Hollywood's pampered heroes are used to California sunshine, first class travel, luxury hotels and fawning fans. The closest most of them have come to real inconvenience in years was when the battery ran out on their cell phones. Actors routinely prattle on about suffering for their art, of crawling inside the skin of a character to understand how to truly play a part. Few have suffered like those in *Saving Private Ryan*.

Tom Hanks, along with tough guy actor Tom Sizemore, who starred in *Heat* and *Natural Born Killers*, New York director/actor Ed Burns, and independent-film stalwarts Jeremy Davies, Barry Pepper, Giovanni Ribisi, Adam Goldberg and Vin Diesel all jumped at the chance of working with master film-maker Steven Spielberg.

But none of them — not even Tom — had realised what the director had in store for them.

Spielberg's chief aim in making the film was to be as accurate as possible in recreating the nightmare of D-Day — 6 June 1944 — and the story of an American officer and his squad searching behind enemy lines for an elusive GI in the days after the Normandy Invasion. So he sent his actors to boot camp. The director remained at his Hamptons, Long Island, estate while his 'soldiers' went off to war in England, at an old British Aerospace site outside Hatfield, Hertfordshire.

The man whose job it was to test them to the limit, Captain Dale Dye, a 21-year veteran of the American Marine Corps, had already worked with the movie industry. Through his Warriors Inc. company, he had taught Tom how to throw a grenade in *Forrest Gump* and shown Tom Cruise how to search a Vietnamese hut for *Born on the Fourth of July*. He had also worked as a consultant on Oliver Stone's *Platoon* in 1985.

This time, his mission was simple: to erase any hint of Hollywood phoniness from the movie and the men starring in it. 'Most war movies are the biggest collection of rotten dog shit that I have ever seen,' he growls. He is not a man to mince words.

'This is not a high school play,' Dye barked at his troops. 'And if you think you are going to be actors who can fake your way through three months of shooting a movie about our fallen comrades, you are wrong.'

The men were forced to refer to each other only by their movie names, a dictum punishable with painful push-ups if forgotten. Anyone mentioning anything contemporary could expect similar excruciating penalties.

As well as the extreme demands of the daily routine — dawn exercise, mock battles, long hikes — there was the atrocious weather to add to the men's woes.

'It was utterly freezing,' Tom — or Turd Number One, as Captain Dye called him — told *The Times*. 'The only thing that we couldn't do was to go to the bathroom in the woods. The nature conservancy in Hatfield wouldn't allow us to do that, so we had to use an outhouse which was not a pleasant place.

'You have a brand of pitch blackness in England that I've never quite experienced.'

Given all they had to endure, something had to happen. And it did — there was the vote on them staying there to have more of it flung at them, or going home. And as we saw at the very beginning of this book, it was the leader — Tom Hanks, playing Captain John Millar — who turned the situation round.

As we have seen, Tom was persuasive and to the point: 'Of course, we all felt like a bunch of idiots after that,' Adam Goldberg told *People*. 'Tom made a very strong case for sticking it out and turned us all around.'

Ed Burns added: 'The boot camp was, I think, the toughest thing any of us had ever done in our lives. You hated every second of the experience. But the minute it was over, you were just so happy that you got to be a part of it. You felt such a sense of accomplishment and you really felt like, "Hey, I did something here that a lot of people will never get the opportunity to do."'

To Tom, the arrested mutiny was a defining moment that helped bind the men into their roles. 'We got yelled at a lot and it was very physically gruelling and the food wasn't any good. We were very, very tired.'

But, quoting war historian Stephen Ambrose, consultant to the film, he said: 'There is nothing more terrified than a veteran going into combat.' And he went on: 'I wanted that to be a palpable thing that I could draw on as an actor, as opposed to some anonymous intellectual choice that I made.

'We were scared so much that we can still go back and remember the time we had to walk for an hour through the pitch-black darkness of the woods, only to be ambushed by Dye and his gang in a moment of absolute sheer terror. And not only did it scare us to death at the moment, but for 20 minutes we were walking with our hearts beating as though we were running a marathon.'

Tom told *The Times-Picayune* that the experience 'was only a cheesy microcosm of what really happened in World War II, but nonetheless as actors we had never been in that position before, and it was very important for us to go through it.

'It was five days of very little sleep at night. It was not even a fraction of what anybody in the service goes through. But for us, whose job it is to protect that — it was the most important thing we did.'

Over the campfire towards the end of the week, Dye opened up to his recruits, giving them some of his first hand knowledge of what it feels like to go to war. Asking them what they think it must feel like to watch a comrade die in front of you, the actors gave him the response he expected. They talked of sadness, rage and grief. 'Bullshit, bullshit, bullshit,' he stormed at them. 'You feel joy! You feel joy that the guy got it and you didn't. And shortly thereafter, you feel shame.'

Irrespective of his Oscars and his long, proven track record, Tom's officer rank gave him the right to remain aloof from his fellow actors, all of whom were both less experienced entertainers and under his command in the film. He was also best friends with the director, a fact not lost on the entire cast and crew. But, true to form, when the cameras stopped rolling there was no star trip. He stayed close to the other actors, eating lunch with them and they spent off time chatting in each other's trailers.

Matt Damon, who by the time the film was in cinemas had won an Oscar himself for *Good Will Hunting*, said: 'What Hanks does is lead by example, whether by working long, hard hours or simply by eating off the catering cart like everybody else. He could have ordered cracked crab from Alaska every day, because this business really does indulge people. But he didn't want the special treatment.'

Added Ed Burns, known for directing and starring in his self-financed *The Brothers McMullen*: 'A lot of us hadn't been in such a big Hollywood film. Tom kind of took us under his wing. This is one of the biggest stars in the world, and he's not bossy or arrogant and is nice to everybody. Without being hokey, we all felt lucky to work with him and become his friends.'

Tom's leadership earned him a glowing recommendation from Captain Dye, who told *Time* magazine: 'The guy could be, should have been, a professional soldier. He has the mind, the motivation, the spirit and the body to make a good officer. He is inquisitive and highly intelligent. Strip away the Hollywood crap and he's like Captain Miller: a common man in uncommon circumstances who rises to uncommon levels.'

The idea of a Spielberg-Hanks collaboration came after both men read the *Saving Private Ryan* screenplay without the other's knowledge. 'Both of us just thought it was fantastic,' said Tom.

The result is a gripping two-and-a-half hour opus that showcases Hollywood's premium talents. The first half an hour of the movie — a raw, unvarnished bird's eye view of the stark horror of the Allied landing at the codenamed Omaha Beach — shocked even the most hardened cinema-goer with its blood-soaked carnage. Many veterans simply couldn't bear to watch, so realistic were the images conjured by the magic of Spielberg's cameras. Tom's understated performance held together the narrative with an equal intensity.

The concept of being an ordinary man caught up in extraordinary circumstances is one Tom had often used to explain his vaunted position as a millionaire movie star. It is no coincidence that his one spectacular failure in *The Bonfire of the Vanities* saw him struggling and failing to capture the elitist East-Coast attitude of Sherman McCoy, the WASP who watches his privileged life disintegrate. Now he was bringing his everyman hero to his part as Captain John Miller in *Saving Private Ryan*.

The dedicated but conflicted Miller is duty bound to put himself and seven of his men in harm's way in order to rescue a young soldier, played by Matt Damon, whose three brothers have all been killed in battle.

Although the return home of a surviving sibling is a US military tradition dating back to Abraham Lincoln's time, Miller's distaste at first losing two of his men, then facing an aborted mutiny from the others to find one man while others are dying all around them becomes a central theme of the film.

Miller, the consummate officer, finally reveals himself to his men as a schoolteacher with just one ambition — to return to the classroom. But duty is duty and orders have to be carried out if any sense was to be made of it all.

Critics hailed Tom's pivotal performance for reminding the shell-shocked audience that war is ultimately about people, many of them questioning what they are doing and why. Most of them terrified out of their lives.

'Heroes are cigar-chomping, leatherneck guys who against all the odds save the day,' Tom told *The Times*, 'I don't play anybody like that. I play guys who are scared, guys who've probably made some mistakes, guys who wonder how any of this stuff went wrong and guys who are just trying to do the right thing moment by moment. That's like 99 per cent of the people on the planet.'

Filming revealed another essential difference between Tom and many of Hollywood's most famous leading men. At one point, the script called for Tom's enigmatic captain to suddenly launch into a long speech revealing his innermost feelings to his stunned soldiers. It was, as Tom said, 'a monologue any actor would kill for' — the kind of breakout speech that attracts Academy Award judges. But Tom didn't want to drop the mantle of mystery that surrounded the captain's private life. On the spot, just as the cameras were about to roll, he cut the speech.

He told Spielberg he felt it would 'cheapen the character and compromise the integrity of who he is throughout the entire movie.'

Although a maddening perfectionist with definite views about his characters, Tom had developed over the years a way of changing directors minds in the nicest possible manner. He usually got his way.

Tom understandably had high hopes going into the film, but he was still unprepared for the emotional scope of the finished article.

He told *The Times-Picayune*: 'We were shooting for something, but I was shocked that the end result was what it was. I was amazed and broken up by it. I think we were hoping to have something that was going to be palpably emotional to the audience, but I think we did something that's much, much greater than we even could have imagined.

'When I saw the movie for the first time, I had the luxury of being in a room by myself, so I wept openly for a long time. I have never cried harder at a movie, or almost in real life, than at the end of this one — it was just so painful. I think an absolutely unbelievable thing has occurred here, and I am part of it, and I sort of can't believe it.'

Unlike other Oscar winners, like Nicholas Cage, a fine actor who turned to action movies for a new thrill — and a bigger fee — Tom says: 'I am sick of machine guns, cop chases and airplanes crashing into buildings. I'm sick of films where someone fires a gun along a crowded street, but you don't see innocent bystanders getting shot, only the bad guy.

'In *Saving Private Ryan*, all the violence has consequences. None of it is there just because it looks cool. Sure, it's grim. But it's brutally honest. It does not discount the fact that every time a trigger is pulled, someone's head may shatter into a million pieces.

'Kids who play Mortal Kombat computer games should see the film because it might just make them weep.'

The same Hatfield countryside where Hanks and co. fought their own private battles with Captain Dye was later transformed from scratch into a fictional French village, where the second wave of combat in the film was shot. A beach in Ireland's County Wexford doubled as Omaha Beach and 850 members of the Irish Army worked on the film.

Spielberg's attention to detail was such that his team discovered the American company which made the soldiers shoes during the war was still in business and still had a batch of the old dye it used at the time. The firm was immediately commissioned to make 2,000 pairs of shoes. Veterans told the director they remembered thousands of dead fish washing up as they tried to take the beach. One recalled seeing a Bible floating past him in the water. Both touches were added to the film.

A yard full of Nazi gear was found in London. Tanks were bought from the Czech Republic and Allied landing boats were discovered languishing in the desert site of a California dealer.

Said one technician: 'If someone had their legs blown off, Spielberg wanted a man without legs to do the scene. Plastic arms and legs were fitted to real life amputees and blown off.'

The production suffered its own casualties. On set on Ballynesker Beach, in County Wexford, 14 Irish reservist extras were taken to hospital with exposure after being in the sea too long. One extra strayed out of line and a dummy bomb blew him 10 feet into the air, breaking one of his legs.

Another was hurt when a dummy mine exploded under him as he crawled on the sand. And two more were reported to have broken legs when they were run over by a jeep. Tragically, one 17-year-old was killed in a car crash on his way home from the set. According to aides, the director was mortified and sent personal condolences 'and more' to the family of the young movie hopeful who had only just passed his driving test.

The army reservists had worked the previous year on Mel Gibson's *Braveheart* and were paid £44 a day for 14-hour shifts in hostile conditions. Spielberg worked even longer hours — albeit for better money — overseeing every scene himself.

While most of the cast and crew stayed in local inns, Tom and Spielberg took over half of one of Ireland's most exclusive small hotels, Marfield House, in Gorey, about 20 miles from the set, living in suites backing on to a private nature reserve.

Tom had Rita and all four of his children with him. Spielberg brought wife Kate Capshaw and several of their children.

After filming had finished, a pensive Tom walked alone along the French beaches recreated so chillingly in *Saving Private Ryan*. Among the many small identifying plaques that litter the shoreline, he found one dedicated to the Second Battalion, C Company of the US Rangers, the company his character led in the movie. 'I looked up in disbelief at those bunkers, some of which are still there,' he told *Daily Variety*'s Army Archerd. 'I walked where they died, where some put on dry socks for the last time.' Overcome with emotion, lost in the silence where once there had been such a terrible cacophony of sound, Tom lay down and slept dreamlessly before walking back to his car and the present.

There is little dispute that the movie is the most authentic cinematic depiction of the World War II in Hollywood history, towering above its closest rival, Darryl Zanuck's *The Longest Day*.

It's a remarkable compliment to Tom's career that the public that once delighted in him as an overgrown boy who ends up working for a toy company in *Big* would accept him ten years later as a war-weary captain close to collapse.

World War II veterans werre strongly affected by *Saving Private Ryan*. Some old soldiers couldn't even bear to sit through the unrelenting drama of the D-Day landings portrayed in the first section of the movie. To others, it enabled their loved ones to understand fully for the first time the hell they survived.

Veteran groups in the US and Europe hailed the first 17 minutes of the film as the single most accurate depiction of field battle ever captured on film. And they found they were suddenly getting a new measure of respect from later generations. 'It's had a catalytic effect in terms of getting younger people interested in World War II,' said Leland Bellot, a history professor at California State University in Fullerton. 'This might have been something that would have happened without *Private Ryan*, but there are a lot of kids who really want to know about war right now who probably wouldn't have been interested if they hadn't seen it.

But there were some dissenting voices. Les Stapleton, who fought in World War II, came out from seeing the film, saying: 'Why does anybody need the detail? I've been though that, and I'll tell you it's not something that should be in a movie.' Travel agent Hal Ryder, a retired Lieutenant Colonel who fought in France in 1944, added: 'Why should I pay money to see something I've been trying my whole life to forget.' In addition, black, World War II veterans were also angry that the film denied African–American soldiers 'our rightful place in history'.

Nonetheless, the overall response to the project was remarkably enthusiastic. The film took $30 million on its opening weekend in America in July 1998, a record for a summer movie. That was even after Spielberg had warned that teenagers under 14 might find it too gruesome and Tom declared his younger kids would not be watching it. After 17 days, word of mouth and critical praise and pushed the box office up to $100 million and at Christmas of that year, it was over the $180 million mark — an incredible achievement for a three-hour epic with a R-Restricted rating, no romance and hideous violence. Feeling there was still an audience — and giving the movie an extra nudge towards the Oscars — *Saving Private Ryan* was also rereleased across cinemas in the US in February, 1999.

Further proof of the film's popularity came on the Internet, where by the Monday after the opening, America Online's message boards were receiving 25 messages a minute praising it, totalling over 10,000 by the end of the day — a figure only beaten once, the occasion of Princess Diana's death.

On Tuesday, 9 February 1999, Tom got word that he had been nominated for his fourth Best Actor Oscar for his portrayal of Captain Miller. He was on his way to a film shoot in Fiji when the nominations were announced, reserving him yet another prime seat at the Dorothy Chandler Pavilion the following month, and the chance of a historic first ever hat-trick of golden Best Actor statuettes. Tom made one of his traditional short, but sweet, thank you pronouncements, saying: 'Making *Saving Private Ryan* was a life experience for all of us. To be nominated is a very great honour, to be nominated for *Saving Private Ryan* all the more. I am delighted and proud.'

Despite already winning two Academy Awards for *Philadelphia* and *Forrest Gump* and being pipped at the post for *Big*, Tom was still hot favourite among his fellow 71st academy nominees Ian

McKellen, Roberto Benigni, Nick Nolte and Edward Norton. A third win would put him on a plateau no other actor had ever reached. Previously, actor Walter Brennan won three Best Supporting Actor awards and Jack Nicholson has won two Best Actor Oscars and one for Best Supporting Actor.

The first call Tom received was from an equally jubilant Steven Spielberg, who told him their film had won an astonishing 11 Oscar nominations, including one for Spielberg in the Best Director category.

Spielberg was in Berlin to attend the Golden Camera awards and was so nervous he had asked his assistant to watch the nominations being read out on live television from Hollywood. She knocked on his door shortly after 5.30pm and breathlessly read out the list to her boss. 'I was flabbergasted; I just leaned against the wall,' said Spielberg, who has been nominated for five Best Director Oscars, including an emotional win for *Schindler's List*.

'I never, ever get blasé about this. This day is always indelibly tattooed on the frontal lobe of my brain. I'm usually never nervous about these kinds of things but this always makes me so nervous. I was very anxious this year. In fact, I think I set a new record for anxiety this year.'

Spielberg said the success of *Saving Private Ryan* was far from a foregone conclusion, even with Hollywood's most bankable star on board. 'Actually, just the opposite was true,' he added. 'Two weeks into the shooting of the Omaha Beach scenes which open the film, I turned to the entire cast and crew and told them, "At this point in the movie, every single Tom Hanks fan is going to stand up, leave the theatre and never come back. This film is going to cost Tom a lot of fans."

'The fact that the film has done so well is thrilling to me. The people have spoken. They said they were ready to go back a half-century to a blasphemous time and have the courage to experience *Saving Private Ryan*. I think their courage was remarkable.'

The nominations, along with two for the animated feature *The Prince of Egypt*, were the first for the DreamWorks movie studio owned by Spielberg, David Geffen and Jeffrey Katzenberg and a major boost to the fledgling company.

For Tom, seven hits out of seven meant he no longer agonised over his film choices. As he headed out on a wearying promotional tour for the film, he said: 'I don't fight with myself over which movie to do next. I don't try to top myself with every new movie I make. If I specifically set out to do that, I would be making terrible, artificial films. What am I supposed to do? Die of another horrible disease?

'All the audience cares about is watching a decent movie. They don't care how good your last movie was. They want to see a good movie NOW.

'Being an actor can be fun. The people around you are funny, and you get sandwiches whenever you want some. Still, at the end of the day, you have to tell yourself that, well, it's the end of the day. So, you drive home to your family, have a nice dinner and watch a dart competition on TV. Some actors flog themselves to death. Me, I do not treat my job as if it is a circus act. You do not have to perform around the clock.'

With the movie completed, an unreserved triumph, with the reputations of both Tom and Spielberg further enhanced, there was an added bonus. The friendship between the two men had not only survived, it had flourished in the work environment.

Spielberg had this to say about Tom: 'It was wonderful working with my friend, and even better that we stayed friends after the experience. I've always had tremendous respect for Tom, and this project enhanced my respect for him, both as an actor and a human being. He offered great suggestions that benefited the film and was completely open to my ideas about his character.

'Tom Hanks represents to me what is best about idealised America. Tom is Gary Cooper and Jimmy Stewart. He is what I think is America.'

And Tom repaid the compliment: 'Making this movie was like walking into Thomas Edison's laboratory. You're in the presence of this genius who in real life is this badly dressed, nebbishy kinda guy who talks in tangents and only vaguely answers a question. But seeing him on the set, he's a dynamo, a source of incredible vision and information that's hard to keep up with.

'Steven is even more of a mystery to me now than he was before we had this experience. I think he probably gets about four hours sleep because he is always up thinking about stuff. I think he lives his regular life at the same pace that he lives his movies, except that when he's making a movie he's actually got something to occupy his time, whereas when he's not, he's just got to foment stuff. I mean, who is Albert Einstein's good friend? That's the way I look at it.'

To keep their friendship free of cash concerns — and shave about £30 million from the budget — the two men sacrificed their usual salaries in return for a share of the grosses. Although it was never going to touch the phenomenal box office of *Forrest Gump*, Tom would still recoup his requisite £15 million fee, with some quite considerable change.

There was only one disappointment in all this. Despite being a hot favourite to win his third Best Actor Oscar, Tom lost out to Italy's maverick comedian Roberto Begnini, who climbed on chairs and talked on stage in broken English how thrilled he was to win for his film tragi-comedy about the Holocaust, *Life is Beautiful*.

Tom, sporting a fuzzy beard, grown for a forthcoming project, kept a low profile with wife Rita as *Shakespeare in Love* beat out his *Saving Private Ryan* for the lion's share of the Oscars. Tom's only public comment on the day was that he prepared by taking his kids out to a toy shop and an In-and-Out fast food burger restaurant. The Miramax comedy took Best Picture, Best Actress for Gwyneth Paltrow and Best Supporting Actress for Judi Dench among its seven Oscars.

Out of its 11 nominations, *Saving Private Ryan* culled five statuettes, including Best Director for Steven Spielberg. The four other Oscars were for Cinematography, Editing, Sound and Sound Effects Editing. In spite of his denials, Spielberg looked put out at the tally and there was a heated row in the press over whether *Shakespeare in Love* studio Miramax had bamboozled voters by spending a fortune on publicity to promote its film heavily.

Apart from industry awards, however, there were other aspects of *Saving Private Ryan*'s success. Amid the publicity hoopla, Tom also found time to lend a cash-raising hand in aid of the World War II Memorial, a £70 million project to built a lasting tribute in Washington DC to those who lost their lives. After pitching the memorial while picking up a gong at the national televised People's Choice Awards in America, more than 30,000 calls were logged in less than 24 hours, raising £200,000. The plea 'hit a responsive chord,' said memorial spokesman Mike Conley.

Tom and Steven Spielberg have also quietly helped finance a D-Day museum in New Orleans. Founder Stephen Ambrose, the historian who worked with both men as a consultant on *Saving Private Ryan*, said they jointly donated hundreds of thousands of pounds to save the project. The museum was due to open on 6 June 2000, the 56th anniversary of the Normandy invasion.

With all its success, *Saving Private Ryan* had been a wearing project with a lot on the line, not least of those his friendship with Steven Spielberg and the unspoken need to further earn his respect.

Even many of the wisecracks traditional to most Hollywood war films had been swept from the original script, mainly at the insistence of Tom, who asserted there was little to laugh about when you were terrified out of your wits.

It was time for some fun. And who better to have some fun on screen with than with another of his close friends, Meg Ryan.

16

Tom and Meg

It was a private moment that best defined the deeply-rooted connection that has made two stars of considerable individual accomplishment a partnership to match any of the great pairings of Hollywood's golden past.

Meg Ryan and her actor husband Dennis Quaid were guests at a Fourth of July barbecue being thrown by Tom and Rita at their Los Angeles home. As Tom heated up the coals, his 'bohemian' neighbours were celebrating rather more rowdily a few feet away. 'Those were the people who intimidated me in high school,' said Ryan, with the characteristic mixture of bemusement and insight that have preserved her place in movie stardom since that famously faked orgasm in *When Harry Met Sally*.

Tom, a friend of Ryan's since their first film together, 1990's *Joe Versus the Volcano*, told *People* magazine he was charmed by the Proustian realisation. 'It's not everybody,' he said, 'who can remember exactly how disconnected she felt in those primal stages of adulthood.'

It was meant as a throwaway comment for a magazine cover story on one of his closest friends. But the point was that Tom had recognised something in Ryan that he knew existed in himself. Tom could certainly remember how disconnected he felt for most of his life until he met Rita.

Like him, Ryan had a troubled family life growing up, which had extended into adulthood.

Like him, her parents split when she was a child, leaving her lonely and confused — and being brought up by her father.

And like him, she found a partner she felt had 'saved' her, and built up her own family around that new nucleus.

That connection, consciously or not, has cemented a chemistry between them that radiates onto the screen.

Spencer Tracey and Katherine Hepburn had it. So did Fred Astaire and Ginger Rogers. And James Stewart and June Allyson. Call it on-screen romantic chemistry. Or a mystical blending of two distinctive personalities into something unique and memorable. But in the Hollywood of the 1990s, Tom Hanks and Meg Ryan had it too.

Both come across on screen as ordinary people, the boy and girl next door. In this sense, they are classic movie stars, perfect for pictures patterned on earlier Hollywood romances. Two of their three films together were indeed based on old favourites: *Sleepless in Seattle* is a revision of Cary Grant and Deborah Kerr's *An Affair to Remember* and *You've Got Mail* is a loose reworking of *The Shop Around the Corner*, which starred James Stewart and Margaret Sullavan.

We know how Tom came to this point. To better grasp the genesis of the Hanks-Ryan partnership it is necessary to examine Ryan's background and the upbringing that provides the shared foundation for their understanding.

To her adoring fans, she has that girl-next-door image and sweet smile that women want to copy and men can't resist. But Margaret Hyra, or Peggy, as she was known in the little town of Bethel, population 15,000, where she grew up in Connecticut, 60 miles north of New York, certainly hasn't had a conventional life.

Her parents split up when she was 16 and still at school, a traumatic parting that continues to have ramifications today. Her father, Harry, was a mathematics teacher and sports coach at the nearby Danbury High School. Her mother, Susan, was an actress who settled down as a housewife and mother to their four children, of which Margaret was the second oldest.

When the marriage unravelled it was Susan who left the family home, leaving Harry with the children until she could find a job and take them to live with her. As she packed her bags into the back of her old Ford Pinto car, a sobbing Ryan begged her to stay. Although she remained living in Connecticut while she commuted into Manhattan to try and find acting work, Susan says her daughter never forgave her for leaving.

Like Tom, Ryan ended up being cared for by a father who was not really fully equipped to handle the job. Friends say she found the new chapter in her life painful and upsetting. Her father, trying his best to be both mother and father to four children, says now he had trouble giving them enough time and attention. 'Maybe Meg felt out on her own,' he confessed.

By the time Susan had found a steady teaching job and was ready to take her children back three years later, Ryan had left home to go to the University of Connecticut, doing TV commercials to help pay her fees.

Echoing stories from Tom's youth, Ryan's old school friend Tracy Parsons told *People* magazine that her classmate didn't even tell her about her parents' break-up until a year had passed. 'She didn't want to let other people in on her pain,' said Parsons. 'She had to take care of herself. Her father tried, but it was overwhelming for him.

'It was hard for her not to have her mother at home, in terms of proms and first dates and first kisses. She was very unhappy. Susan never left the family, just the house. Still, Meg got the idea that her mother abandoned her.'

After university, relations between mother and daughter improved, with Susan helping the then Margaret Hyra to get her acting union card and giving her daughter her maiden name — Ryan — which she took as her own in tandem with the more cosmopolitan Meg ...

The relationship again became tense when Susan married writer Pat Jordan, whose strong personality conflicted with his headstrong stepdaughter.

Shortly after Ryan met roguish actor Dennis Quaid on the set of the 1988 thriller *D.O.A.*, the slender bond was broken for good. Susan, angry at continually being cast as the bad mother by an unforgiving daughter, said Ryan refused to talk to her after she tried to warn her about Quaid's drug-taking. The star of *The Big*

Easy and the Jerry Lee Lewis biopic *Great Balls of Fire* later went into rehab to beat his cocaine use when Ryan gave him an ultimatum that he must give up drugs before she would marry him.

Ryan denied the drug confrontation with her mother was the reason for the impasse. She told *Vanity Fair* in 1995: 'It's a very long story. It's 32 years of stuff with this woman.'

The two women have not seen each other since 1990 — Susan has never seen grandson, Jack — and Ryan has rebuffed all attempts at a reconciliation. 'All I have of my grandson is a photograph,' said Susan. 'It is like looking at a total stranger. It breaks my heart.'

After a two-year stint in New York on the daytime soap *As the World Turns*, Ryan had a small role as Anthony Edwards' wife in Tom Cruise's *Top Gun* and then her big breakthrough in *When Harry Met Sally* opposite Billy Crystal.

She first met Tom by chance in a hotel lift in New York in 1987. 'He was with his wife Rita and I had just seen him in *Punchline* and blurted out that I thought it was one of the best things he'd done,' said Ryan. 'He was so gracious and humble and that's exactly how he turned out to be when I worked with him.'

Ryan teamed up with Tom for the first time in 1990's poorly received *Joe Versus the Volcano* and the two hit it off at once. The chemistry was a bit confused as although Ryan was playing Tom's leading lady, she was also playing two other women in the film as well.

It was really *Sleepless in Seattle*, released three years later, that established the romantic comedy partnership.

Tom and *Sleepless* director Nora Ephron immediately thought of Ryan when they began looking for an actress for the part of Annie Reed, a reporter who falls in love with the voice of Tom's character, Sam Baldwin, on the radio. Tom felt they had clicked in *Joe Versus the Volcano*, even if the film hadn't quite come together. Ryan felt the same.

Perhaps the most unusual thing about the love story is that the two principals do not actually meet until the very final moments of the film. They only actually spent one week filming together because their characters spend the entire movie just searching for one another. Ryan would later describe the whole film as 'foreplay'.

The couple would pass each other on the set and ask how the other's half of the movie was going. 'I got to thinking how nice it would be to work with Tom,' Ryan said.

Director Nora Ephron raved about both of her favourite stars, saying they were 'without vanity. They will do anything that is required.'

She added: 'When you do a romantic comedy, any romantic comedy, Tom and Meg are the ideals. They're intelligent and they have incredible instincts for comedy. I know Tom's wife and Meg's husband, but when I'm making these movies, I get to the point where I actually think Tom and Meg should be together. They are from the same food group.'

Rita even gave the onscreen romance her blessing, saying: 'Meg is one of the all time great people I know. It is a lot nicer when you know that it's your good friend kissing your husband.'

It is interesting to think that while Ryan gels so well with Tom on screen, she has found happiness with a complete opposite away from the cameras. She has made three movies with Quaid, none of which has touched the success of *Sleepless* or *You've Got Mail*. But after helping her husband beat his drug demons, she has revelled in family life, to the extent of turning down a plethora of good roles after their son, Jack, was born in favour of staying at home.

She would hire a plane to hoist a huge 'Happy Birthday Dennis' banner for him in the sky over his film set. He one-upped her by sending a marching band to send a similar message when she was off on location. Once a month they planned mystery weekends where one made the romantic engagements and the other came along for the surprises.

Quaid gets Ryan away from her books and out of the house, just as Rita Wilson does with Tom. And they also try to be parents first, actors second. 'We don't have a nanny because I want to cook Jack's meals, wash and mend his clothes and put him to bed. Dennis is great about being there for him at school and at play and we read to him every night. A family is a very important unit,' Ryan told the *Calgary Sun*.

She added: 'Dennis is a doer. I'm a watcher. He flies a jet plane. He doesn't just golf — he's an amazing golfer. Dennis is also very sentimental and romantic and I'm not. Dennis is the one who picks the cards. I just mail them. I definitely believe in fate and destiny. I think my life proves it. My life may look orderly on the surface, but I know I could never have imagined, let alone engineered anything this fantastic.'

In spite of his Tom 'Hankies' reputation in the aftermath of his emotional Oscar speeches, Tom wouldn't claim to be romantic either. He says he never sends flowers and resists Rita's attempts to get him to watch old weepie movies. 'My favourite movie couple is R2D2 and C3PO,' he joked.

But he does advertise his love for his wife in interviews and speeches that reach millions — a hard feat for most romantics to beat. And he knows how to put a smile on his wife's face in the morning.

'Well, I do make breakfast for Rita,' he says. 'I guess that's romantic. I'm the morning guy. I can make a morning the most delightful thing that you could experience. How do I do it? There's a way to wake people up. There's a way to make French toast with just the right amount of powdered sugar. Listen, I can't make lunch or dinner to save my life but breakfast, man, I got that covered.'

When Tom had wrapped *Saving Private Ryan*, he was looking forward to a change of pace. Romantic comedies were, in effect, the only remnants of his previous, pre-Oscar, career and when Nora Ephron showed him her *You've Got Mail* script, he knew there was only one person who could play New York bookstore owner Kathleen Kelly. He called up Ryan and she agreed on the spot to do the film. To get an instant decision from the notoriously picky Ryan, that was a feat in itself and a testament to Tom's pulling power.

In the old days of the all-powerful Hollywood mogul, even the biggest stars could be virtually forced into continuing partnerships because most of them were contractually tied into studios.

With the greater freedoms of the century's last three or four decades it was much more difficult first to find a durable star pairing and then to keep them together. Studios largely found it easier to flog solo action star vehicles such as *Rocky*, *Rambo* or *Die Hard*, or team up male buddy partnerships such as *Lethal Weapon*'s Mel Gibson and Danny Glover for big money productions.

The producer of *You've Got Mail*, Lauren Shuler-Donner —

married to *Lethal Weapon* director Richard Donner — said the Hanks-Ryan team is the only one filling a major public demand for old-fashioned romantic comedies. 'I don't think you can quite put your finger on the chemistry,' she said. 'They are both very intelligent and they have a remarkable gift for comedy. They are both unafraid on screen. They're willing to be clowns, and that leads to a certain vulnerability. But beyond that ...'

Ephron, who wrote the *You've Got Mail* script with sister Delia — the sisters also co-wrote *Sleepless* — defines the chemistry as 'two brains falling in love'.

Tom cannot rule out the sexual connection. He told the *Ottawa Citizen*: 'I think a bona fide amount of attraction is there. When you're into the dynamics of man-woman stuff, I don't really think you can fake it.

'Obviously, Meg is very attractive. She's easy on the eyes. She's also inspiring, so there's this intellectual thing there at the same time. I don't think there is a man in America who doesn't have a crush on Meg Ryan, but on top of that for me she's a really tight kind of friend and there's something very attractive in that as well.

'I don't want to go into the cheesy analogy mode, but it's like if you are going to play tennis with someone who's really good, you know it's going to be a good tennis game.'

He continued: 'Meg is very smart. She is a friend. It's getting together with a competitor, yet there's no competition to it whatsoever. What's truly good about it is that I don't think we can get stale because we don't really do it unless we love it. We don't do it unless it's going to be fun. It's not some forced union. It's almost a crime that we get paid for doing it because it is not like working.'

Ryan adds: 'This is a strange genre because it's not ha-ha-hilariously funny and it's not like real drama. There's this weird little tightrope you walk on.'

She is not much better at putting a finger on what makes the partnership work so well. 'I feel it's not really for me to say,' she says. 'I have such an incredibly easy time. I just love being around him. I feel it's like stealing money from the studio. It's just a great time. I liked going to work in the morning and I was sad when the movie was over.'

'All I know,' she says, 'is that it was easy from the first moment of the first day. One of the great things about Tom is that he could, by all rights, be on an Elvis trip. He could come to the set with all these things and people, but he's just this guy that you feel like you know, and you probably do. Even after all this stuff that has happened to him, he's gracious enough to feel lucky. I love the way he is in the world. He's a great example for all of us.'

She told *Entertainment Weekly*: 'Chemistry is a really weird thing. Sometimes you feel like you don't have it, but it ends up on the screen anyway. Other times you feel a really strong connection, and it ends up looking flat and dead. So the thing with Tom — I don't think it behooves me to examine it too closely. If I started trying to dissect it, it might go away.'

In *You've Got Mail*, Ryan's character runs a cosy, family bookshop on New York's West Side driven out of business by the dreaded Fox Books, a chain store offering a huge range and discount prices, that bulldozes its way into the neighbourhood. Tom plays Joe Fox, the ruthless chain store boss with, you guessed it, a heart of gold.

The rivals meet and fall out, becoming enemies as Ryan tries in vain to fight back at the big-brother book chain. But at the same time as they are bickering in person, they are unwittingly falling in love over the Internet, E-mailing each other anonymously after meeting in an America Online chat room. His sign-on, if you are interested, was NY152. Hers was Shopgirl.

The final scene, to the surprise of no one, has the couple sharing a big, juicy kiss having belatedly discovered what their mutual cursors looked like in the flesh.

Once again, the stars spend much of the time on screen avoiding one another, just missing each other or corresponding to each other on the Internet. 'I'm dying to do a movie with Tom where we are in every scene together. This is getting ridiculous,' Ryan laughed after wrapping their third film.

But she added: 'I don't think this is the last time we'll work together.' That's quite likely because as well as being a lot of fun, Tom and Ryan are handsomely rewarded for their services, to the tune of £15 million for him and £7.5 million for her.

The bonhomie of good friends working together was clearly

evident on location in New York, where Tom happily waved at gawkers who stopped to watch some of the street scenes being shot. The crew, many of them well used to working with spoiled prima donnas, spoke of 'a nice reunion' feeling about the shoot.

While taking a break at Starbucks coffee shop, Tom went behind the counter to learn about making the drinks while his co-star quietly sipped her skim-milk mochaccino.

On another time-out, during a long night scene, the couple dropped into the gourmet food store Zabar's, where Tom had Ryan doubling up with laughter. The shop's general manager, Scott Goldshine said: 'We have a loud PA system in the store and Tom Hanks would pick up the microphone and yell, "Meg Ryan to cheese! Meg Ryan to coffee!" He had her in hysterics.'

Not that it was all fun and games. 'It's movies like *Mail* that wear you down,' Tom told *Entertainment Weekly*. 'Going into a dark soundstage every day, stepping over cables and ladders, getting your hair done for three hours, shooting the same shot from so many different angles. And having to be so aggressively fresh for every scene.

'That's when it almost feels like you're working for the post office.'

In real life, Tom surfs the waves, but rarely surfs the net. 'I do occasionally search for those nude pictures I did 20 years ago,' he laughed. 'Thank God, I have yet to find them.' He does, however, have a passion for typewriters. In *You've Got Mail*, Ryan's Luddite boyfriend, played by Greg Kinnear, gets a gentle ribbing for going on about his collection of old typewriters. Tom actually has up to 20 old portable typewriters, some of them worth several thousand pounds, and most of them in working condition. He first found an old Hermes 2000 in a Cleveland junk shop, loved its Swiss-made preciseness, and became hooked.

You've Got Mail lived up to expectations and opening as America's number one film just before Christmas 1998. the pairing had worked its magic again, making eight hits out of the last eight films Tom starred in.

It generally got good reviews, but there was a feeling that some critics may be tiring of the Hanks–Ryan formula. 'This romance is pleasant but not extraordinary. Even Ryan is reportedly

tired of these silly soufflés which force critics to invoke the word
"twinkly",' said the *Pittsburgh Post-Gazette*. However, such opinions
were not the norm. *Patch Adams*, the Robin Williams comedy about
an offbeat doctor, was released on the same day as *You've Got Mail*,
and eventually grossed $20 million more than the E-mail romance,
but even so, this Hanks–Ryan project delivered exactly what most
cinema-goers had wanted.

Nonetheless, as Tom tests his range with future projects, it is a
comfort that movie-making with Meg Ryan, Nora Ephron, etc. can
still be fun.

And there will always be an audience waiting for the next
Hanks–Ryan romantic comedy.

17
President Hanks?

The talk of the party was the similarity in hue of Hillary Clinton's Pamela Dennis gown and the Ronit Zilkha ensemble worn by Britain's first lady, Cherie Blair. Among the 240 guests invited to the White House reception for Prime Minister Tony Blair — a high-wattage mix of Hollywood celebrities and Beltway bigwigs — the M-word was strictly forbidden.

It was just days after the Monica Lewinsky scandal had exploded onto the world's front pages and the humiliation of Bill Clinton's prime-time confession and the ensuing impeachment was still many months away.

A few brave souls dared to joke under their breaths that Elton John, who was providing the entertainment, should serenade his host with 'Scandal in the Wind', but otherwise the theme was very much business as usual.

Dining in the East Room on an eclectic menu of honey mango chicken, grilled salmon and chocolate replicas of Big Ben, Tom and Rita were in their element. They had, of course, stayed in the White House as guests of the Clintons three times in the past five years and were among the President's most fervent supporters.

Blair and his wife mingled happily among guests like Secretary of State Madeleine Albright, who was with Jackie Onassis's longtime beau Maurice Tempelsman, John F Kennedy Jnr and senior Democrats. The starstruck Blairs were introduced to actor Harrison Ford — who played a save-the-day president in *Air Force*

One, by Clinton with the quip: 'This guy's got a better plane than I do.'

But every eye was on a select Hollywood group that had aligned itself at Clinton's side from the beginning. 'This is a night to have a good time,' said Rita, setting the agenda. 'We sent the Clintons our message of support a week-and-a-half ago.' Her husband, with his Gump-like ability to be in the heart of the action, enthused: 'This is an exciting place to be.' Steven Spielberg, with wife Kate Capshaw, noted quietly that the President's through-the-roof approval ratings 'are exactly as I feel about him'. And Barbra Streisand, whose name had been closely linked to the President in the past, insisted: 'Whatever he does behind doors is his business. We did elect him President, not Pope.'

Clinton, happily unaware of the knife-turning twists the Lewinsky affair had in store for him, danced with Hillary until 1.00am. To the President, with the eyes of the world watching his reaction to the latest sex allegations against him, the mere presence of such vaunted guests at such a difficult time spoke volumes. 'This has been a great night,' he said. 'Hillary and I are very grateful.'

Before the year was out, Hollywood's strict party line in full-blooded favour of the bad-boy President would be broken by one of this select group. Who would have dreamed back then that it would be Tom Hanks?

But then Tom has always been able to see the bigger picture.

He turned down the chance of playing America's most disgraced President in one film and passed on the chance to portray the nation's most debased President in another.

But does the actor who, as we saw, named his youngest son Truman Theodore after two other former Presidents have a more serious role in mind? Having tried the White House guest bedroom out for size on three occasions, does Tom have aspirations of moving into the master suite? As President Hanks?

Like a good politician-in-waiting, he didn't rule it out. And then he did. But along the way, perhaps just as he had intended, the suggestion was out there that Tom Hanks just possibly, some way down the line, could be tempted to forsake his position as the most powerful actor in Hollywood to try his hand at being the most powerful man in the world.

Hadn't Ronald Reagan managed the same feat and served his country with aplomb? And he wasn't even a very good actor.

Tom Hanks may not have much of a history in politics, but his campaigns had earned his fair share of votes from the Academy Award judges over the years. If it had been Tom's intention to test the water by talking openly of running for presidential office, it certainly succeeded. Newspapers and TV stations around the world picked up on his comments in an interview with *New Yorker* magazine — and no one was laughing.

Even an alleged about-face comment to the same publication that he regretted giving financial support to help the cash-strapped President Clinton to fight his way out of the mire of sexual allegations involving Paula Jones and Monica Lewinsky was perceived as a strategic and politically astute move to distance himself from a fatally damaged leader.

Surprised at the furore his comments caused, Tom immediately denied ever having any intention of running for office and made the expected jokes about movie star as president and how anybody in their right minds could think he was serious about it.

Nevertheless, he is certainly not a stupid or naïve man and he is extremely well-versed in the ways of the media. Rarely does anything pass his lips that wasn't carefully thought out beforehand, even if it does all appear to be off the cuff.

Tom has always had very forthright political views even if, as he says, they are largely kept around the kitchen table. He remains, either by luck or design, the most trusted star of his times. And despite all he has achieved, he is still driven by ambition and new challenges. What better way for a child once tagged Number Eight to show that he really could become Number One? Friends of the actor say privately that they believe Tom would make an excellent President, perhaps even following Reagan's route by first serving as governor in his native California.

Ronald Reagan was not just President of the United States, he was one of the country's most beloved Presidents. Peggy Noonan, the writer who scripted some of Reagan's best speeches, said in 1994 that there was one Hollywood actor who shared a lot of her old boss's characteristics. His name was Tom Hanks.

It is interesting to examine exactly what Tom said to his *New Yorker* profiler Kurt Andersen, an experienced American writer and editor who himself moves in influential media circles.

The article appeared in the prestigious magazine just before Christmas in 1998, when President Clinton was at the height of his 'Sexgate' troubles. His claim that he did not have sex 'with that woman' had come back to haunt Clinton, who was accused of lying under oath about his affair with White House intern Monica Lewinsky. Facing certain impeachment and fighting a rearguard action to save his political skin, the last thing the President needed was another attack by a high-profile 'supporter', particularly one that the American public identified with.

On Tom, Andersen wrote: 'The man who still believes in heroes and the old-fashioned virtues also maintains a faith in politics, and what he unselfconsciously calls "the good fight".

'His own politics are almost oxymoronic: He's a moderately conservative Hollywood Democrat. He's a death penalty proponent who said "God bless America" at the end of an Oscar speech but finds the "religious right that controls the Republican Party kind of scary".

'He's an actor-director-producer who decries the "despicable, shallow" run of Hollywood entertainment and "pornography delivered to the home" on cable TV. Yet he believes in "this concept that the government can do work that is really good. And it's not just building roads and bridges. I think that the government can do things that truly do better society and give people a hand up and still let them do what they want to do."'

At first, Tom seems to be merely playing down his relationship with Clinton, who had played host at Tom's three overnight stays at the White House saying: 'I'm friendly with him. But I don't think I've ever had a true connective conversation with him. I just can't. I'm still too much in the "Jeepers, creepers, he's talking to me" kind of thing.'

Andersen mentions the widespread rumours that had been circulating in both Washington and Hollywood circles for some time, namely, that a house Tom had bought recently in Los Angeles was being reserved for his friend the President's retirement. A parallel rumour — that Tom and Clinton's mutual friends Steven

Spielberg, David Geffen and Jeffrey Katzenberg also had a job ready for the President with their DreamWorks studio as well as a possible position at Tom's Playtone production company when he left office — was also given a wider airing.

Tom says the new house was bought for his growing family. But he goes on to court further controversy. Saying he wrote a cheque for Clinton's legal defence fund, he said he regretted making the donation.

Andersen reported Tom as saying: 'We gave ten thousand bucks. Very early on. In all honesty in the light of events since, it would be awfully hard to say now, "Oh, here, let me help you out with this problem." Or buy him a house.

'But — well, the other side has plenty of figures that pony up an awful lot of dough, too. So you try to fight fire with fire, or something.

'But he ain't getting that house. I'll tell you that, right now. Forget it. And he ain't working at the Playtone Company [Tom's production company], either.'

Andersen said he quizzed Tom over a potential career in politics, only half-seriously suggesting a spell in the US Senate followed by a run for the presidency. Said the writer: 'I expected a snort, a roll of the eyes, an emphatic disavowal. But instead he said, vaguely, 'I'd have to know more about law or economics.'''

Andersen said Tom later sent him an E-mail that was a 'squishy non-denial of political ambition'. It actually reads like a campaign statement: 'My image is a really good one,' he wrote. 'I made a nice acceptance speech on TV a couple of times. I handle myself pretty well in the glare of the entertainment media. The actual ideology that anyone can glean as projected by my appearances on TV is that America is good because we are all so different and respecting each other is not so hard a thing to do.

'Not a bad platform, I suppose, to run for some office.'

The comments — particularly those about his friend the President — put Tom on the front page of the *New York Post* the morning after the *New Yorker*'s publication, and the story was followed in Britain and around the world.

His comments were all the more surprising in the light of a

previous interview in which he had criticised celebrities who turned to politics. 'When I saw Sonny Bono at the Republican National Convention with Gerald Ford in 1976 all I could think of was, What the hell is he doing there? he said in the *New York Times*. 'I was 18 years old and thought that was the stupidest, dumbest thing I had ever seen. I don't feel that anybody is influenced in any way by the fact that a public figure on the show business level embraces any sort of political cause. The images just balance out after a while. For every Warren Beatty, there's a Charlton Heston.'

Nevertheless, the story was mushrooming around the world. The *Guardian* headlined its report 'Wholesome Hanks turns his back on the Clintons' and started the story: 'Tom Hanks, one of Hollywood's biggest stars, tore apart the curtain of celebrity shielding President Clinton yesterday when he said that he regretted giving financial support to the former governor of Arkansas.'

The *Daily Mail* asked: 'Hanks hints at lofty ambition — is Forrest Gump in line for President?'

The *New York Post* put it more prosaically: 'Gump dumps on his buddy Bill — Tom Hanks is first Hollywood defection.'

Maureen Dowd, a much-respected former White House correspondent for *The New York Times*, devoted a whole column to Tom's apparent political aspirations, saying: 'A slap from Tom Hanks must sting the President more than a slap from Congress.'

She wrote: 'Tom Hanks will have some explaining to do before we elect him President. We'll want to know if he enjoyed wearing that dress in *Bosom Buddies*. We'll want to know exactly what happened under the blanket with that stewardess in *Nothing in Common*. We'll want to know what possessed the man who went to the moon to moon in the December *Vogue*.* We'll want to know if he is truly contrite about making *Turner and Hooch*.

'But on the other hand, he would have definite assets as a candidate. He served in World War II, Vietnam and the Peace Corps. He brought *Apollo 13* back safely. He learned about suffering

---

* The December 1998 edition of *Vogue*, with Hillary Clinton on the cover, has a photo inside, taken by famed photographer Herb Ritts, of Hanks mooning to readers with a 'not particularly trim' bottom.

in *Philadelphia*. He got that magic handshake from J.F.K. in *Forrest Gump*. And he has a catchy campaign slogan "Life is a box of chocolates".'

'Jeepers, creepers, as Mr Hanks likes to say, why not? In Washington, we've had no-one to root for in a very long time. A *faux* hero would be better than no hero. We have a groupie for President. Why not have a star.'

She said the campaign donation controversy was 'a striking reversal. It used to be that Hollywood was drawn to Washington's issues, and Washington to Hollywood's sex appeal.'

Dowd goes on: 'Hollywood will soon realise: Why give millions to prop up Democratic candidates when it can field its own? With President Hanks, at least the stars sleeping in the Lincoln bedroom would be real friends.

'President Clinton has increased our appetite for entertainment to the point where we may not even be satisfied with Tom Hanks the person. We may need to go all the way and elect Tom Hanks the character.'

Carefully thought out, or carelessly ad-libbed, Tom's debut into the political arena had caught fire.

The very next day, however, Tom was rapidly backtracking, realising perhaps that his comments put him at odds with his Hollywood cabal of close friends. Spielberg, his wife, Kate Capshaw, Barbra Streisand, Michael Douglas and Ron Howard had all, like Tom, contributed $10,000 to the Clinton fund. Streisand, in particular, had been vociferous in her public support for the beleaguered President. Tom's $10,000 was the maximum allowed under the rules of Clinton's second legal defence fund — the first fund allowed only $1,000 and was shut down because it didn't rake in nearly enough money to help pay the mountain of lawyer's bills that were growing daily.

Clinton, who was spending most late nights alone in his office flicking through the TV channels to gauge his standing in the polls — his main hope for survival — was said to be deeply upset and hurt by Tom's outburst, which came at a crunch time days before a vote in the House of Representatives' judiciary committee on whether to impeach or censure the President. Tom may have played more heroes than anyone since John Wayne, but a fourth invitation to the world's most exclusive bed and breakfast now looked unlikely.

Rather than moan about the magazine taking what he said out of context and deflecting any criticism the way of the media, the usual path of attack for embarrassed politicians and film stars, Tom took the upbeat approach. He still said his comments had been taken out of context, but said he 'loved' the interview and enjoyed the novelty of creating a stir. 'I love being controversial … I've never been controversial before,' he told a local cable TV station in New York as he was about to be honoured at an AIDS benefit.

He went on to enthusiastically reaffirm his support for Clinton, saying: 'You couldn't get a bigger supporter of the President than I am. He is doing a great job.'

Having told Andersen he wished he hadn't given cash to the President, he was doing a complete volte face and telling TV reporter Eleanor Mondale, a close friend of Clinton: 'Well, I tell ya, as a person, as an American, as a voter, who has supported the President, still continues to support our President, there's been a couple of times over the last year or so where sitting, reading the morning paper, I slapped myself upside the head and said, "What the heck is this?" You know, I ponied up 10 grand for our President's legal defence fund, and if I had never done that and he asked me today, I'd probably give twice as much.'

But he did add: 'For a moment or so I might have questioned my original intentions in donating to the defence fund. I do regret the country is still going through the entire affair.' Tom carried on yanking his foot out of his mouth in a *Time* magazine interview several weeks later. He supposedly went 'all stammery' as he tried to explain: 'Look, if I hadn't given it then, I would have given it now. As a guy who supports the President of the United States, I think he's doing a fabulous job and I'm glad I gave him the money.

'In the vast, surrealistic expanse of the Story of the Year, who didn't at one point or another slap themselves upside the head and say, "Holy smoke! Holeee smoke! Can you believe this?" And you can't believe it, but it's the reality. But you know what? He's my guy.'

On the question of becoming the new Ronald Reagan, he

insisted: 'I'm not running for the President of the United States. I'm an actor who makes movies, and that's how I was answering the questions.

'Good Lord Almighty! This is how trivial the times we are living in are. I don't even want to talk about it! Arggggghhhh!'

Tom's big brother, Larry, was equally disbelieving, saying: 'The President? Oh boy! That's not going to happen. That was a real media thing.'

Tom's attempt to defuse the controversy once more showed his deft touch with the media.

Everyone knows what an uncontroversial image Tom has, so by claiming to enjoy the sudden notoriety brings a smile rather than a grimace to the faces of the assembled media hordes and to the audience it represents.

He didn't appear rattled or aggrieved at the attention even though he completely changed his stance while laughing about the speculation launched by his original claims.

The outcome was exactly as he had intended. He was seen as an unconcerned fisherman casting about ideas, rather than as a worm wriggling on the hook of public opinion. A born politician?

The controversy was all the more surprising because the friendship between Clinton and Tom was widely thought to be the at the root of Hollywood's unswerving (until now) support of the President.

Even before the Lewinsky scandal, Tom had turned down the plum role of the randy, slick-talking Southern governor based on Clinton in the movie *Primary Colors*. The book by Joe Klein had caused a sensation as a thinly veiled, fictionalised account of Clinton's 1992 White House election campaigning. The book depicts the central character, Jack Stanton, as a habitual and remorseless philanderer.

President Clinton, knowing the film was being made with director Mike Nichols at the helm, made it clear who he wanted to play Stanton. He even said Tom would be his choice as an actor if they did a movie version of the William Jefferson Clinton story. 'If I had to cast it today just in an instant, I'd like Tom Hanks to play me. I mean, we don't look alike, and we're not the same size or shape or anything, but I know him and respect him as a person and an actor, very much,' Clinton said in an interview with CBS in America. 'And I think he has shown a range of capacity that's quite remarkable, and if someone were trying to play me and actually go through this job, in the kind of roller coaster way that life takes you, I would want a person with a lot of range and a lot of feeling.'

Tom was also thanked profusely from the stage by Clinton for his support after the actor, with all his usual charm and savoir faire, emceed a star-studded 1996 Hollywood benefit for the President at Green Acres in Los Angeles that raised an estimated £2 million. In spite of the glowing references, Tom still passed on *Primary Colors* and the role went to his friend John Travolta.

Tom strenuously denied his decision was because of his close ties with the President. 'It's a hilarious amount of ink for a story that's not true,' he said. 'I've met the President — that's a big difference between being friends with him.'

He claimed the real reason he turned tail on the film was that he was simply too busy. 'I went to Mike and said, "You know, I can no longer do this thing because life has caught up with me. You're going to have to cast someone else,"' he said.

But he still insisted that being in the film, which co-starred Emma Thompson as the Hillary-like wife, would not have offended Clinton. 'I was at an event with him recently,' he said. 'He joked, "It's okay with me if you do *Primary Colors*." I laughed harder than anybody else did.'

Muddying the waters slightly, he also told *The Times*: 'I was interested in doing *Primary Colors*, but I never saw the script. In all honesty, I'm a supporter of the President and I wouldn't have gone off and attempted to obviously slag off the President of the United States. It probably would have been a very different movie had I been involved.'

Tom had also rejected Oliver Stone's overtures for him to play Richard Nixon, a subject and an era that would normally have interested the baby-boomer star. The 1995 film, in which Sir Anthony Hopkins played the villain of Watergate as a foul-mouthed and manipulative drunkard, courted controversy, sparking protests from Nixon's daughters and supporters.

Whether or not Tom will now admit to any ambition for high office, the *New Yorker* episode has shown that the public — and the media — will take him at his word. They will also take him seriously, no mean feat for an actor once shrugged off as lightweight and goofy.

As strange as it may seem, for a restless man with an incisive, inquiring mind it may no longer be enough to be regarded as the best film actor of his generation. It may not even be enough to have a loving, intelligent, beautiful wife and a settled, satisfied family.

His comments on the presidency may have unwittingly allowed us a glimpse into a game plan that looks long beyond the next two or three movies.

He calls himself 'the luckiest man in the world', but maybe Tom's most important role will not be left to chance. The world of politics is beckoning even now. Tom may never get to play a President in the movies.

Perhaps it is his destiny to play one in real life. Whether he likes it or not, his comments have already started the ball rolling — fans at the 1999 Academy Awards held aloft signs and placards reading 'Tom Hanks For President'.

18

The Coolest Man in the World

The little boy sat on his grandfather's lap, just as his father had done, trying desperately to stretch out his legs far enough to reach the accelerator pedal. The old man fretted that perhaps the family ritual would be lost on his grandson, who had probably seen more of the world in his few years than all of his ancestors combined. This was a boy, after all, who had taken the pilot's seat on a supersonic flight from New York to London on Concorde as a special birthday treat.

It was the first time Amos Hanks had taken grandson Colin — Tom's eldest child — to visit the family burial plot at Paskenta Cemetery in Northern California. But he needn't have worried. Amos had the boy in his thrall as he showed him how to drive the car, talked about his love for hunting and his admiration for the books and lifestyles of his heroes, Hemingway and London, authors who wrote of the wild side of life, a far cry from the razzamatazz of Hollywood.

And, just as he did with Tom and his sister and brothers, Amos led Colin around the graves where his ancestors were buried. The poignancy of the moment was not lost on the misty-eyed grandfather, remembering Tom's dramatic graveside performance many years before.

How could he have guessed back then at the heady heights his second son would rise to?

For Colin, the path would be clearer. Growing up with both parents and a stepmother as actors and with the likes of Spielberg, Ryan, Travolta and Streisand popping over for dinner or joining the car pool, Hollywood was fluttering her eyelids from an early age.

Tom, Rita and Susan have gone to great lengths to protect their children from the constant spotlight that comes with being associated with a star of Tom's magnitude in this instant-access era. But they have never tried to pretend it isn't fun to be a megastar. So when Colin told his parents he wanted to leave school to be an actor, they could hardly complain. In fact, both older children appeared in *That Thing You Do!* and Elizabeth had a small part in *Forrest Gump*.

A fiercely protective father, Tom said his children were rarely starstruck. 'My work doesn't make much of a blip at the house,' he told *Time*. 'There is always a hubbub of activity because we are going somewhere, but they don't say, "Hey, Dad, you're on TV!"'

'All my kids can look and see what I do for a living and see that it's really fun. It produces a vast amount of joy. It's hard work if you can get it, but it's great work too.'

Sometimes, even for the most grounded children, the line between Hollywood and reality can become a little blurred. When Chester was four, he was sitting at home watching his father in *Turner and Hooch* on cable television and at the end of the film he went over and stood by the door, waiting for Tom. 'Isn't that sweet?' said his proud dad. 'I was done in the movie — so I must be coming home.'

Tom praises his children for helping to keep life in perspective. 'If you haven't sorted it out by the time you have your fourth kid, if you are actually going to be undone by the fact that they're not sleeping through the night or down with the measles, you should never have had number two,' he said.

'It also helps to keep you grounded. You come home and you've got an eight-year-old who wants to wrestle on the floor and a teenager who's having trouble at school — they don't care if you couldn't pull off a tracking shot. They just want you to be a dad. It keeps life real, and the attention where it should be.'

Having been hanging around film sets his whole life, Colin knew enough to work at his father's production company. At 20, he was cast in a TV show being produced by Fox, Rupert Murdoch's US TV network. The concept was every much as bizarre as his father's small-screen breakthrough as a cross-dressing advertising executive in *Bosom Buddies*. Colin was chosen by *Star Trek* producer Jonathan Frakes to star in his *Roswell High* series — as one of six American teenagers — three of whom are aliens — set to debut in the US towards the end of 1999.

Meanwhile, his father was busy working on his image. The man who described himself as 'a geek, a spaz' at school was set to become 'the coolest man in the world'.

Tom and John Travolta had long been looking for a project they could work on together. Like Tom, Travolta's career had been through its ups and downs and they had a shared history with some parts. Travolta, another space buff, had particularly coveted Tom's role in *Apollo 13* and he had happily taken the lead in *Primary Colors* when his friend dropped out of the running. The two had even been Oscar rivals, with Tom's *Forrest Gump* winning out over Travolta's dramatic comeback in *Pulp Fiction*.

Now they had found the perfect project. *Dino*, the story of the legendary Dean Martin, was to be directed by Martin Scorsese, with Tom being pencilled in for the lead. Travolta was being courted to play Frank Sinatra, and comics Jim Carrey or Adam Sandler, (fresh from the blockbuster success of his knockabout comedy *The Waterboy*), were being lined up as Joey Bishop, the only Rat Packer left alive after Ol' Blue Eyes's death in 1998.

Putting together such star-studded packages had often come undone in the past and there was no guarantee Tom and Travolta would finally get to work together.

Why would Tom want to play Dino? 'Because I want to be the coolest man in the world,' he answered.

In true Hanks fashion, he had three other, vastly different, projects simmering for what must already be the coolest job in the world.

Pairing America's favourite actor with America's most twisted author will certainly be one of the strangest film combos.

In the screen adaptation of Stephen King's 1996 serialised horror novel *The Green Mile*, however, Tom doesn't look cool at all.

He looks fat. He packed on more than 30 pounds for his role as prison guard Paul Edgecombe in the death row thriller set in a grim prison in America's Deep South in 1935.

The film tells Edgecombe's flashback recollections of magical goings-on during his stint as a death row guard at the Louisiana State Penitentiary, Cold Mountain. The head cell-block guard develops an unusual relationship with a gentle giant of a man who is convicted of raping and killing two little girls and sentenced to death in the electric chair. The 'green mile' refers to the line of green linoleum on the floor of death row.

Edgecombe relates his strange tour-of-duty watching over a quartet of convicted killers awaiting execution. Michael Clarke Duncan, who was in the Bruce Willis action flick *Armageddon* and Warren Beatty's *Bulworth*, also stars as John Coffey, the seven-foot-tall inmate convicted of murder whose caring, naïve nature and weird powers raise questions in Edgecombe's mind about his guilt.

The film marks Frank Darabont's return to the director's chair for the first time in five years. He wrote and directed *The Shawshank Redemption*, which received seven Oscar nominations, including one for Best Picture.

In a far from glamorous role, Tom doesn't look any better in the opening and closing sequences of the film, when his character is supposed to be 90 years old. Tom spent most of the second half of 1998 shooting the film, travelling between Tennessee and Stage 3 at Warner Bros studios. It didn't help that the film fell well behind schedule and Tom spent much of it with a painful ear infection.

The delays did not wear too well with the film's star and, even before its release, it was gaining a reputation as what the sinister Hollywood lexicon calls 'a troubled project'.

Tom told the *San Diego Union-Tribune* in December, 1998: 'It is still going on. It's just one of those movies that is taking this much time. Some movies you can just crank out — this isn't one of them.

'*Green Mile* is a death row movie. We're on death row for a long time, and you've got to have that look a little different every time. It was never going to be easy to make, and it's not — that's just the way it is.'

He added later: 'We're a month over shooting schedule, but it seems like three months. It's a death row movie that seems like eternity.'

But there was one major advantage. 'The great thing is I get to eat a few more cheeseburgers, which is fine with me,' he said. 'I get to be fat because I'm playing a prison guard in 1935. You don't want to look like you have buns of steel.'

Right up to the film's US release date in December 1999, there was a mystery over whether it would be completed in time.

Several months before it was due to hit cinema screens the film's beginning and ending still hadn't been shot, special effects were being created and the musical score wasn't ready. Bad weather had prevented the opening and closing sequences of Tom's character looking back over his life from being shot the previous autumn and were further delayed because the star was committed to another project early in 1999.

To make matters worse, Tom's make-up test was a disaster. He simply did not look old enough. At the end of the film, his character is supposed to be 90 years old. But Darabont told *Entertainment Weekly*: 'When the angle was just right, old Tom looked completely credible. Then he'd turn three inches and suddenly he'd look like Condom Head. When we saw him in sunlight, he looked like the Elephant Man.'

In the end, Darabont chose to cast veteran actor Dabbs Greer as the ancient Hanks.

Whispers of a jinx were further fuelled by author Stephen King's near-fatal accident, when he was knocked down by a minivan while walking near his summer house in North Lovell, Maine, in June, 1999. King landed in a ditch 14 feet away and suffered multiple broken bones in his right leg, a collapsed lung, cracked ribs, a fractured hip, and cuts to his head. Five life-saving operations later he was allowed out of hospital to begin a long rehabilitation.

Shortly before the accident, King was pondering publicly over whether *The Green Mile* director Darabont, who he hand-picked to helm the movie, should consider cutting it by 15 minutes or so after he saw a working print.

'I think it's maybe 15 minutes too long,' King said to *Entertainment Weekly*. 'Frank's very adamant about not cutting it. He won't cut the film on the basis of what I say. But if he thinks about it for a while, I think he might.'

Darabont, putting the final touches to one of the most highly-charged electric chair scenes ever shown on the big screen, insisted: 'Everything's under control.'

The second project on Tom's calendar has one of the most unusual filming schedules in film history — and will ensure the star who professes his abiding hobby to be watching his weight will work off the flab he so happily gained for *The Green Mile*.

He was heading to Fiji to begin work on *Castaway* in February 1999 when his Best Actor nomination was announced. The film unites Tom with *Forrest Gump* director Bob Zemeckis. A joint project between DreamWorks and 20th Century Fox, it was already being given a £80 million price tag before a frame was shot.

The reason is the lengths Tom and the film-makers were prepared to go to make his performance look realistic.

In *Castaway*, Tom plays a courier for an international company similar to Federal Express. *En route* home with an agonising toothache, his plane crashes onto a deserted island. Tom's character is the only survivor and manages painfully to extract his infected tooth. But as he does so, he blacks out and the picture fades to black with him.

When the audience sees Tom again, it is supposed to be months and months later, and he is looking emaciated, a shadow of his former self.

Rather than use camera trickery or make-up to create the effect of losing weight, Tom and Zemeckis decided the star would lose weight the old-fashioned way — through dieting and exercise. So they spent eight weeks through January and February of 1999 filming and then packed away the cameras while Tom went on a crash (*sic*) diet. Tom was planning to start work on *Dino* during the enforced sabbatical from *Castaway* and Zemeckis scheduled another movie *What Lies Beneath*, a supernatural thriller with Harrison Ford and Michelle Pfeiffer.

Tom grew the beard he was sporting at the 1999 Oscars ceremony for this film. At an American Museum of the Moving Image fête for Hanks at the beginning of May, he was looking beefier than usual, and admitted he needed to lose 40lb by the autumn. He said he wasn't dieting. 'Not yet,' he added, 'as I have just eaten everything on my plate — I start again tomorrow.'

When he loses enough weight, an extremely thin Tom Hanks will then fly back out to Fiji in the year 2000 with the director and crew to resume filming. As Tom explained to the *Chicago Sun-Times*: 'I'm going to make half a movie with Robert Zemeckis. Then we're going to shut down for a year and a half. Bob's going to make another movie. I'm going to make the *Dino* movie. Then we'll revisit *Castaway* and film the second half after I lose 40 pounds.

'It's insanity,' he admitted. 'I mean, what if somebody dies? Whoops, I shouldn't say that.'

The multi-million-pound gamble relies on Tom staying out of harm's way during the hiatus, as most of the crew would have to be kept on salary the whole time.

The gamble didn't start out too well when Tom almost had to cancel his visit to the 1999 Oscars after his right knee became infected by a bacteria he picked up in Fiji on the *Castaway* shoot which, if left untreated, could have ultimately led to amputation.

At first, physicians at St John's Hospital in Santa Monica, California, couldn't work out what was wrong with the star, who was in excrutiating pain. But they diagnosed the ailment as cellulitis, a bacterial infection that had caused his knee to become painfully swollen.

Filming long hours in the warm water in Fiji, where he was unable to keep a blister properly dressed in the tropical climate, he returned to Los Angeles and was given antibiotics by his doctor. But he had to be admitted to hospital under a false name when the infection spread.

Because of his illness, the actor missed the pre-Oscar luncheon with his fellow nominees. But he made it to the big night and the condition soon cleared up under treatment.

Zemeckis told the *New York Times*: 'The Tom Hanks character has to emotionally and physically survive many years of loneliness. He doesn't have anything to eat but fish and coconuts. Tom had to transform his body.

'We have to do things this way. There's no way to hide the different looks of his body. When Tom read this, he said, "This is a great story, but how do you do it? How do you show a modern guy in a movie becoming emaciated?" This is what we came up with. It will end up believable because it's so real.'

The director was worried that Tom's dramatic weight loss midstream in the movie might dominate publicity. But it won't be the first time his star has lost weight for a role. The last time he slimmed down, he took home an Oscar for his troubles.

'Mind you,' said Tom, 'the last time I lost this kind of weight was for *Philadelphia*, but that was six years ago and my metabolism has definitely changed. I will have to go away with dietitians and trainers and lose the weight.

'It's a risk. There's a lot of money at stake. But they're trusting us to do it, so we're going to try.' The film is expected to co-star another Oscar winner, Helen Hunt, from TV's *Mad About You*.

Larry couldn't resist a brotherly jab at Tom: 'It has got to be good for him to lose all that weight. He had too many fat roles in a row. He had to put the weight on for the parts he was playing. But I am sure he enjoyed the eating.

'If someone would give me $1 million (£616,408) to lose a few pounds, I would do it too. There is some kind of inspiration in that. It is certainly one way to lose weight.'

As if he hasn't got enough on his plate, Tom has also scheduled another project for release late in the year 2000, or early in 2001.

Following the success of the Hanks-Spielberg allies in their first sortie, the *Saving Private Ryan* vets are launching another war project, this time for TV. They are returning to the World War II battlefield to produce a 13-hour multi-million-pound mini-series based on the best-selling combat tome *Band of Brothers*.

The 1993 book by historian Stephen Ambrose — who acted as special consultant on *Saving Private Ryan* — will be put on the small screen by DreamWorks and Tom's Playtone Company. Much of the filming will be done in Europe.

Brothers tells the story of the 'Easy Company', an elite group of paratroopers formally known as the 506th regiment of the 101st Airborne Division. The series will follow the unit's tough journey through the Second World War, from their tortuous training in Georgia to their landing in France on D-Day, and through the Battle of the Bulge. It will go on to show how the paras liberated the Dachau concentration camp and captured Adolf Hitler's Eagle's Nest compound at Berchtesgaden, in the Alps.

Tom is co-writing the series, using Ambrose's book as a 'bible', and is likely to pull back on his uniform to help attract attention to the project, which could be the most expensive TV drama ever filmed, leap-frogging the actor's pet Emmy-winning *From the Earth to the Moon*.

Tom and Spielberg will be serving as executive producers in the series, which will also incorporate elements of another Ambrose book on World War II, *Citizen Soldier*.

Conclusion

So here he stands. An actor in his prime in every sense of the word. The most bankable star in Hollywood. He will tell you there are bigger stars. He said to *The Sunday Times*: 'If you're going to go just by the box office, Tom Cruise is bigger than me; Robin Williams and Harrison Ford — all much bigger. I've just had a good run the last few years.' Take no notice. The total gross for his 25 films is fast approaching $2 billion and Tom is leading an elite band of actors who can command more than £16 million a movie. Yet he is still a Hollywood oddity because he will not chase glamorous parts just to make him look macho or sexy. Instead, having carefully learned all the lessons of his earlier, more spotted, career, he picks characters who have a history, a connection — characters that consequently have a great appeal to audiences.

Backers know that if Tom Hanks's name is attached to a project, they can more than quadruple their money at the box office — and they may even be able to boast an Oscar or two to boot.

While other stars squabbled with studios about on-set perks and scrabbled for position to make themselves look good, irrespective of the overall look of the film, and watched their status go down the drain as a result, Tom has meticulously guarded the honesty of a project, even to the extent of sacrificing showy facets of his own parts.

The laid-back, Mr-Nice-Guy quips are left in the trailer when he goes to work. Directors quickly learn that he is a perfectionist and a stickler for accuracy. He not only turns up on time to hit the mark himself, he expects others around him to do the same. And because he is a decent reasonable man with an unparalleled track record, they usually do. He doesn't rant and shout and show off, but that doesn't mean he can't be insistent with a steely resolve that few would argue with.

Producer Brian Grazer, Ron Howard's partner and a longtime friend of Tom, said the actor is strong-willed and competitive. He told *The Sunday Times*: 'If you think he is easygoing, you should see him make a movie. He's like the truth police. He's intense, precise and judgemental. He judges everyone around him. If he thinks something in the movie isn't right, he says, "This is bullshit."'

Even Spielberg once remarked: 'For an Everyman, he's pretty damned opinionated.'

Yet directors line up to work with him again. The reason is simple. In a town where money rather than quality is often the dominating factor, Tom can deliver both. He will make a film better. He will treat both fellow cast members and the lowliest gofer on the set with respect. And he will return the trust the public has conferred upon him.

'He's so versatile and has such range,' said Frank Darabont, director of *The Green Mile*, 'that you don't have to take the character to him. He brings the character to the screen.'

Occasionally, he allows a small insight into his competitiveness, such as with his very rare public comments about fellow stars like Cruise, Gibson and Costner being movie stars rather than actors. Tom's heroes are the old professionals, such men as Jason Robards and Robert Duvall.

He spoke glowingly about Duvall to *Screen Actor* magazine, saying: 'Though he is not particularly a chameleon, it took me a long time to recognise him from one movie to another. He is not unique looking — doesn't put a hump in his back or do much more than walk a little different. Yet this man keeps entire movies together, as in *The Godfather* pictures. As Boo Radley in *To Kill a Mockingbird*, he stood behind a door and committed something worse than your worse nightmare. He made you feel sorry for him too. To me, this is a film actor: a man who conveys so much without saying anything.'

It is interesting to note that Tom made those comments in 1989, when he was still thought of as a more physical actor. Ten years later his acting was far more understated. In both *Saving Private Ryan* and even *You've Got Mail*, he was able to convey so much simply by sitting in a bomb shelter reading with a shaky hand, or pondering over a computer as he typed out an E-mail love letter. He had clearly been watching and learning from actors like Duvall, even as he conquered the movie industry.

Perhaps the most pertinent comparison would not be with the megastars of his day, but the icons from the golden days of Hollywood, an era which, in some ways, Tom has recreated for his fans.

Like the celluloid heroes of a bygone time, Tom has an unwritten pact with an audience.

There is no sex in a Tom Hanks movie, you can take that as a given. You may have seen him in his Y-fronts once or twice, or reading the paper in bed, but that's about as revealing as it gets. Even when he gets the girl at the end, the kiss looks like one of those black-and-white smooches when the lips lock without ever moving and the couple seems more engrossed in moving so the camera angle zooms in on the back of their heads. Asked why he doesn't do sexy scenes, Tom is happy to quote James Garner, an actor who has straddled old and new Hollywood and who says: 'I don't do horror movies!'

He is most definitely a leading man, but not on the modern sense of the word. Tom Cruise, Brad Pitt, Mel Gibson, Sly Stallone, Bruce Willis, Kevin Costner, John Travolta, Harrison Ford and even Jim Carrey have the brands of good looks — pretty, rugged, chiselled, or downright sexy — expected in a screen hero. With the exception of perhaps Robin Williams, Tom is the only superstar of his day who has none of those things.

The fact that Tom is the most successful of all of these extremely accomplished stars says much about the cinema-going audience as the curtains closed on the 20th century, particularly in America, where the public tried its very best to turn its eyes from the excesses of its President, even when they were being force-fed detail by lurid detail. Bewildered by the personal weaknesses of its leadership, an embarrassed nation craved a strapping six-footer, a vulnerable but honest hero with moral spirit.

The people wanted someone strong and steady who would do the right thing whatever the circumstances, a character to put up on a pedestal, to admire and to be proud of. They needed someone who had grown up with them, someone they could trust. America, as it has many times before, found the man they were looking for at the movies. His name was Tom Hanks.

Whether he was running across America in that ridiculous straight-backed hurdle, or flying to the moon, or trying manfully to make sense of the World War II, Tom's words and actions counted for something.

He has been compared with Jimmy Stewart and Cary Grant throughout his career. And for good reason. There is a similarity in style between the three actors. His diffident humour has echoes of Grant and the basic decency of the characters he often plays is reminiscent of Stewart. And, although he tries to play down the comparisons, he has, after all, starred in loose remakes of films made famous by both legendary stars.

But as his career moves into the new millennium, it is another American icon who comes most to mind. For four decades, John Wayne was the American hero, embraced for the true grit strength and patriotism he epitomised as his country blossomed into a superpower.

With the passing of the sixties, a confident young audience was looking for surprises in Hollywood and if the end results were sometimes erratic and the stars unreliable, then it was still worth the ride. Or at least the price of admission. Sitting on top of the world, America could stand a little retrospection, even a little criticism, as long as Hollywood remembered the boundaries.

But with the dawning of the nineties and the uncertain future of a new century, who better to look to than a man who ended two successive Oscar acceptance speeches with the sincere, if not very trendy 'God bless America.'

If the world recognised a great actor in those two films, *Philadelphia* and *Forrest Gump*, America recognised a hero who was truly one of their own in those emotional speeches. Tom Hanks may have been a gifted, intelligent, well-travelled star. But first and foremost, he was an American.

Unashamedly patriotic, he once said he was told by an astronaut there are just six flags on the moon, all of them American. 'I must say I feel proud about that,' he added. 'pure and simple.'

And Tom has not let anyone down. He has lived the American dream, coming all the way from a dank basement in Reno to being courted by Princesses and Presidents. He has a loving wife, a happy family and, as he puts it: 'I don't F a lot of starlets.'

As a result, the tabloids have never made him a target. 'There is nothing particularly glamorous about me,' he adds. 'I don't go to clubs. I'm not that much of a jet-setter. So the best they can do is take pictures of me when I'm on vacation with my family and talk about how fat I've gotten. That's as bad as it gets, and that's not too bad.'

He has also starred in quality film after quality film, all of them making a mint of money.

Saving Private Ryan, in particular, established Tom as a heavyweight of the grandeur of John Wayne, rather than simply another leading Hollywood star, at a time his country was again questioning its place in the world. With his added weight and muscle, he even looked like Wayne during some of the formidable action sequences. His friend, producer Walter Parks, affectionately dubbed Tom 'John Wayne Gump'.

You can be sure that Tom has never seen himself as another John Wayne, but he hasn't been able to ignore comparisons with the likes of Grant and Stewart, comparisons that have been made by such illustrious friends as Spielberg and Nora Ephron, among many others. If he has to choose, Tom sees himself more in the James Stewart category. 'Jack Lemmon I can understand. Jimmy Stewart I would love to be compared to. Another Cary Grant? I can't see it. Cary Grant was Cary Grant,' he said to *Connoisseur* magazine.

'Sure, I'd like to have the class of a Cary Grant. I would like to have the enthusiasm of a Jack Lemmon. But above all, I would like to be like Jimmy Stewart. He's not the most handsome man in the world, and he has a kind of geeky voice, but it doesn't matter — there are women out there who are rabidly in love with him, and men who admire him. Mostly, without a drastic altering of look or personality, you believed him in everything he did. If he is playing the sweetheart at the Savings and Loan, if he is playing the tough guy who has to shoot someone, if he's playing the funny guy who thinks he sees a rabbit six feet tall — no matter what, you believe him.'

Once again, the way Tom described James Stewart back in 1986 could easily be the way a critic or a fan would describe the Tom Hanks of today.

While he is happy to recreate the good old days of Hollywood in his comedies, it is his unerring ability to choose the right subjects for his more contemporary movies that have made him so unique.

The ability to plug into the baby-boomer psyche is not lost on Tom, who told an interviewer at the Venice Film Festival: 'I think I represent the sensibilities of my generation.'

And what is the perspective of the leading film critics on this rather unlikely superstar?

Alexander Walker, film critic for the London *Evening Standard*, noticed something darker behind Tom's Mr Nice Guy image. He wrote: 'There's something a bit creepy about Tom Hanks. Yes, he's direct and decent; but also, you feel, somehow devious and even dangerous — as if some emotional injury in childhood has mended well on the outside but left the inner man remote and watchful.'

Yet Walker perceives the way Hollywood, and Tom Hanks in particular, have tapped into the public consciousness in America. 'The movies form opinions, set attitudes and provide a self-image for people who find their elected leaders less vivid and immediate than their box-office icons,' he wrote. 'Tom Hanks hardly seems a name made for such elevation. Yet this cheerful, likeable son of a broken home and a father who was an itinerant cook, has achieved a Hollywood ascension that puts him closer to the mood of America than even the man in the White House.'

Walker goes on: 'Hanks is living proof that what matters most in movie-making is timeliness. Talent counts but other people have that — more, perhaps, than he has. A rare asset for an actor is making the right choice at the right time.

'His ascension to being his country's unlikely spokesman coincided with the decline of one-time American icons like Stallone and Schwarzenegger. The muscle-flexing grandiloquence of S & S now seemed hollow and impotent in a country dazed by internal violence, confused about its external role.

'Ordinary people achieving extraordinary things: the stoicism of an AIDS victim; the faith of a Gump; the ingenuity of a space-missionary. It's fallen to the unlikely talent of Hanks to incarnate this trilogy — and provide his country with the fictions it needs these days to face reality. But that's what stars are for.'

The *New Yorker*'s inimitable Pauline Kael, in a compilation titled *Hooked*, says of Tom's starring role in *Big*: 'Hanks gets by with his little-boy act: he doesn't hit any wrong notes, and he doesn't make you want to hide your face. You feel his essential boyishness all the time. Of course, you feel the kid in just about all of Hanks's roles, though generally it's a wise-guy adolescent. I prefer him that way. As a child, he's too predictably "spontaneous".'

Many of Tom's closest friends and admirers, a crowd of more than 800 people, gathered at the New York Waldorf-Astoria in April, 1999, for the American Museum of the Moving Image's tribute to the star, the youngest ever to be thus honoured.

Speakers tried to put their finger on Tom's elusive, yet undeniable appeal. Spielberg called his friend 'the most moral man I have ever known' and spoke with great affection about the special friendship the two men share.

But it was another old friend, Sally Field, who perhaps captured best the unconventional blend of talents that have so beguiled the public over the years. She told the crowded Grand Ballroom audience: 'I first met Tom Hanks in 1986. We had lunch and he talked about his wife, his kids, his girlfriend, Rita, and his world. Every once in a while he'd break away from his crabcakes ... I thought he was half Goofy, half Nureyev. And then when he got up to leave, I realised his fly was open and his shirt was hanging out.'

Intriguingly, the *New Yorker* tried to build up a case against the world's most likeable star in an article, 'The Tom Hanks Phenomenon — How Did He Pull It Off?' In fact, it didn't amount to a lot. After much research and questioning of Tom's closest friends and the actor himself, the magazine presented the dark side of the saint next door:

1) He tried cocaine while starring in the sitcom *Bosom Buddies*.

2) During one six-year period he starred in *Bachelor Party*, *Volunteers*, *The Money Pit*, *Dragnet*, *The Burbs*, *Turner and Hooch*, *Joe Versus the Volcano* and *The Bonfire of the Vanities*.

3) He was rude and unco-operative with a magazine reporter in 1986; his publicist gave the excuse that his marriage was falling apart.

4) His first marriage fell apart.

5) He gets 'a little peevish' about comparisons with James Stewart, despite the fact that his recent movie *You've Got Mail* was a remake of Stewart's *Shop Around the Corner*.

6) At the Venice Film Festival, when his *Saving Private Ryan* co-star Tom Sizemore thanked him for sharing some press attention, he replied, his mouth full of pasta, 'Yes, I'm throwing you the bones — and I had a boner as I was throwing them.'

7) He made a large donation to Bill Clinton's legal defence fund.

8) He thinks the comedy *Friends* is 'hilarious'.

The article goes on: 'That is the extent of the case against Tom Hanks. In other words, he is, as billed, the most disarming and successful of American movie stars.'

If one has to compare Tom with Hollywood's other superstars, the name of Harrison Ford is most likely to come up. Both have won the trust of a worldwide audience with their reliability and an underlying sense of decency, on and off the screen.

It is interesting to note that while many of their more flamboyant A-list rivals, like Sylvester Stallone, Arnold Schwarzenegger and Bruce Willis, have stumbled at the box office and, in some cases, sought critical acceptance with low-budget cameo appearances, Hanks and Ford, the steady superstars, have rolled from one hit to another. Only Tom Cruise remains with them at the very top of the heap. And in many ways, Cruise and Ford have more in common with each other than they do with Hanks.

For a start, they have the looks, usually regarded a must in Hollywood. As scrupulously as they choose their scripts and projects, there is no getting away from the fact that millions are drawn by Cruise's all-American clean-cut hunkiness and by Ford's smouldering charm. Both also starred in major action blockbusters: Cruise in *Top Gun* and Ford in the *Star Wars* and Indiana Jones films.

Tom's route to the top was very different and probably had more in common with the path taken by Robin Williams, a small rung down from Hanks on the superstar ladder. Like Tom, Williams made his name initially on a TV show, *Mork and Mindy*, and managed to crossover from his manic comedy to Oscar-winning dramatic performances. And like Tom, the *Mrs Doubtfire* star could hardly be described as a hunk.

There is little argument that every actor in Tom's league is sexier and more handsome than he is. Black Armani suits that are supposed to look clunky and cool look merely clunky on him. A double chin is always waiting to inflate, as is his waistband. He seems intent on playing down his fame rather than playing up to it.

Yet his star continues to rise. The reason, I believe, is that his very ordinariness — and his skilful ability to appear that way on screen — has allowed him to tap into the sensibility of the everyman in a way Cruise, Ford, Travolta, and even Williams never could. With their good looks, superhuman heroism or quickfire comic genius, they shine too bright to be real people. They are all Hollywood, however earnestly they pretend to be otherwise.

After no small number of false starts, Tom has discovered the trick of combining his stock character with scripts that place his ordinary man in extraordinary circumstances. His characters don't climb buildings or save the world single-handed. They do their best. Usually, in films like *Sleepless*, *You've Got Mail* and *Forrest Gump*, things work out. Sometimes, as in *Saving Private Ryan*, they don't. But we can always see the better parts of ourselves in a Tom Hanks character. And he usually provides the moral core to the subject central to the movie.

That is why Tom has shrewdly shied away from villainous characters. There is no way he would ever have accepted the kind of part his friend John Travolta took in *Pulp Fiction*. He wouldn't have even considered portraying a disillusioned vampire, as Tom Cruise did in Anne Rice's *Interview with the Vampire*.

By playing a character without any redeeming virtue, he knows he risks losing his core audience — because he knows that would break an unwritten agreement he has with his fans. They don't want to see their own reflections turn sour in a Tom Hanks movie. They may not demand a happy ending, nor do they insist on a clean-cut hero bleached free of flaws. But they do want to see an ultimately decent Tom Hanks try to do the right thing.

Referring to himself as a form of franchise or brand name, Tom told the *New Yorker*: 'You've got to be really careful. You've got to protect it. Because otherwise ... You don't want to become that brand that nobody — You don't want to become Palmolive soap.

'The thing that is most powerful is the power of the new. If you're not being new somehow, there's something wrong.'

In the same article, *Forrest Gump* director Robert Zemeckis said: 'Male stars who achieve mega-stardom have the quality of being attractive to women and non-threatening to men. For you to be a giant male star, men have to want to have a beer with you.'

Richard Schickel, *Time* magazine's film critic, said of Tom: 'Intelligence always manifests itself as a form of restlessness. Obviously there was a restlessness there that was not content with doing *Turner and Hooch*.

'Some smart actors blessed by the huge success showbusiness can bring have an awareness of their own ordinariness. It might even be a measure of movie stars' mental health that those who realise the margin between success and failure is very thin are far better off than the guys who think, "Hey, I made it because I'm so fabulous ..."

'I think Tom Hanks is very much in touch with the not-very-promising kid that he once was, who was drifting around. That's a sign of his quality as an actor. And one of the reasons Tom Hanks is visibly a decent guy.'

Perhaps the most difficult thing about being so successful is that Tom knows he could play any role he wants. All he has to do is ask. 'I could get on the phone now and manufacture the chance, the job, to go off and play anything you want; a rough and tumble cop, a psychotic killer,' he told *The Independent*. 'But that's not going to be an organic choice on my part. The material isn't going to be the right thing for me.'

Tom has been so adept at picking winners that he has inevitably drawn criticism for showing a lack of adventure in his choices. After winning his Best Actor Oscar as a hopeless drunk in the low-budget *Leaving Las Vegas*, Nicholas Cage successfully tried his hand at becoming an unlikely action hero and has continued to cut a quirky, unpredictable — and largely successful — swathe through Hollywood. Another Academy Awards regular, Meryl Streep, has continued to challenge herself with her wide choice of movies, from a love-lorn housewife in *The Bridges of Madison County* to an imperious vamp in *Death Becomes Her* and a white-water action hero in *The River Wild*.

Tom and his 'crack team of showbusiness professionals' could argue that his four Oscar-nominated performances — in *Big*, *Philadelphia*, *Forrest Gump* and *Saving Private Ryan* — are all very different characters. Certainly, Gump was a risky role, and not a very flattering one. At the time of *Philadelphia*, Tom was putting his career on the line by playing a homosexual. But both films still stayed true to the Hanks not-so-secret formula, giving us an unheroic hero we could feel for and cheer on.

It has to be said Tom has never stepped totally out of his range to play a historical character, a foreigner or a bona fide villain, although, to be fair, he did play a toy cowboy who pushed an astronaut out of the window. 'I'm always dealing with "When are you going to play the bad guy?"' he told the *New Yorker*. 'And the answer is so simple: as soon as I find one I understand.'

He has an advantage over his Hollywood rivals in that neither he, nor his audience, are particularly concerned about his leading man looks. Brad Pitt's directors may feel duty bound to linger the camera lovingly on his blond hair and blue eyes and Tom Cruise has to be sure to look, well, like Tom Cruise. But an extra few pounds or a naff haircut aren't going to turn off Hanks fans. Don't they themselves sometimes feel a little overweight or regret a trip to the barber's?

It is interesting to note that, like another thinking woman's favourite, Harrison Ford, Tom rarely acts with women who have a strong presence. His romantic comedies with Meg Ryan follow a by-now familiar pattern, with neither of them spending more than the odd climactic scene on screen with the other. Robin Wright had very much a supporting role in *Gump*, as indeed did Antonio Banderas, his partner in *Philadelphia*. Daryl Hannah, while a fine actress, wasn't exactly required to act her tail off in *Splash*. The only time he shared serious screen time with a leading lady was with Sally Field in *Punchline*, and the relationship proved to be the chief hiccup in an otherwise impressive film.

But while he may veer away from sharing the screen with the likes of Sharon Stone, Tom has no fear of working with the industry's best directors. As well as his friend Steven Spielberg, Tom has worked with a 'Who's Who' of top directors, including Robert Zemeckis, Jonathan Demme, Ron Howard, Richard Donner, Nora Ephron, Joe Dante, Penny Marshall and Brian De Palma. He has also signed on to make Dean Martin's life story with Martin Scorsese.

Indeed, the quality of direction may have done as much as anything to elevate him into the film industry's acting elite. With the notable exception of *That Thing You Do!*, it also helped eliminate costly vanity projects from his resumé. He is shrewd enough to know good directors produce good films — and at the same time offer him a serious challenge to impress his peers.

$$*\qquad\qquad *\qquad\qquad *$$

Ten years ago, Tom was on a similar level to stars like Jim Belushi, Steve Guttenberg and Jeff Daniels. Curiously, it may have been the *Bonfire* disaster that set him on a path apart from many of his comedy contemporaries.

As we have seen, he took time off from churning out movie after movie to take stock of his position. He realised that he wasn't desperate for money any more and he had a good measure of fame. What he needed was job satisfaction. And from that point on, the projects were chosen very carefully to ensure that not only did they have good scripts and the right sort of character for him, but also that he had some level of control over the quality of what he was being asked to do.

The end of 1998 saw Tom as the top box office earner in the world. Between them, *Saving Private Ryan* and *You've Got Mail* had earned more than £334 million in just 12 months.

Tom beat pretenders to his Hollywood crown, such as Jim Carrey and Leonardo DiCaprio, to become the magnetic attraction of the year — the third time he topped the list.

The survey covered every country where the films were released. But Tom still had some way to go to catch two old hands who have topped the annual list most often. John Wayne won four times and appeared 19 times in the top ten, while Clint Eastwood had scored five wins and 15 top ten places.

The full list — with such superstars as Jack Nicholson, Tom Cruise and John Travolta dropping out from the previous year — is an interesting guide to the calibre of actors being put in the shade by Tom's domination of the film industry.

1) Tom Hanks, £334 million, in *Saving Private Ryan, You've Got Mail.*
2) Jim Carrey, £212 million, in *The Truman Show, Simon Birch.*
3) Leonardo DiCaprio, £175 million, in *Titanic, The Man in the Iron Mask, Celebrity.*
4) Robin Williams, £171 million, in *Patch Adams, What Dreams May Come.*
5) Meg Ryan, £163 million, in *City of Angels, Hurlyburly, You've Got Mail.*
6) Mel Gibson, £161 million, in *Lethal Weapon 4.*
7) Adam Sandler, £124 million, in *The Waterboy, The Wedding Singer.*
8) Eddie Murphy, £97 million, in *Holy Man, Doctor Dolittle.*
9) Cameron Diaz, £94 million, in *There's Something About Mary.*
10) Julia Roberts, £86 million, in *Stepmom.*

So what drives Tom Hanks? He doesn't need the money. Although he has more in the bank than he will ever need, friends believe him when he says that has never been motivated by his monster paydays. There was a time when he was tempted by £3 million fees, even when he knew the scripts were excruciating. But those days are long gone. When his contemporaries were driving around in Ferraris and Rolls Royces, Tom was tooling around LA in a VW Jetta. He's never bothered with boats and planes. On friend John Travolta's state-of-the-art Airstream trailer, Tom says simply: 'If I had one like that, I would never want to leave it to go to work.'

Although he could afford to hire a regiment of household staff, Tom and Rita prefer to care for their children themselves, taking them and picking them up from school and helping them with their homework. He certainly doesn't spend his money on clothes. At one point, he would only buy shirts that didn't have designer labels, not an easy task in many of LA's finer retailers.

Neither is Tom being driven by the need to be recognised by his peers. Back-to-back Oscars put paid to any such worries long ago and the wide variety of his roles means no one could ever accuse him of being a one-trick pony.

Interestingly, Tom shows little sign of taking cameo parts in art-house or *auteur* movies. Perhaps he feels he doesn't need to impress anyone with his acting prowess. He may have felt burned by his unbilled role in 1992's *Radio Flyer*, which he narrated and appeared briefly in at the beginning and the end. The film bombed, making a huge loss.

Asked in a *New Yorker* interview if he would ever star in a $9 million independent film. He said: 'I'm open to any sort of suggestions. The problem is I read those things and say, "Look, I don't get it. This is just the same scene over and over and over again. You don't get any credit from me because it's only a $9 million movie."'

He adds, in a mock *artiste* voice: 'What do you mean? Don't you want to be a renegade?

'If someone had come to me and said, "Do you want to make *Fargo*?" I'd have said, "Well, yeah." But I didn't get to read that. I can tell in seven pages of reading a screenplay if I'm interested in doing it. More often than not, you read stuff that just doesn't work. It has no surprises in it. The character to me always has to have some logic to him that I understand.'

No, the reason Tom Hanks is still making such an impact on Hollywood is simply that he finds the job fun.

He told the *Mail on Sunday* in 1998: 'No one believes me when I say it, but this is still just as fun and challenging as it was when I was in the high school play. And I still feel like I did when I saw my name on the cast list for *Night of the Iguana* in 1971 at Skyline High School in Oakland, California.

'Every time I take a job it's the most exciting thing in the world, because this is the greatest job in the world.

'I don't do it for the money or the power or anything else. I do it because it is fun.'

He added that he doesn't have any goals. 'I just try to make it through the next job. I mean, the communists had goals, you know, the five-year plans. Look where it got them.'

As a child, forever glued to the television, Tom dreamed of being an astronaut, of being a soldier, of getting the beautiful girl. He would never have dared dream of doing all of those things, particularly as he was not overly bright at school, not especially brave or tough and rather plain-looking with a perpetually bad haircut.

Through acting, all his dreams came true, and more besides. There wasn't just one beautiful girl. There were lots of leading ladies — one being his wife.

His success hasn't come without a price. The collapse of his first marriage, he blames chiefly on spending so much time away from his family on location, making his way in a business that doubles as a marital graveyard. He has known failure too. *The Bonfire of the Vanities* débâcle was far more of a setback at the time than it now seems in the wake of his ensuing triumphs.

And it wasn't really until he was into his 30s — and had met Rita Wilson — that he could truly put his itinerant childhood to rest. Like many children who grow up too soon, he couldn't help but carry over his misgivings into adulthood.

Even now, close friends like Steven Spielberg and Meg Ryan admit they don't truly know Tom. The only residue of the lonely, confused boy from Northern California remains in the silent reveries he can fall into even in a crowded room.

It is like a switch being flicked in his head, taking him away from the present to somewhere no one — not even Rita — can reach.

In those moments, Tom Hanks the movie star is gone. He's little Tommy reaching for the pedals in his father's car.

Trying to see how far he can go ...

Filmography

He Knows You're Alone (1980) Director: Armand Mastroianni. Producer: George Manasse. Executive producers: Edgar Lansbury and Joseph Beruh. Screenplay: Scott Parker. Director of Photography: Gerald Fell. Editor: George T. Norris. Art Director: Susan Kaufman. Music: Alexander and Mark Peskanov. Released by: Metro Goldwyn Mayer. Running time: 94 minutes. Cast: Don Scardino (Marvin), Caitlin O'Heaney (Amy), Elizabeth Kemp (Nancy), Tom Rolfing (Killer), Lewis Arlt (Gamble), Patsy Pease (Joyce), James Rebhorn (Professor), *Tom Hanks (Elliot)*.
Fee: $800
US Box Office: N/A
Plot: A reluctant wife-to-be is stalked by a serial killer who only targets brides and the people around them. While her friends get knocked off one by one, a renegade cop whose own bride was killed years before tries to hunt down the murderer before it is too late. Cliché-ridden slasher movie with Tom in small part as a smarmy psychology student. The role is so tiny he doesn't even get a gruesome death scene, which put him in the minority in this film.

Rona Jaffe's Mazes and Monsters (1982) Director: Steven H. Stern. Producers: Tom McDermott and Richard A. Briggs. Teleplay: Tom Lazarus. Director of Photography: Laszlo George. Art Director: Trevor Williams. Editor: Bill Parker. Music: Hagood Hardy. From the novel by Rona Jaffe. Released by: CBS-Lorimar (for television).

Running time: 103 minutes. Cast: *Tom Hanks (Robbie Wheeling)*, Chris Makepeace (J.J. Brockaway), Wendy Crewson (Kate), David Wallace (Daniel), Susan Strasberg (Meg), Vera Miles (Cat), Anne Francis (Elle), Lloyd Bochner (Mr Wheeling).
Fee: N/A
US Box Office: TV only
Plot: In Tom's first starring role in a film, he plays a student hooked on the fantasy game Dungeons and Dragons. The made-for-TV movie was based on a real life case, when police searching for a missing student found a maze of tunnels and caves beneath a college campus. Tom's character 'flips into the game' and becomes convinced he is 'Pardieu the Holy Man'.

Splash (1984) Director: Ron Howard. Producer: Brian Grazer. Executive producer: John Thomas Lenox. Screenplay: Lowell Ganz, Babaloo Mandel, Bruce Jay Friedman. Screen story: Bruce Jay Friedman based on an idea by Brian Grazer. Director of Photography: Don Peterman. Underwater Director of Photography: Jordan Klein. Production designer: Jack T. Collis. Editors: Daniel P. Hanley, Michael Hill. Costume Designer: Mary Routh. Special Visual Effects Supervisor: Mitch Suskin. Mermaid Design and Construction: Robert Short. Music: Lee Holdridge. Released by: Touchstone. Running time: 111 minutes. Cast: *Tom Hanks (Allen Bauer)*, Daryl Hannah (Madison), John Candy (Freddie Bauer), Eugene Levy (Walter Kornbluth), Dody Goodman (Mrs Stimler), Shecky Greene (Mr Buyrite), Richard B. Shull (Dr Ross), Bobby DiCicco (Jerry), Howard Morris (Dr Zidell), Tony Di Benedetto (Tim the doorman).
Fee: $80,000
US Box Office: $69.8 million
Plot: Tom gets the chance to show his value as a comic actor in this fantasy co-starring Daryl Hannah as a beautiful fish out of water. Hannah's landlocked mermaid falls in love with Tom and gets a taste of Manhattan as she dines on lobster — shells and all — while her hero tries to keep her out of hot water. The film that made Tom and Daryl Hannah stars.

Bachelor Party (1984) Director: Neal Israel. Producers: Ron Moler, Bob Israel. Executive Producer: Joe Roth. Screenplay: Neal Israel, Pat Proft. Story: Bob Israel. Director of Photography: Hal Trussel. Art Directors: Kevin Conlin, Martin Price. Editor: Tom Walls. Music: Robert Folk. Released by: 20th Century Fox. Running Time: 106 minutes. Cast: *Tom Hanks (Rick Gassko)*, Tawny Kitaen (Debbie Thompson), Adrian Zmed (Jay O'Neill), George Grizzard (Mr Thompson), Robert Prescott (Cole Whittier), William Tepper (Dr Stan Gassko), Wendie Jo Sperber (Dr Tina Gassko), Barry Diamond (Rudy), Gary Grossman (Gary), Michael Dudikoff (Ryko), Brad Bancroft (Brad), Martina Finch (Phoebe), Deborah Harmon (Ilene), Tracy Smith (Bobbi).
Fee: $60,000
US Box Office: $38.6 million
Plot: As Tom says, it's not *Richard III*, but this distinctly low-brow comedy keeps the dumb and dumber laughs going with an *Animal House/Police Academy*-style slapstick frenzy. Amidst it all, Tom, as the goofy groom-to-be who promises to behave himself at his bachelor party, stays slightly above the grossness and comes out smiling.

The Man With One Red Shoe (1985) Director: Stan Dragoti. Producer: Victor Drai. Screenplay: Robert Klane. Director of Photography: Richard H. Kline. Production Designer: Dean E. Mitzner. Editors: Bud Molin, O. Nicholas Brown. Music: Thomas Newman. Based on the French farce *The Tall Blond Man With One Black Shoe*, written by Francis Veber, Yves Robert. Released by: 20th Century Fox. Running time: 92 minutes. Cast: *Tom Hanks (Richard Drew)*, Dabney Coleman (Cooper), Lori Singer (Maddy), Charles Durning (Ross), Carrie Fisher (Paula), Edward Herrmann (Brown), Jim Belushi (Morris), Tom Noonan (Reese), Gerrit Graham (Carson), David L. Lander (Stemple).
Fee: N/A
US Box Office: $8.7 million
Plot: Tom is a symphony violinist and eccentric composer mistaken for a spy in this so-so comedy. The Georgetown musician is unwittingly caught up in a game of CIA one-upmanship, with one spy, Lori Singer, luring him into bed, and Carrie Fisher turning up as a bedmate with a weakness for Tarzan-and-Jane games. The shoe doesn't really fit casting Tom in this comedy of errors.

Volunteers (1985) Director: Nicholas Meyer. Producers: Richard Shepherd, Walter F. Parkes. Screenplay: Ken Levine, David Isaacs. Story: Keith Critchlow. Director of Photography: Ric Waite. Production Designer: James Schoppe. Editors: Ronald Roose, Steven Polivka. Music: James Horner. Released by: Tri-Star. Running time: 106 minutes. Cast: *Tom Hanks (Lawrence Bourne III)*, Rita Wilson (Beth Wexler), John Candy (Tom Tuttle), Tim Thomerson (John Reynolds), Gedde Watanabe (At Toon), George Plimpton (Lawrence Bourne Jnr), Ernest Harada (Chung Mee), Allan Arbus (Albert Bordonaro).
Fee: N/A
US Box Office: $20.2 million.
Plot: When his rich, stuffy dad won't give him any cash to pay his gambling debt, Tom's Lawrence Bourne III switches places with a roommate and heads to Thailand with the Peace Corps. In the jungle, he finds love and himself and, naturally, saves the day. Most memorable for Tom as the film where he met future wife Rita Wilson.

The Money Pit (1986) Director: Richard Benjamin. Producers: Frank Marshall, Kathleen Kennedy, Art Levinson. Executive Producers: Steven Spielberg, David Giler. Screenplay: David Giler. Director of Photography: Gordon Willis. Production Designer: Patrizia von Brandenstein. Editor: Jacqueline Cambas. Special Effects Supervisor: Michael Wood. Music: Michael Colombier. Released by: Universal. Running time: 91 minutes. Cast: *Tom Hanks (Walter Fielding)*, Shelley Long (Anna Crowley), Alexander Godunov (Max Beissart), Maureen Stapleton (Estelle), Joe Mantegna (Art Shirk), Philip Bosco (Curly), Josh Mostel (Jack Schnittman), Yakov Smirnoff (Shatov), Carmine Caridi (Brad Shirk), Jake Steinfeld (Duke).
Fee: $750,000
US Box Office: $37.5 million
Plot: Hapless homeowners Tom and Shelley Long buy a £1 million house for a fraction of the cost and regret it for the rest of the film as everything possible goes wrong in the house from hell. A less-than-successful attempt to update the Cary Grant classic *Mr Blandings Builds His Dream House*.

Every Time We Say Goodbye (1986) Director: Moshe Mizrahi. Producers: Jacob Kotzky, Sharon Harel. Screenplay: Moshe Mizrahi, Rachel Fabien, Leah Appet. Story: Moshe Mizrahi. Director of Photography: Giuseppe Lanci. Editor: Mark Burns. Music: Philippe Sarde. Released by: Tri-Star. Running time: 97 minutes. Cast: *Tom Hanks (David)*, Cristina Marsillach (Sarah), Benedict Taylor (Peter), Anat Atzmon (Victoria), Gila Almagor (Lea), Monny Moshanov (Nessim), Avner Hiskyahu (Raphael), Caroline Goodall (Sally), Esther Parnass (Rosa), Daphne Armony (Clara), Orit Weisman (Mathilda).
Fee: N/A
US Box Office: $300,000
Plot: Tom's first real break-out straight drama role as a World War II pilot who falls in love with a beautiful Jewish girl, much to the chagrin of her devout family. A beautifully filmed love story shot on location in Israel.

Nothing in Common (1986) Director Garry Marshall. Producer: Alexandra Rose. Executive Producer: Roger M. Rothstein. Screenplay: Rick Podell, Michael Preminger. Director of hotography: John A. Alonzo. Production Designer: Charles Rosen. Editor: Glenn Farr. Music: Patrick Leonard. Released by: Tri-Star. Running time: 118 minutes. Cast: *Tom Hanks (David Basner)*, Jackie Gleason (Max Basner), Eva Marie Saint (Lorraine Basner), Hector Elizondo (Charlie Gargas), Barry Corbin (Andrew Woolridge), Bess Armstrong (Donna Mildred Martin), Sela Ward (Cheryl Ann Wayne), Cindy Harrell (Stewardess), John Kapelos (Commercial Director), Carol Messing (David's Secretary).
Fee: $1 million
US Box Office: $32.5 million
Plot: Tom is a cocky advertising executive whose life turns upside down when his parents break up and his father falls seriously ill. The father-son bonding between Tom's character and his dying dad is the central, touching theme. It was American TV legend Jackie Gleason's last film.

Dragnet (1987) Director: Tom Mankiewicz. Producers: David Permut and Robert K. Weiss. Executive Producer: Bernie Brillstein. Screenplay: Dan Aykroyd, Alan Zweibel, Tom Mankiewicz. Director of Photography: Matthew F. Leonetti. Production Designer: Robert F. Boyle. Editors: Richard Halsey, William D. Gordean. Music: Ira Newborn. Released by: Universal. Running time: 110 minutes. Cast: Dan Aykroyd (Joe Friday), *Tom Hanks (Pep Streebek)*, Christopher Plummer (Reverend Whirley), Dabney Coleman (Jerry Caesar), Alexandra Paul (Connie Swail), Harry Morgan (Captain Bill Gannon), Elizabeth Ashley (Commissioner Kirkpatrick), Jack O'Halloran (Emil Muzz), Kathleen Freeman (Enid Borden), Bruce Gray (Mayor Parvin), Lenka Peterson (Granny Mundy).
Fee: $1.2 million.
US Box Office: $57.4 million
Plot: Tom plays second banana to Aykroyd's no-nonsense Joe Friday in a spoof of the Los Angeles-based cops and robbers show that ran for more than a decade in the '50s and '60s. The odd couple's chief mission is to tame the PAGANS (People Against Goodness and Normalcy). But they don't manage to scare up too many laughs.

Big (1988) Director: Penny Marshall. Producers: James L. Brooks, Robert Greenhut. Co-producers and Screenplay: Gary Ross, Anne Spielberg. Director of Photography: Barry Sonnenfield. Production Designer: Santo Loquasto. Art Directors: Tom Warren, Speed Hopkins. Editor: Barry Malkin. Music: Howard Shore. Released by: 20th Century Fox. Running time: 104 minutes. Cast: *Tom Hanks (Josh Baskin)*, Elizabeth Perkins (Susan Lawrence), John Heard (Paul Davenport), Jared Rushton (Billy Kopeche), Robert Loggia ('Mac' MacMillan), David Moscow (Young Josh), Jon Lovitz (Scotty Brennen), Mercedes Ruehl (Mrs Baskin), Josh Clark (Mr Baskin), Kimberlee M. Davis (Cynthia Benson), Oliver Block (Freddie Benson).
Fee: $1.75 million
US Box Office: $114.9 million
Plot: Tom plays a 12-year-old boy in a 35-year-old man's body and spends much of his time, hilariously and sensitively, trying to get back to his childhood. Whether he is astonishing the other grow-

ups with his childlike sincerity or beguiling toy company colleague Elizabeth Perkins with his innocent charm, it is a big, big leap for Tom, who was rewarded with his first Academy Award nomination.

Punchline (1988) Director: David Seltzer. Producers: David Melnick, Michael Rachmil. Screenplay: David Seltzer. Director of Photography: Reynaldo Villalobos. Production Designer: Jack DeGovia. Editor: Bruce Green. Music: Charles Gross. Released by: Columbia. Running time: 128 minutes. Cast: Sally Field (Lilah Krytsick), *Tom Hanks (Steven Gold)*, John Goodman (John Krytsick), Mark Rydell (Romeo), Kim Greist (Madeline Urie), Paul Mazursky (Arnold).
Fee: $1.5 million
US Box Office: $21 million
Plot: Tom called it the closest had had come to playing 'an unredeemable character'. Playing a stand-up comedian, he takes Field, as a New Jersey housewife, under his wing as they both try and break into the tough New York comedy circuit. Tom moves from comic glibness to manic intensity with an understated ease that makes it a powerful performance, even if Oscar-winner Field is miscast.

The Burbs (1989) Director: Joe Dante. Producers: Michael Finnell, Larry Brezner. Screenplay: Dana Olsen. Director of Photography: Robert Stevens. Production Designer: James Spencer. Editor: Marshall Harvey. Music: Jerry Goldsmith. Released by: Universal. Running time: 103 minutes. Cast: *Tom Hanks (Ray Peterson)*, Bruce Dern (Mark Runsfield), Carrie Fisher (Carol Peterson), Rick Ducommun (Art Weingartner), Corey Feldman (Ricky Butler), Wendy Schaal (Bonnie Rumsfield), Henry Gibson (Dr Warner Klopek), Brother Theodore (Uncle Reuben Klopek), Courtney Gains (Hans Klopek), Gale Gordon (Walter), Dick Miller, Robert Picardo (Binmen).
Fee: $3.5 million
US Box Office: $36 million
Plot: Dull suburbanite executive takes a holiday to get a little excitement into his life and goes to war with his loony neighbours

against the new family on the block. With lots of lame jokes, explosions and screaming, the haunted-house spoof has too much going on for such a thin script and wastes its leading man.

Turner and Hooch (1989) Director: Rodger Spottiswoode. Producer: Raymond Wagner. Executive Producer: Daniel Petrie Jnr. Screenplay: Dennis Shryack, Michael Blodgett, Daniel Petrie Jnr, Jim Cash, Jack Epps Jnr. Story: Dennis Shryack, Michael Blodgett. Director of Photography: Adam Greenberg. Production Designer: John DeCuir Jnr. Editor: Garth Craven. Music: Charles Gross. Released by: Touchstone. Running time: 98 minutes. Cast: *Tom Hanks (Scott Turner)*, Mare Winningham (Emily Carson), Beasley (Hooch), Craig T. Nelson (Chief Hyde), Reginald VelJohnson (David Sutton), Scott Paulin (Zack Gregory), J. C. Quinn (Walter Boyett), John McIntire (Amos Reed), David Knell (Ernie).
Fee: $3.5 million
US Box Office: $71.1 million
Plot: Hooch, Tom's big, drooling canine co-star, witnesses his owner's murder and leads our hero, a compulsively clean small-town cop, to solve the crime. Includes a couple of scenes with Tom in black briefs. But don't expect a sequel — the dog gets it in the end.

Joe Versus the Volcano (1990) Director: John Patrick Stanley. Producer: Teri Schwartz. Executive Producers: Steven Spielberg, Kathleen Kennedy, Frank Marshall. Writer: John Patrick Shanley. Director of Photography: Stephen Goldblatt. Production designer: Bo Welch. Editor: Richard Halsey. Music: Georges Delerue. Released by: Warner Bros. Running time: 102 minutes. Cast: *Tom Hanks (Joe)*, Meg Ryan (De De/Angelica/Patricia), Lloyd Bridges (Graynamore), Robert Stack (Dr Ellison), Abe Vigoda (Chief of the Waponis), Dan Hedaya (Mr Waturi), Amanda Plummer (Dagmar), Ossie Davis (Marshall), Carol Kane (Hairdresser).
Fee: $3.5 million
US Box Office: $39.4 million
Plot: Tom's hypochondriac character throws in his boring job for a South Seas adventure after being diagnosed with a fatal disease. In the course of his hi-jinks he meets and falls in love with Ryan for

the first of many times — even though she is playing three parts in the one movie — and discovers, surprise, surprise, that he is not going to die after all.

The Bonfire of the Vanities (1990) Director and Producer: Brian DePalma. Executive Producers: Peter Guber, Jon Peters. Co-producer: Fred Caruso. Screenplay: Michael Cristofer. Director of Photography: Vilmos Zsigmond. Production Designer: Richard Sylbert. Editors: David Ray, Bill Pankow. Music: Dave Grusin. Based on the novel by: Tom Wolfe. Released by: Warner Bros. Running time: 125 minutes. Cast: *Tom Hanks (Sherman McCoy)*, Bruce Willis (Peter Fallow), Melanie Griffith (Maria Ruskin), Kim Cattrall (Judy McCoy), Saul Rubinek (Jed Kramer), Morgan Freeman (Judge White), John Hancock (Reverend Bacon), Kevin Dunn (Tom Killian), F. Murray Abraham (D.A. Weiss), Donald Moffat (Mr McCoy), Robert Stephens (Sir Gerald Moore), Alan King (Arthur Ruskin), Beth Broderick (Caroline Heftshank), Mary Alice (Annie Lamb), Rita Wilson (PR Woman).
Fee: $5 million
US Box Office: $15.7 million
Plot: Tom simply doesn't fit the William Hurt-type role as the WASPy broker whose millionaire lifestyle goes down the pan after he becomes involved in an accident with his mistress on the wrong side of town. Never lives up to the promise of Wolfe's best-selling novel.

Radio Flyer (1992) Director: Richard Donner. Producer: Lauren Shuler-Donner. Executive producers: Michael Douglas, Rich Beieber, David Mickey Evans. Screenplay: David Mickey Evans. Director of Photography: Laszlo Kovacs. Production Designer: j. Michael Riva. Art Director: David Frederick Klassen. Editor: Stuart Baird. Music: Hans Zimmer. Released by: Columbia. Running time: 114 minutes. Cast: Lorraine Bracco (Mary), John Heard (Daugherty), Adam Baldwin (The King), Elijah Wood (Mike), Joseph Mazzello (Bobby), Ben Johnson (Geronimo Bill), *Tom Hanks (Unbilled, Mike as adult)*.
Fee: $2 million
US Box Office: N/A

Plot: Tom serves as the narrator of an unsettling story about two boys who dream of flying away from their drunken, abusive stepfather.

A League of Their Own (1992) Director: Penny Marshall. Producers: Robert Greenhut, Elliot Abbott. Co-producers: William Pace, Ronnie Clemmer, Joseph Hartwick. Executive Producer: Penny Marshall. Screenplay: Lowell Ganz, Babaloo Mandel. Director of Photography: Miroslav Ondricek. Production Designer: Bill Groom. Editor: George Bowers. Music Hans Zimmer. Based on a story by Kim Wilson, Kelly Candaele. Released by: Columbia. Running time: 128 minutes. Cast: *Tom Hanks (Jimmy Dugan)*, Geena Davis (Dottie Hanson), Madonna (Mae Mordabito), Lori Petty (Kit Keller), Jon Lovitz (Ernie Capadino), David Strathairn (Ira Lowenstein), Garry Marshall (Walter Harvey), Megan Cavanaugh (Marla Hooch), Rosie O'Donnell (Doris Murphy), Bill Pullman (Bob Hanson).
Fee: $5 million
US Box Office: $107.5 million
Plot: Tom changes gear completely to play baseball coach Jimmy Dugan, an overweight alcoholic given the job of coaching a wartime women's baseball team because of his past glories. The dedication of his team — Madonna, Geena Davis, Rosie O'Donnell, etc. — finally sobers him up enough to care again and strike up a meaningful, if platonic, relationship with his star catcher, Davis.

Sleepless in Seattle (1993) Director: Nora Ephron. Producer: Gary Foster. Executive Producers: Lynda Obst, Patrick Crowley. Screenplay: Nora Ephron, David S. Ward, Jeff Arch. Director of Photography: Sven Nykvist. Production Designer: Jeffrey Townsend. Editor: Robert Reitano. Music: Marc Shaiman. From a story by: Jeff Arch. Released by: Tri-Star. Running time: 104 minutes. Cast: *Tom Hanks (Sam Baldwin)*, Meg Ryan (Annie Reed), Bill Pullman (Walter), Ross Malinger (Jonah Baldwin), Rosie O'Donnell (Becky), Gaby Hoffman (Jessica), Rita Wilson (Suzy), Rob Reiner (Jay), Victor Garber (Greg), David Hyde-Pierce (Dennis Reed).
Fee: $7.5 million
US Box Office: $126.5 million

Plot: Get your hankies out. He's sleepless in Seattle, grieving over his lost wife. She's baffled in Baltimore, obsessed by the widower she knew only through his voice on a late night radio talk show. It takes them the whole movie to get together on top of the Empire State Building, but it's worth the wait.

Philadelphia (1993) Director: Jonathan Demme. Producer: Edward Saxon, Jonathan Demme. Executive Producers: Gary Goetzman, Kenneth Utt, Ron Bozman. Screenplay: Ron Nyswaner. Director of Photography: Tak Fujimoto. Production Designer: Kristi Zea. Art Director: Tim Gavin. Editor: Craig McKay. Music: Howard Shore. Released by: Tri-Star. Running time: 126 minutes. Cast: *Tom Hanks (Andrew Beckett)*, Denzel Washington (Joe Miller), Jason Robards (Charles Wheeler), Mary Steenburgen (Belinda Conine), Antonio Banderas (Miguel), Joanne Woodward (Sarah Beckett), Anna Deavere Smith (Anthea Burton), Lisa Summerour (Lisa Miller), Ron Vawter (Bob Seidman), Charles Napier (Judge Garnett).
Fee: $8 million
US Box Office: 77.3 million
Plot: The story of a bright, up-and-coming young lawyer whose life and career is blighted by AIDS was a watershed in Hollywood's handling of the disease. Tom's brave character takes his homophobic bosses to court and wins, but he cannot beat the AIDS virus that ravages his body in front of our eyes. Tom lost up to 30 pounds in weight for his Oscar-winning performance.

Forrest Gump (1994) Director: Robert Zemeckis. Producers: Wendy Finerman, Steve Tisch, Steve Starkey. Screenplay: Eric Roth. Diector of Photography: Don Burgess. Production Designer: Rick Carter. Special Visual Effects Supervisor: Ken Ralston. Editor: Arthur Schmidt. Music: Alan Silvestri. Based on the novel by: Winston Groom. Released by: Paramount. Running time: 142 minutes. Cast: *Tom Hanks (Forrest Gump)*, Robin Wright (Jenny Curran), Gary Sinise (Lt Dan), Mykelti Williamson (Bubba), Sally Field (Mama Gump), Michael Humphreys (Young Forrest), Hanna Hall (Young Jenny).
Fee: Eight per cent of gross. Estimated at up to $60 million
US Box Office: 356.8 million

Plot: Life is a box of chocolates for Tom's Forrest Gump, a naïve simpleton whose remarkable journey through contemporary American history touched a nerve around the world. Like the man who plays him — Tom got his second Oscar here — Gump is always at the right place at the right time, making you laugh and cry and, always, care.

Apollo 13 (1995) Director: Ron Howard. Producer: Brian Grazer. Executive Producer: Todd Hallowell. Screenplay: William Broyles Jnr, Al Reiner. Director of Photography: Dean Cundey. Production Designer: Michael Corenblith. Visual Effects Supervisor: Rob Legato. Editors: Mike Hill, Dan Hanley. Music: James Horner. Based on the book *Lost Moon* by: James Lovell and Jeffrey Kluger. Released by: Universal. Running time: 136 minutes. Cast: *Tom Hanks (Jim Lovell)*, Kevin Bacon (Jack Swigert), Bill Paxton (Fred Haise), Gary Sinise (Ken Mattingly), Ed Harris (Gene Kranz), Kathleen Quinlan (Marilyn Lovell), Mary Kate Schellhardt (Barbara Lovell), Emily Ann Lloyd (Susan Lovell), Jean Speegle Howard (Blanch Lovell), Clint Howard (Eecom White), Joe Spano (NASA Director), David Andrews (Pete Conrad), Chris Ellis (Deke Slayton). Fee: $15 million
US Box Office: $172 million
Plot: The crew of *Apollo 13* may have never landed on the moon, but the story of the ill-fated mission and the incredible rescue of a spacecraft literally almost lost in space makes a spellbinding story — and Tom, a lifelong space nut, knew he was born to play Lovell, the cool-hand veteran who helps bring his crew home safe.

Toy Story (1995) Director: John Lasseter. Producers: Ralph Guggenheim, Bonnie Arnold. Executive Producers: Edwin Catmull, Steven Jobs. Screenplay: Joss Whedon, Andrew Stanton, Joel Cohen, Alec Sokolow. Supervising Animator: Pet Docter. Editors: Robert Gordon, Lee Unkrich. Music and songs: Randy Newman. Based on an original story by: John Lasseter, Pete Docter, John Ranft, Andrew Stanton. Released by: Disney. Running time: 80 minutes. Voices: *Tom Hanks (Woody)*, Tim Allen (Buzz Lightyear), Annie Potts (Bo Peep), Don Rickles (Mr Potato Head), Jim Varney (Slinky the Dog), John Ratzenberger (Hamm), Wallace Shawn (Rex),

John Morris (Andy), Erik Von Detten (Sid), Laurie Metcalf (Mrs Davis), R. Lee Ermey (Sergeant).

Fee: $200,000

US Box Office: 191.7 million

Plot: Andy's toys are happy with Woody the cowboy as their leader until the little boy gets a flashy new toy for his birthday. Buzz Lightyear's arrival in the bedroom sets the toy caste system out of sinc and jealous Woody tries unsuccessfully to dispose of his rival, turning the other toys against himself in the process. But, hey, it's a Disney movie, so it all turns out all right in the end.

That Thing You Do! (1996) Director: *Tom Hanks*. Producers: *Tom Hanks*, Jonathan Demme, Gary Goetzman, Edward Saxon. Associate Producer: Terry Odem. Screenplay: *Tom Hanks*. Cinematography: Taki Fujimoto. Production Designer: Victor Kempster. Art Director: Dan Webster. Visual Effects Supervisor: Steve Rundell. Original Music: Adam Schlesinger (title song), Howard Shore. Released by: 20th Century Fox. Running time: 110 minutes. Cast: Tom Everett Scott (Guy Patterson), Liv Tyler (Faye Dolan), Jonathan Schaech (James 'Jimmy' Matingly II), Steve Zahn (Lenny Haise), *Tom Hanks (Mr White)*, Ethan Embry (The Bass Player), Charlize Theron (Tina), Giovanni Ribisi (Chad), Peter Scolari (Troy Chesterfield), Rita Wilson (Marguerite), Chris Isaak (Uncle Bob), Holmes Osborne (Mr Patterson).

Fee: N/A

US Box Office: $46 million

Plot: Tom only makes a brief appearance as the manipulative manager of a pop group that hits the top of the charts with 'That Thing You Do!', a catchy pop ditty that has the girls screaming. But not for long. The group goes into the annals of one-hit-wonder bands when the honeymoon ends and they break up. Tom may not do much acting, but he wrote, directed and produced this charming '60s period piece.

Saving Private Ryan (1998) Director: Steven Spielberg. Producers: Steven Spielberg, Ian Bryce, Mark Gordon, Gary Levinsohn. Co-Producers: Bonnie Curtis, Allison Lyon Segan. Screenplay: Robert Rodat. Director of Photography: Janusz Kaminski. Editor: Michael

Kahn. Costume Designer: Joanna Johnston. Production Designer: Tom Sanders. Music: John Williams. Released by: DreamWorks Pictures/Paramount. Running time: 170 minutes. Cast: *Tom Hanks (Capt Miller)*, Tom Sizemore (Sgnt Horvath), Edward Burns (Private Reiben), Barry Pepper (Private Jackson), Adam Goldberg (Private Mellish), Vin Diesel (Private Caparzo), Giovanni Ribisi (Medic Wade), Jeremy Davies (Corporal Upham), Matt Damon (Private Ryan), Ted Danson (Capt Hamill), Paul Giametti (Sgnt Hill), Dennis Farina (Lt Col Anderson), Joerg Stadler (Steamboat Willie).
Fee: Percentage of gross. Estimated at $20 million
US Box Office: $190 million
Plot: When you have recovered from the intensity of the first half hour, which shows the slaughter on World War II's Omaha Beach in the most realistic and shocking detail ever seen on the big screen, you regroup to discover Tom's Captain Miller leading his men on a dangerous mission behind enemy lines to find the only surviving one left of four brothers who went to war for their country. A powerful film and a powerful, understated performance from its star.

You've Got Mail (1999) Director: Nora Ephron. Producers: Nora Ephron, Lauren Shuler Donner. Executive Producers: Delia Ephron, Julie Durk, G. Mac Brown. Screenplay: Nora Ephron, Delia Ephron. Cinematography: John Lindley. Music: George Fenton. Released by: Warner Bros. Running time: 119 minutes. Cast: *Tom Hanks (Joe Fox)*, Meg Ryan (Kathleen Kelly), Parker Posey (Patricia Eden), Greg Kinnear (Frank Navasky), Jean Stapleton (Birdie), Steve Zahn (George Pappas), David Chappelle (Kevin Scanlon), Dabney Coleman (Nelson Foz), John Randolph (Schuyler Fox), Heather Burns (Christina).
Fee: $20 million
US Box Office: $111.1 million
Plot: Hard to believe it, but Tom and Meg hate each other when they meet. His character is a take-no-prisoners bookstore-chain boss. Hers is a caring owner of a small, family children's bookshop being driven out by the newcomer on the block with its vast range and big discounts. Unbeknownst to both, they are falling in love via the Internet, chatting anonymously by E-mail. By the end of the film (just) all is revealed and everyone goes home happy.

The Green Mile (1999) Director: Frank Darabont. Producer: David Valdes. Based on a novel by Stephen King. To be released by: Castle Rock. Cast: *Tom Hanks (Paul Edgecombe)*, Patricia Clarkson (Melinda Moores), James Cromwell (Hal Moores), Michael Clark Duncan (John Coffey), Graham Greene (Arlen Bitterbuck), Bonnie Hunt (Janice Edgecombe), Barry Pepper (Dean Stanton), Sam Rockwell (William 'Wild Bill' Wharton), Gary Sinise (Burt Hammersmith), Harry Dean Stanton (Old Toot Toot).
Fee: $22 million
US Box Office: Unreleased
Plot: Tom's grisly prison guard reflects on his bizarre tour-of-duty on death row in the 1930s and his relationship with a convicted rapist and killer whose gentle, healing nature leaves his captor wondering about his guilt and worrying whether he deserves to go to the electric chair.

Dino (1999) Director: Martin Scorsese. Screenplay: Nicholas Pileggi. To be released by: Warner Bros. Cast: *Tom Hanks (Dean Martin)*.
Fee: $22 million
US Box Office: Unreleased
Plot: Based on the life and times of screen legend and singer Dean Martin. The film is titled *Dino* because of his real name, Dino Crocetti.

Toy Story 2 (1999) Directors: Colin Brady, Ash Brannon. Producer: Ralph Guggenheim. Executive Producers: Steve Jobs, John Lasseter. Music: Randy Newman. To be released by: Disney. Voices: *Tom Hanks (Woody)*, Tim Allen (Buzz Lightyear), Don Rickles (Mr Potato Head), Annie Potts (Bo Peep), Jim Varney (Slinky), Wallace Shawn (Rex), John Ratzenberger (Hamm), John Morris (Andy).
Fee: $350,000
US Box Office: Unreleased
Plot: Unknown

TOM HANKS

Director Filmography

From the Earth to the Moon — TV mini-series — 1998
That Thing You Do! — Feature film — 1996
Fallen Angels — TV — 1993
A League of Their Own — TV series — 1993

Writer Filmography

From the Earth to the Moon — TV mini-series — 1998
That Thing You Do! — Feature film — 1996

Producer Filmography

From the Earth to the Moon — TV mini-series — 1998

Television Credits

I Am Your Child — Host — 1997
Bosom Buddies — Kip 'Buffy' Wilson — 1980-82
Saturday Night Live — Guest Host — 1985-96
The Naked Truth — Himself — 1995
Family Ties — Uncle Ned — 1982
Taxi — Gordon — 1978
The Love Boat — Rick Martin — 1977
Happy Days — The Fonz's old 'friend' — 1974